Christian Hübsch

Flexible Application-Layer Multicast in Heterogeneous Networks

Flexible Application-Layer Multicast
in Heterogeneous Networks

by
Christian Hübsch

Dissertation, Karlsruher Institut für Technologie (KIT)
Fakultät für Informatik
Tag der mündlichen Prüfung: 29. Juni 2012

Impressum

Karlsruher Institut für Technologie (KIT)
KIT Scientific Publishing
Straße am Forum 2
D-76131 Karlsruhe
www.ksp.kit.edu

KIT – Universität des Landes Baden-Württemberg und
nationales Forschungszentrum in der Helmholtz-Gemeinschaft

KIT Scientific Publishing 2013
Print on Demand

ISBN 978-3-7315-0021-6

Flexible Application-Layer Multicast in Heterogeneous Networks

zur Erlangung des akademischen Grades eines

DOKTORS DER INGENIEURWISSENSCHAFTEN

der Fakultät für Informatik
des Karlsruher Instituts für Technologie (KIT)

genehmigte

Dissertation

von

Dipl.-Inform. Christian Hübsch

aus Oldenburg in Holstein

Tag der mündlichen Prüfung: 29. Juni 2012

Erster Gutachter: Prof. Dr. Martina Zitterbart
                                 Karlsruher Institut für Technologie (KIT)

Zweiter Gutachter: Prof. Dr. Torsten Braun
                                 Universität Bern

FÜR MEINE
FAMILIE

Danksagung

D<small>IE</small> vorliegende Arbeit entstand während meiner Zeit als wissenschaftlicher Mitarbeiter am Institut für Telematik des Karlsruher Instituts für Technologie (KIT). An erster Stelle gilt mein Dank Frau Prof. Dr. Martina Zitterbart, die mir durch die Anstellung die Promotion erst ermöglichte. Darüber hinaus hat sie das Erstreferat der Arbeit übernommen und mich über die Jahre fachlich begleitet und angeleitet. Die Erfahrungen, die ich in dieser Zeit im Umfeld der Forschung und auf internationalen Konferenzen sammeln durfte sind für mich von unschätzbarem Wert. Herrn Prof. Dr. Torsten Braun von der Universität Bern danke ich sehr für die Übernahme des Koreferats.

Allen Kolleginnen und Kollegen des Instituts möchte ich für die gute Zusammenarbeit und die schöne Zeit danken. Selbiges gilt auch für die Kollegen anderer Institute, mit denen ich über die Jahre im Rahmen von Projekten zusammenarbeiten durfte.

Besondere Erwähnung soll das SpoVNet-Team finden, allen voran Herr PD Dr. Oliver Waldhorst, der immer den absoluten Durchblick auch in schwierigen Phasen hatte und ohne dessen Motivation es mit Sicherheit um einiges schwieriger für mich geworden wäre (Danke, Waldy!). Eine ebenso besondere Rolle spielte Herr Dr. Christoph Mayer, der es verstand, einen immer wieder aufzubauen und mit dem ich unglaublich produktive Diskussionen entweder vor dem Whiteboard oder auch auf einem zerknitterten Zettel am Hafen von San Diego geführt habe. Ebenso dankbar bin ich Herrn PD Dr. Roland Bless, der mir als langjähriger Büronachbar immer mit seiner unerschöpflichen Erfahrung zur Seite stand sowie Herrn Dr. Sebastian Mies, mit dem ich die ersten Jahre das Büro teilte und wir versucht haben, unsere Forschungsnischen auszuloten.

Herrn Dr. Jochen Furthmüller danke ich für die philosophischen Gespräche auf der Treppe und das gemeinsame Durchleiden der letzten Etappe. Letztgenanntes gilt auch für Herrn Martin Röhricht, der immer ein offenes Ohr hatte, sowie Fabian Hartmann, der leider viel zu spät zum ITM kam. Herrn Dr. Bernhard Heep möchte ich ausdrücklich für seinen schwarzen Humor danken, es war eine lustige Zeit.

Alle Kollegen, die eine Rolle gespielt haben, können hier leider in Gänze keine Erwähnung finden, aber seid Euch meines Dankes gewiss. Das gilt auch für die Studenten, die zur Arbeit beigetragen haben, hier allen voran Mario Hock, Martin Florian und Daniel Schmidt. Vielen Dank für die Unterstützung.

Nicht zuletzt danke ich natürlich auch meinem privaten Umfeld. Eine Promotion ist meines Erachtens ohne die Unterstützung, die Rücksichtnahme und auch das Zurückstecken von Familie und Freunden gar nicht möglich. Allen voran sei meine Kathy genannt, die mich unzählige durchgearbeitete Wochenenden im Institut hat gewähren lassen und sich (fast) nie beschwert hat. Danke, Maus.

Meinem Bruder Markus und meinem Freund und Büronachbarn Moritz Killat danke ich dafür, dass sie immer mit guten Ratschlägen für mich da waren, und meiner Mutter Ulrike für ihre Unterstützung, auf die ich immer zählen konnte (und kann) und die den Weg für die akademische Schiene seinerzeit geebnet hat. Und allen nicht explizit genannten Freunden danke ich für die wichtige Zerstreuung in der verbliebenen Freizeit!

Nicht zuletzt möchte ich den Foo Fighters für gute Musik im Büro und Red Bull für das nötige Quäntchen Energie zu später Stunde danken.

Karlsruhe, im März 2013

Christian Hübsch

Zusammenfassung

Das Internet spielt heute in fast jedem Bereich des täglichen Lebens eine Rolle. Viele der eingesetzten und neu aufkommenden Anwendungen im Internet realisieren eine Kommunikation von einem Server zu einer *Gruppe* von Teilnehmern (z.B. Spiele, Chat, Videostreaming). Da eine derartige Gruppenkommunikation in den meisten Fällen durch das einzelne Versenden der Daten zu jedem Teilnehmer realisiert wird, ist das Netz (und die verwendeten Server) einer hohen Verkehrslast ausgesetzt. Im Zuge des stark wachsenden Marktes der mobilen Endgeräte erfasst diese Lastproblematik auch die mobilen Zugangsnetze: Hier klagen immer mehr Dienstanbieter über Ausfälle durch zu viele Teilnehmer mit hohen Bandbreitenansprüchen, die neuere Geräteklassen (z.B. Smartphones) in der Lage sind zu verarbeiten. Ein Ansatz zur Entlastung der Server liegt in sog. Peer-to-Peer-Techniken (P2P), bei denen Endgeräte direkt untereinander in logischen Overlay-Netzen kommunizieren. Mit diesen Techniken lässt sich (trotz der Nichtverfügbarkeit eines entsprechenden globalen Netzdienstes) eine Gruppenkommunikation realisieren (Application-Layer Multicast, ALM). ALM-Protokolle weisen allerdings – verglichen mit ursprünglichen Ansätzen wie IP Multicast – i.d.R. schlechtere Leistungswerte auf, etwa höhere Paketverzögerungen oder höhere Netzlast. Daher ist es umso wichtiger, die eingesetzten Mechanismen im Hinblick auf den jeweiligen Anwendungsfall zu optimieren und zu spezialisieren. Die meisten ALM-Ansätze gehen von einem homogenen Netz aus und differenzieren nicht explizit zwischen verschiedenen Zugangstechniken. Dieses Verhalten steht in Kontrast zu einer zunehmenden Diversifikation im heutigen Internet: Neue Zugangstechniken werden verfügbar und drahtlose Netze in wachsender Zahl ermöglichen direkte, spontane Kommunikation zwischen Teilnehmern. Um mit diesen Entwicklungen Schritt zu halten bedarf es ALM-Protokollen, die flexibel und adaptiv an sich ändernde Bedingungen anpassbar sind und sich auf unterschiedlichen Endsystemen und in verschiedenen Anwendungsszenarien verwenden lassen.

In dieser Dissertation werden verschiedene ALM-Protokolle beschrieben und analysiert. Um Einblick in das Verhalten typischer ALM-Protokolle in großen und dynamischen Netzwerkungebungen zu erhalten wird das Cluster-basierte Protokoll NICE analysiert. Im Gegensatz zu existierenden Arbeiten, die vor allem den Einfluss auf das Netzwerk betrachten, fokussieren die Untersuchungen dieser Arbeit auf die Leistungswerte des Protokolls aus Perspektive der Endsysteme. Überdies wird das Protokollverhalten in Szenarien mit realistischer Knotenfluktuation betrachtet. Die Studien belegen, dass NICE gute Skalierbarkeitseigenschaften und eine hohe Robustheit aufweist, sofern es entsprechend konfiguriert wird. Desweiteren wird eine Erweiterung vorgeschlagen, die NICE eine autonome Reparametrisierung zur Laufzeit ermöglicht, um sich an ändernde Netzwerksituationen anzupassen.

Mit CMA (Capacity Matching ALM) wird ein Protokoll vorgeschlagen, das im Kontext eines Livestreaming-Szenarios die Verkehrslast in zellulären Zugangsnetzen berücksichtigt. CMA verwendet einen baumbasierten Ansatz, der mittels einer gewichteten Summe die Verteilstruktur wartet und periodisch neue Elternknoten für jeden Teilnehmer sucht. Dem Ansatz liegt das vorgestellte Konzept der Kapazitätsadaption zugrunde, das sich – entgegen dem oft verfolgten Ziel der Topologieadaption in Overlay-Netzen – primär an den Weiterleitungskapazitäten der Zellen orientiert. Umfassende simulative Untersuchungen von CMA belegen, dass das Protokoll dabei helfen kann, Kapazitätsengpässe in mobilen Zugangsnetzen zu vermeiden, sofern genug Kapazität in alternativen Zellen in der Umgebung vorhanden ist. Dabei wird gezeigt, dass eine durch CMA hervorgerufene erhöhte Empfangsverzögerung durch geeignete Parametrisierung auf unter 10% gehalten werden kann. Die Untersuchungen beziehen sich dabei auf ein Netzwerkmodell, das sich an heutigen 3G-Netzen orientiert.

Obgleich CMA ein Verteilen von Netzlast auf unterschiedliche Zugangsnetzzellen ermöglicht, wird trotzdem durch das ALM-Protokoll zusätzliche Last induziert. Ein Weg, um die Last auch über unterschiedliche Zugangstechniken hinweg zu balancieren, besteht in der dedizierten Berücksichtigung und Integration dieser Techniken im ALM-Protokoll. Mit WIMP (Wireless Multi-Access Proximity Probing) wird ein Mechanismus entwickelt, der es ermöglicht, gegenseitige Erreichbarkeit von Teilnehmern in drahtlosen lokalen Netzen zu erkennen. In dieser Arbeit wird der WIMP-Mechanismus sowohl in NICE als auch in CMA exemplarisch integriert. Hierzu werden beide Protokolle konzeptionell um die Berücksichtigung drahtloser lokaler Netze erweitert. In NICE werden für Teilnehmer in drahtlosen Netzen neue Rollen definiert, die zu weniger Protokollverkehr in drahtlosen lokalen Netzen führen. Überdies wird die Broadcast-Fähigkeit dieser Domänen genutzt, um Verkehrsaufkommen zu reduzieren. Die Berücksichtigung drahtloser lokaler Netze in NICE führt zu einer verbesserten Anwendbarkeit des Protokolls in heterogenen Netzumgebungen mit Hinblick auf erzeugte Netzlast und Weiterleitungsverzögerung. In CMA wird WIMP genutzt, um zelluläre Netze von Datenverkehr zu entlasten, indem öffentliche drahtlose Netze in dichten urbanen Umgebungen integriert werden. Die Integration dieser in großer Zahl verfügbaren lokalen Netze stellt eine vielversprechende Strategie zur Entlastung der stark genutzen mobilen Zugangsnetze dar.

Schließlich wird in der Dissertation ein Rahmenwerk präsentiert, das die Entwicklung und Ausbringung von Overlay-basierten P2P-Netzen unterstützt: Die SpoVNet-Architektur verbirgt komplexe Eigenschaften des Netzes vor dem Entwickler (z.B. NAT-Boxen, Verbindungsabbrüche bei Mobilität oder Protokollheterogeniät) und bietet somit eine einfach zu verwendende Plattform für die Entwicklung von P2P-Netzen. Die vorgestellten ALM-Protokolle können in der SpoVNet-Architektur realisiert werden. Darüber hinaus können über eine spezielle Schnittstelle auch unmodifizierte Anwendungen von der SpoVNet-Architektur profitieren.

Die in dieser Dissertation präsentierten Ansätze sind ein Schritt in Richtung flexiblerer ALM-Protokolle, die mit den technischen Änderungen und neuen Anwendungsanforderungen im Internet durch eine hohe Flexibilität, Konfigurierbarkeit und Erweiterbarkeit besser umzugehen vermögen als existierende Ansätze. Die Evaluationen der Protokolle unterstützen die These, dass P2P-Protokolle vielversprechende Eigenschaften für die flexible Ausbringung neuer Kommunikationsdienste im Internet bieten und sogar zur Milderung von Lastengpässen in mobilen Netzen beitragen können. Somit können sie potenziell nicht nur vorteilhaft von Endbenutzern ausgebracht und eingesetzt werden, sondern sollten auch als Zusatztechnologie für die kostengünstige Verteilung bestimmter Inhalte von Seiten der Provider erwogen werden.

Table of Contents

List of Figures

List of Tables

List of Algorithms

List of Symbols

Chapter 5 (CMA)

CHAPTER 6 (WIMP)

Part I

Introduction & Fundamentals

1. Introduction

The Internet plays an important role in nearly every domain of daily life: Since its commercial launch in the early nineties it has become the major communication platform for economics, but also for private and social exchange. A large number of Internet applications employs communication among a group of users, like e. g. games, chat applications, or video streaming. Due to the non-availability of an Internet-wide network support for such group communication applications data is often sent to each participant separately via a single data transmission. Unfortunately, this results in increased traffic load on Internet servers as well as in the network due to the need to forward the same data multiple times.

In recent years Peer-to-Peer (P2P) communication gained attention as a way to flexibly unburden centralized servers from their load by establishing direct communication links between end-systems (peers). No centralized servers have to be involved. P2P protocols help to deploy novel services without relying on dedicated support in the underlying network: E. g., P2P approaches can be used to provide end-system-based group communication through so-called *Application-Layer Multicast (ALM)* protocols. Here, participating peers implement all group communication logic.

Most existing ALM protocols assume a homogeneous Internet and do not explicitly differentiate access networks. This approach contradicts the growing diversification in today's Internet. New access technologies come up that coexist in parallel, offering a range of ways to access the Internet. Also, wireless technologies enable end-systems to communicate directly and spontaneously

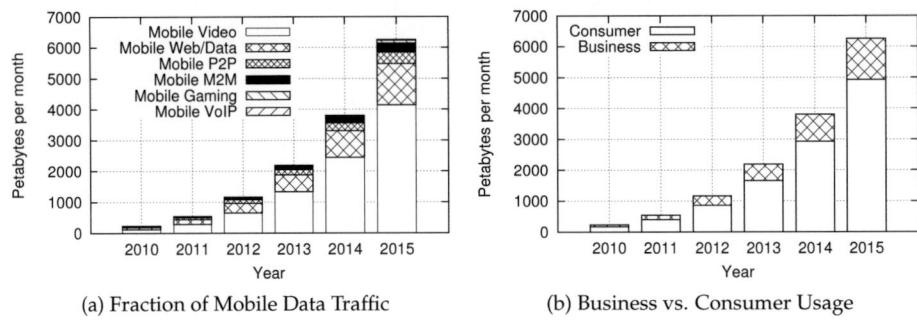

(a) Fraction of Mobile Data Traffic

(b) Business vs. Consumer Usage

Figure 1.1 Global Mobile Traffic Forecast 2010-2015 (Cisco VNI [41])

in local areas. Further technical developments in the communication sector and a huge business market push advancements forward, leading to ongoing miniaturization and growing end-system capabilities. To keep pace with these developments in the context of ALM, protocols must flexibly adapt to changing network conditions, consider different access technologies, and provide means to be deployed in various group communication scenarios and on diverse end-systems.

With diversification in end-systems and Internet access new problems arise in today's access networks. For instance, the generated traffic load is dramatically increasing.

High-end mobile devices like laptops, smart phones, and tablets are key sources of data traffic in mobile access networks. They offer the consumer content and applications not supported by the previous generation of mobile devices [41]. According to Cisco, mobile data traffic will increase 26-fold between 2010 and 2015 and more than 66 percent of the world's mobile data traffic will be video streaming by then (cf. Fig. 1.1(a)). The number of mobile users (especially private consumers, cf. Fig. 1.1(b)) will grow as well as the contents they consume. Mobile access networks like e. g. 3G/4G are not designed to support this radical growth in bandwidth consumption (*"The networks which could easily withstand a garden-hose flow of data are now being subjected to a pressure from a fireman's hose"* [96]) and become bottlenecks in communication service provision. Even higher-capacity technologies like LTE will most likely not solve the ongoing growth of bandwidth consumption. First access providers in the U.S. already faced service outages due to high numbers of concurrent users consuming broadband contents [9]. In order to attack these problems and mitigate the traffic load bottleneck providers make high investments in access network technology upgrades. Unfortu-

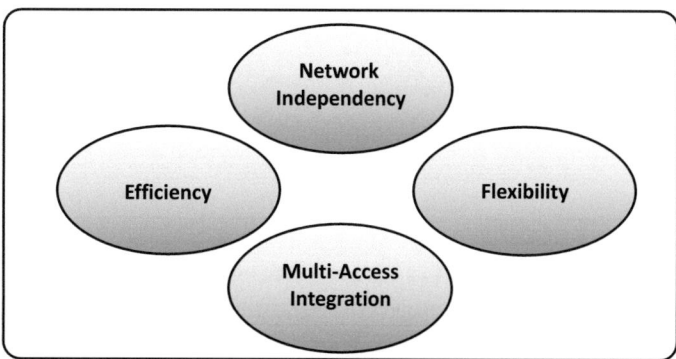

Figure 1.2 Characteristics for ALM Solutions developed in this Thesis

nately, such investments have technical limitations, weakening their suitability to be an adequate solution for the ever-increasing bandwidth demand.

In this thesis a set of P2P-based ALM protocols and mechanisms is described and analyzed as an end-system-based approach to provide Internet-wide group communication. The protocols follow three different communication aspects: First, they bypass the need for a globally available native group communication support in the Internet. Second, they are used to approach the problem of high traffic load in access networks by adapting the ALM protocols to the network situation. Third, they help to mitigate the need for expensive network investments from providers' side by increasing the number of supportable concurrent users.

Two different classes of ALM protocols (cluster-based and tree-based) are examined in order to get insights into their expected behavior and properties regarding group communication. The question whether P2P approaches can help to avoid access network bandwidth bottlenecks is investigated. Mechanisms are proposed that can be used to consider direct wireless reachability among participating end-systems in order to further support network congestion avoidance, if possible. Finally, a framework for easy overlay service creation and deployment is described that can be used as a basis for integrating the proposed ALM protocols.

1.1 Goals, Requirements, and Assumptions

The goal of this thesis is the flexibilization of ALM protocols regarding the following aspects: The applicability of ALM protocols should be enhanced by allowing for configuration of different optimization goals and basic protocol mechanisms. ALM protocols should also be designed with heterogeneous networks in mind, providing possibilities to optionally integrate different access technologies in the ALM dissemination structure, where applicable. Third, the designed protocols should be analyzed in the context of the described access network traffic congestion problems. In this thesis the following characteristics are focused for the design of the presented approaches (cf. Fig. 1.2):

- *Efficiency*: ALM group communication services must be efficient from both the user's perspective as well as from the network's perspective. Efficiency from a user's point of view means the provision of a group communication service that fulfills the specific quality demands connected to the application scenario. Efficiency from the network's point of view means the responsible usage of the network's capacities.

- *Flexibility*: The developed ALM protocols and mechanisms should not be bound to a single application scenario but allow to be adapted to different application scenarios. Regarding the ability to use different access technologies flexibility is also related to the following "Multi-Access Integration" characteristic.

- *Multi-Access Integration*: The ALM protocols should be able to integrate the end-systems' capabilities to use different technologies in order to access the Internet or be able to connect end-systems directly in a local area network. This requirement is a key to cope with load balancing issues in access networks.

- *Network Independence*: The ALM protocols and mechanisms should follow the P2P approach, i. e. no dedicated network infrastructure except the existing Internet unicast routing is needed in order to deploy them. Only end-systems are involved in establishing the ALM structure and forwarding packets.

This thesis is based on two assumptions:

- *End-to-End Connectivity*: Every peer is able to reach every other peer participating in the group communication service in an end-to-end manner. Hence, no dedicated mechanisms regarding e. g. NAT-traversal, firewalls, or different protocol versions (except the mechanisms in the SpoVNet Architecture, cf. Chapter 3) have to be considered in the ALM protocols.

- *Internet Access*: Every peer is assumed to be able to access the Internet through at least one access technology. A subset of peers may have more than one access technology available. In such cases it is assumed that the technologies can optionally be used concurrently.

1.2 Contributions of this Thesis

The contributions of this thesis to the State-of-the-Art are:

1. The analysis of the cluster-based ALM protocol NICE with respect to its peer-perceived performance in different scenarios. While existing evaluations in literature target NICE's implications on the network, this work provides insights into performance from an end-system's perspective. High numbers of peers are considered in the evaluations as well as aggressive peer fluctuation behavior. Furthermore, means for runtime adaptation of important protocol parameters are presented that can be used to actively react to changing network conditions. The evaluations show that NICE scales well with growing numbers of peers due to limited per-peer overhead while it provides dissemination delays with sublinear growth. Refinement of the dissemination structure during runtime leads to the combination of peers located near to each other in the network in the same clusters. This also optimizes join delays over runtime because peers in smaller clusters can be queried for information faster. In environments with heavy peer fluctuation high data success rates are achievable in NICE using aggressive refinement mechanisms.

2. The design and analysis of a tree-based ALM protocol called *CMA (Capacity Matching ALM)* in the context of traffic load balancing in wireless access networks. A scenario of single-source video stream dissemination is considered. The protocol design targets two main aspects: First, the video source is relieved from high traffic load resulting from high numbers of receiver peers. Second, with help of a heuristic in tree parent determination CMA is able to consider traffic load in access networks in order to build the tree according to the current load status. The concept of so-called *Capacity Matching* (in contrast to common Topology Matching in P2P) is proposed as basis for CMA. Under the assumptions that CMA is able to acquire underlay-related capacity information the evaluations show: Tree-based ALM protocols offer the flexibility to adapt the dissemination structure to defined goals at the cost of inducing additional traffic load in form of outgoing video streams in access networks. This additional load can be balanced to high extent if the capacity situation in the networks allows it. The load balancing comes with increased dissemination delays, but this increase is low (below 10 %) if the protocol is configured accordingly.

3. The development of a mechanism called *WIMP (Wireless Multi-Access Proximity Probing)* which provides reachability information for wireless networks to the peers in an existing ALM tree structure. It can be used

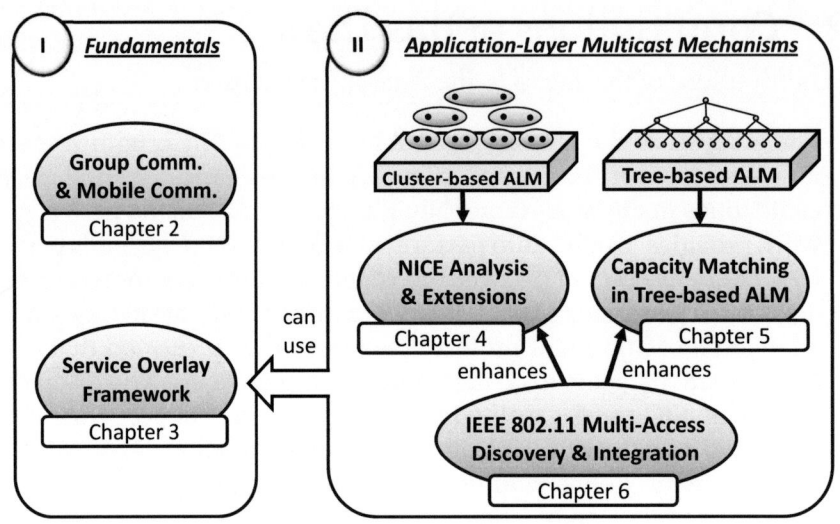

Figure 1.3 Structure of this Thesis

by ALM protocols to look up and integrate wireless peers in the overlay structure with explicit consideration of the wireless access technology. NICE is extended to use WIMP and assign special roles to wireless peers in the overlay in order to avoid high traffic in the wireless domains. The broadcast capabilities of the wireless domains are exploited to increase communication efficiency. Furthermore, WIMP integration in CMA is described in order to allow for the autonomous integration of public IEEE 802.11 domains in the traffic load balancing scenario.

4. The presentation of a service overlay framework that can be used to integrate the described ALM protocols and extensions. The framework aids as an abstraction to the network underlay and offers easy-to-use interfaces. It hides underlay network issues like different protocol versions, link outages, or middleboxes (e. g. NAT-boxes) from overlay service developers and helps to considerably reduce the development complexity of overlay-based services. Through a dedicated legacy interface also unmodified existing applications and services can benefit from the framework.

1.3 Outline

The thesis is structured as follows (cf. Figure 1.3). Chapter 2 gives an introduction to Peer-to-Peer (P2P) networks and group communication with focus on Application-Layer Multicast (ALM). Furthermore, important mobile communication technologies with relevance for this work are introduced. Chapter 3 describes a framework for easy deployment of service overlays which can be employed to integrate the presented ALM approaches. Regarding the class of cluster-based ALM approaches Chapter 4 analyzes the NICE protocol with respect to different scenarios and concerning peer-perceived protocol performance. Chapter 5 focuses on a tree-based approach that is applied to a 3G load balancing scenario. For finding and integrating alternative communication paths via IEEE 802.11 technologies in the ALM dissemination strategies a mechanism for finding peers distributedly in wireless proximity is presented in Chapter 6. It is applied to both presented cluster- and tree-based protocols in order to integrate wireless communication in the overlay structure. The thesis concludes and gives an outlook on possible further research directions in Chapter 7.

2. Fundamentals

This chapter covers fundamentals that are necessary for a complete understanding of this work. It first describes Peer-to-Peer overlay networks which
constitute the general basis for the presented protocols. Then, different forms
of group communication with focus on Application-Layer Multicast are described, before subsequently relevant mobile communication technologies are
introduced.

2.1 Peer-to-Peer Communication

As an alternative to centralized Internet communication (e. g. an end-system
requesting data from a centralized server), Peer-to-Peer (P2P) communication
experienced high interest in the scientific community as well as in the Internet
in recent years. A P2P system is a self-organizing logical network, consisting
of equal participating nodes (peers). Each peer can contribute to the system,
either regarding computation or communication capacity, or by providing
data. Likewise, each peer can use these resources. This way, distributed communication services can be implemented in which all peers incorporate the
role of clients and servers at the same time (so-called *Servents* [204]). Popular
deployed P2P systems in today's Internet are predominantly related to the use
case of *file sharing* (e. g. Bittorrent [25], eMule [65], or KaZaA [124]). However,
a multitude of potential other P2P-enabled communication services has been
considered and partly been deployed, e. g. supporting Internet telephony by
looking up communication end-points distributedly [18], or providing group
communication. The latter builds the basis for the protocols described in this
thesis and will be revisited in Section 2.2.3.

P2P networks avoid the cost and the problem of single-point-of-failure connected to centralized server-based solutions. Furthermore, they provide flexibility to adapt their dissemination structures to the current network situation (if designed accordingly). Finally, while centralized servers have to grow proportionally to the client population regarding their capacities, P2P systems gain further capacities with every participating peer joining the network. Hence, they inherently provide better scalability[1] properties concerning the number of participating peers and regarding data dissemination. A survey on different P2P approaches is provided in [204].

P2P networks are implemented as so-called *overlay networks (overlays)*. Overlays consist of logical communication links between peers, forming a virtual network on top of the physical network topology (the *underlay*). The actual communication is accomplished by using the underlay network's data forwarding capabilities, like e. g. end-to-end routing in the Internet. Hence, a single virtual P2P connection in the overlay abstracts from the physical underlay path that the data between the peers follows. Two classes of P2P networks can be differentiated with respect to the established overlay structure, being *unstructured* and *structured* P2P overlays.

2.1.1   Unstructured P2P Overlays

Unstructured P2P overlay networks have been proposed early and are characterized by full freedom in overlay structure establishment. Each peer can freely choose its position in the overlay, e. g. based on the specific application case's optimization goals. However, this freedom comes with the need for each peer to gain knowledge about the relation to other peers, accomplished through active measurements of relevant metrics between peers. Due to the high overhead for overlay structure establishment and maintenance, the scalability benefit of P2P is often impaired in unstructured P2P approaches. In Narada [40, 98], for instance, peers measure network metrics against all other peers in the overlay, forming a full mesh control structure. Hence, Narada is only usable with small to medium peer populations. Two generations are differentiated in unstructured P2P overlays: Driven predominantly by file sharing motivation, the first generation of proposals used either a centralized instance for database and lookup functionality (e. g. Napster [161]) or used full-mesh overlays (e. g. Gnutella 0.4 [78] or Freenet [43]). The second generation tried to merge aspects from both approaches by assigning different logical hierarchies to the overlay structure: Part of the peers become higher peers, being responsible for local clusters of peers and being interconnected with the other higher peers. These protocols are called *hybrid P2P* approaches

---

[1]The scalability may be limited in case of further reliability mechanisms being used, like e. g. acknowledgements to the sender.

and offer better scalability while avoiding single centralized roles in the network (e. g. Gnutella 0.6 [79] or JXTA [80]).

2.1.2   Structured P2P Overlays

In structured P2P overlay networks, a unique *identifier (ID)* is assigned to each peer. The identifier determines the position of a peer in the overlay, concerning a given base structure (e. g. ring or cube). Gummadi et al. [84] analyzed and compared different routing geometries for structured P2P overlay networks. They found that ring geometries offer highest flexibility and best resilience. Structured P2P overlay networks avoid the high network measurement overhead that is typically connected to unstructured P2P approaches. This is accomplished by the predetermined position of peers in the overlay structure, avoiding the need to measure against many other peers but only requiring to place itself in the right position of the structure. Hence, structured P2P overlay networks offer high scalability and good self-organization properties, but are limited in their adaptability to given optimization goals: In contrast to unstructured approaches, individual peers cannot change their position depending on the current network state easily since their static ID determines the structure. Structured P2P overlay networks are in most application cases employed for the distributed storage and lookup of information. In so-called *Distributed Hash Tables (DHT)*, data is mapped to IDs, determining on which peer the data is stored. For requesting the data it can be looked up by mapping it to the peer's ID. Prominent structured P2P overlay networks are Chord [210], Kademlia [153], or Pastry [193], for instance.

Both structured and unstructured P2P overlay networks are used to provide Internet-wide group communication. A general introduction to group communication is given in the next section, before subsequently a characterization of P2P-enabled group communication approaches is described.

2.2   Group Communication

In today's Internet the prevalent communication form is exchanging data between two single communication devices (e. g. browsing websites or downloading videos). This is also known as *unicast* communication. However, established and upcoming Internet applications—like conferencing, gaming, data sharing, and collaborative work—are inherently based on *group communication*. As those applications communicate in a one-to-many or many-to-many fashion, they make inefficient use of the available unicast-only network infrastructure [97].

Group communication provides means to send data to more than one host with a single transmission, allowing for higher communication efficiency com-

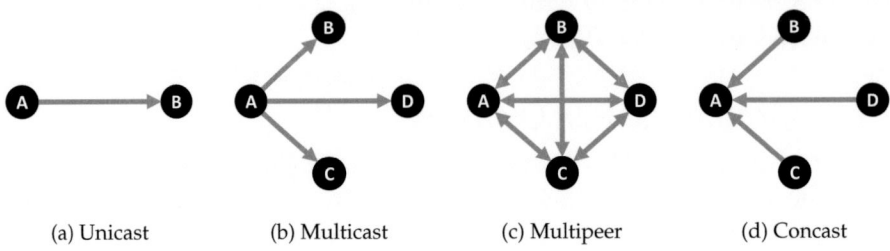

(a) Unicast   (b) Multicast   (c) Multipeer   (d) Concast

Figure 2.1 Different Group Communication Paradigms (based on [232])

pared to sending the same data multiple times via unicast. Thereby, the term group communication represents a whole class of possible communication paradigms [232] (Figure 2.1 shows a selection): Unicast is a special case for group communication where one host sends data to a single receiver host (cf. Figure 2.1(a)). As a growing set of receiver hosts (the *group*) results in many unicast transmissions, this approach does not scale for large groups. *Multicast*, in contrast, allows sending data from one host to a whole group with a single transmission (cf. Figure 2.1(b)). It decouples the group size from the communication overhead the sender and the network experience (as long as no higher reliability mechanisms are used on top of it, cf. Section 2.1). Hence, scalability is considerably higher with growing group size, compared to unicast communication.

Another paradigm is called *multipeer* communication and allows sending data from an arbitrary number of sending hosts to a group (cf. Figure 2.1(c)). It can be emulated through n multicast transmissions (n being the number of senders). Finally, *concast* is a form of group communication where a set of hosts sends data to a single receiver host (cf. Figure 2.1(d)). This paradigm is useful in scenarios where data is collected and transmitted to a sink, for instance.

This thesis mainly concentrates on multicast communication. Multipeer also applies to some scenarios considered in this work, which are explicitly mentioned in the respective chapters. How multicast is accomplished from a network communication point of view is described in the following.

Considering the seven-layer ISO/OSI model for communications [245] (or the corresponding layers in the Internet model [216]) as shown in Figure 2.2, multicast can be integrated as a function in different layers. Multicast implementations in layer 2 (Link Layer) use dedicated Multicast MAC addresses. Receivers in a subnet listen to the respective packets if they are part of the multicast group. Considering wide area group communication (i. e. routing

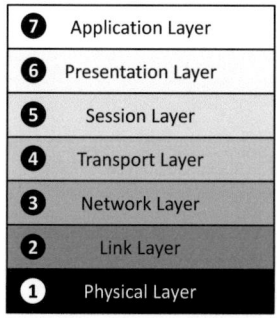
(a) Seven-layer ISO/OSI Model

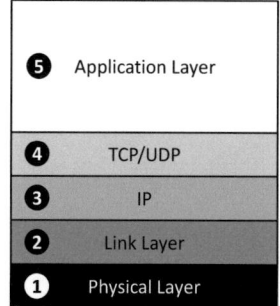
(b) Five-layer Internet Model

Figure 2.2 Common Communication Stack Models

data over different network domains), the layer 3 (Network Layer) fits the multicast paradigm well because packet duplication and forwarding can be accomplished in the network routers. Layer 3 approaches are described in Section 2.2.1. Since provider support and investments are needed to support multicast in the network and this approach is prone to various deployment issues, alternative layers and approaches have been proposed for multicast service provision. They are briefly classified and described in Section 2.2.2, before afterwards the most prominent among them—Application-Layer Multicast—is detailed on in Section 2.2.3 and builds the basis for the protocols and approaches described in this thesis.

2.2.1 Network-Layer Multicast

The first proposals and specifications defining approaches for multicast service provision in communication networks came up in the 1980s already. They target multicast integration in the network layer. Different Request for Comments (RFC)[2] by the Internet Engineering Task Force (IETF) describe mechanisms regarding addressing [56], membership management [53–55], and routing [225]. Since implementing a multicast service in the Internet's network layer requires modifications in the IP protocol [111], this form of multicast is also called *IP Multicast*. Elaborated mechanisms for intra- and inter-network support exist [57]. A survey on related topics is also given by Diot et al. [59] or by Ramalho [179].

---

[2]RFCs describe technical and organizational Internet specifications as basis for discussion and standardization.

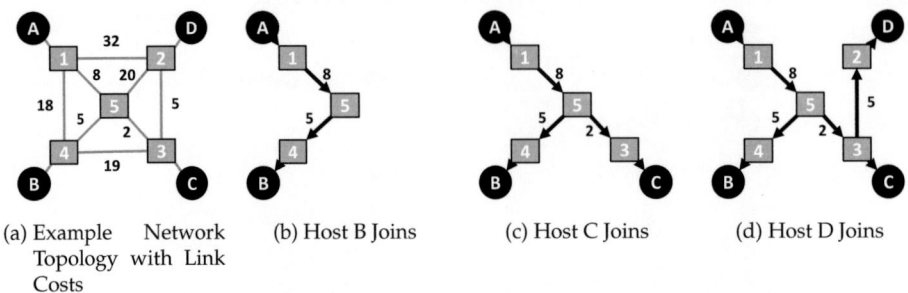

(a) Example   Network   (b) Host B Joins   (c) Host C Joins   (d) Host D Joins
    Topology with Link
    Costs

Figure 2.3 Network of Routers and Hosts with exemplary iterative DVMRP
               Shortest Path Tree Establishment (based on [97])

2.2.1.1   Addressing and Routing

IP (version 4) class A, B, and C addresses are used for point-to-point communication in the Internet and are divided into network and host parts. In
contrast, IP Multicast uses class D addresses for multicast group addressing.
The multicast addresses are in this context often used on a per-session basis [157]. For IP version 6 [52], network addresses can be marked as multicast addresses, and further aspects like e.g. scope and lifetime of the address can be specified. Joining an IP Multicast group is receiver-initiated
and is accomplished using the Internet Group Management Protocol (IGMP).
Different versions have been specified, the most commonly implemented is
IGMPv1 [55]. With IGMP, hosts in a local network can report their group
memberships to an IP Multicast-enabled network router. Afterwards, the
router starts forwarding the respective arriving multicast packets to this local network.

To route multicast data packets IP Multicast establishes dissemination trees
among the IP Multicast-enabled routers. Different protocols have been proposed which are partly derived from distance-vector or link-state unicast routing protocols [170]. Additionally, a new class of shared-tree multicast routing
protocols has been introduced for IP Multicast. Prominent distance-vector
multicast protocols are Distance Vector Multicast Routing Protocol
(DVMRP) [225] and Protocol Independent Multicast Dense Mode
(PIM-DM) [2], while e.g. Multicast Open Shortest Path First (MOSPF) [160]
is based on a link-state approach. Protocols like Protocol Independent Multicast Sparse Mode (PIM-SM) [66] and Core-based Trees (CBT) [11] follow the
shared-tree approach.

To briefly sketch a typical IP Multicast routing scenario Figure 2.3 illustrates a
small example network in which DVMRP is employed to establish a dissem-

ination tree among four hosts (A to D). The hosts are connected to a network topology of five interconnected routers (squares). The goal of DVMRP is to build a spanning tree that is optimal with respect to a given cost metric (e. g. network delay or monetary cost). Each inter-router link in Figure 2.3(a) holds a numeric value reflecting the cost metric on that link. Host A is considered the data source and hosts B to D join the multicast group one after another in Figures 2.3(b) to 2.3(d). DVMRP adds only network links resulting in minimal overall cost to the spanning tree. As a result of this greedy algorithm, a source-specific tree with minimal cost is established that interconnects the source host A with the remaining group members.

IP Multicast is highly efficient in performing multicast data dissemination since it reduces communication costs to a minimum while sustaining short data paths. Despite these benefits there is no global IP Multicast service available in today's Internet.

2.2.1.2   Deployment Issues with IP Multicast

IP Multicast has not yet found widespread commercial deployment by carriers and service providers in the Internet: Although it can be found in network domains controlled by single providers and is integrated in most routers used today, it is not available as a network service across domain bounds. Diot et al. [60] summarized the main reasons for today's unavailability of a global IP Multicast service:

- From a monetary perspective, upgrading routers to support IP Multicast forces providers to replace router hardware, often before their planned longevity.
- Additionally, multicast services require more administrative overhead compared to unicast services. These costs are hard to justify for the providers, as there is no clear billing model defined that could be applied.

Furthermore, some functional aspects were not addressed appropriately:

- Important group management aspects are not fully answered, e. g. sender/receiver authorization, group creation, and security.
- Distributed address allocation for IP Multicast groups is not solved, as is the case for network management, e. g. monitoring, debugging, and planning.
- IP Multicast requires routers to maintain per-group state (and IP Multicast addresses are hard to aggregate), increasing complexity and overhead in routers.
- Running transport protocols on top of IP Multicast induces further complexity. Accomplishing reliability and congestion control with IP Multicast is considerably harder to achieve than in unicast environments. Al-

though further mechanisms for reliability (e. g. SRM [72, 73] and RMTP [142]) and congestion control (e. g. MTCP [188] and PGMCC [189, 190]) have been proposed, they need to be well-understood before wide scale deployment [12].

2.2.2 Alternative Multicast Approaches

To bypass the lack of a globally available native multicast service, approaches that work without a native network service support (like IP Multicast) have been proposed. Compared to IP Multicast, these approaches are less efficient and provide degraded communication performance since they come with longer network paths and higher communication overhead. However, these approaches are often still suitable for many group communication scenarios. El-Sayed et al. [64] provided a survey of alternative multicast strategies. They are classified in the following.

2.2.2.1 Unicast/Multicast Reflectors

In this class hosts have access to an application-layer server (the *Reflector*) to which they send data to be distributed to a group via the available unicast service. The Reflector forwards the data to all (preconfigured) group members. Such a Reflector is usually set up manually for a limited time. In most cases there is one Reflector per group. While the approach offers full control over authorization and multicast session lifetime in the Reflector, it typically comes with a traffic concentration near the Reflector and a single point of failure. Examples are UMTP [71] and Mtunnel [167].

2.2.2.2 Permanent Tunneling

With *Permanent Tunneling*, routing tunnels (via IP-in-IP encapsulation [169]) are established between multicast-enabled networks to bridge network domains not supporting multicast natively. It differs from IP Multicast by requiring administrative privileges and manual configuration. A prominent use of Permanent Tunneling can be found in the Mbone [196], providing a network testbed for multicast communication to the scientific community. The Mbone connects different IP Multicast-enabled network sites through Permanent Tunneling. However, tunnels may be prone to performance problems (high traffic) and the approach is therefore no longer considered a good solution.

2.2.2.3 Application-Layer Multicast

Application-Layer Multicast (ALM) builds the broadest class of alternative multicast approaches. ALM protocols abstract from the physical network by establishing virtual P2P overlay networks (cf. Section 2.1) in which the hosts (peers[3]) accomplish forwarding and group management decisions. ALM protocols can be used to implement a large diversity of group communication objectives. They are described in more detail in Section 2.2.3.

2.2.2.4 Gossiping Approaches

To accomplish group communication *gossiping* strategies can be used as well. Here, hosts send group data to their direct neighbors in a virtual overlay network. In such approaches overlay structures are used that have been established or designed for a different purpose in advance in many cases. Prominent examples are protocols for gossip-based aggregation [116] or the Scribe protocol [36]. Scribe uses gossiping mechanisms on top of the structured P2P overlay Pastry [193]. To multicast data, hosts can send data packets to all their direct overlay neighbors, or to a subset. The neighbors forward the data in similar manner. Rudimentary data distribution can be accomplished with gossiping and no sophisticated (and possibly fragile) distribution overlays have to be refined. However, it is often hard to determine when a data packet has reached all hosts and therefore should no further be forwarded. Although gossiping approaches have been defined as an own class by El-Sayed et al. [64], they are strongly related to ALM protocols.

2.2.3 Application-Layer Multicast

In ALM protocols, data packet forwarding and replication as well as group management is accomplished in the participating peers' application layers. Peers establish virtual overlay networks used for data forwarding and/or control tasks. Hence, only the common unicast routing service is required from the network. ALM protocols constitute a sub-class of P2P overlay network protocols. In contrast to file sharing or distributed data storage they focus on the use case of group communication.

ALM protocols may follow different strategies and maintain diverse overlay structures which come with different properties regarding network impact and peer-perceived communication performance. Figure 2.4 illustrates the difference between network-layer multicast and ALM, showing three exemplary approaches for the latter. The figures each show the same network topology, consisting of four peers (circles) and five routers (squares). In Figure 2.4(a), the network-layer case is shown where the routers replicate the data packets in order to efficiently distribute them to the peers. Figure 2.4(b), in contrast, shows an ALM case where peer A sends the data packets to the remaining peers via three successive single unicast transmissions. Figure 2.4(c) shows a different ALM approach where the involved peers build

---

[3]The terms *host* and *peer* are used interchangeably in the remainder of this work.

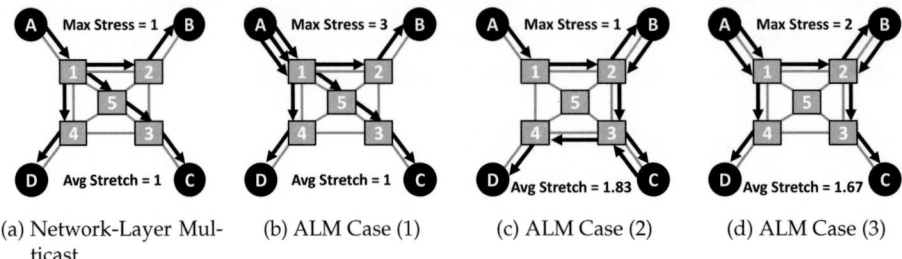

(a) Network-Layer Mul-   (b) ALM Case (1)   (c) ALM Case (2)   (d) ALM Case (3)
ticast

Figure 2.4 Exemplary Network-Layer and Application-Layer Multicast Data
Packet Distribution Strategies (based on [12])

a forwarding chain. Finally, Figure 2.4(d) illustrates an "intermediate" case.
Clearly, ALM allows to accomplish multicast communication following different strategies and approaches with different properties. To compare and
evaluate these properties a set of quality metrics for ALM protocols is described in the following.

2.2.3.1   Quality Metrics for ALM Protocols

ALM approaches typically provide degraded communication performance
compared to network-layer multicast since data packets may traverse the
same link multiple times and end-to-end overlay data paths are in most cases
longer than unicast paths in the underlay. Also, establishing and maintaining
an overlay structure is connected to additional communication overhead for
peers and comes with further implications like e. g. the time it takes to join
the overlay. Widely used ALM performance metrics [64] are:

- **Stress:** The number of identical packets traversing the same network
  link is expressed through the metric *stress*. It's minimum value is 1, being
  the case for every link with network-layer multicast since no redundant
  packet replication occurs. In Figure 2.4 the stress values are provided
  for all example cases, showing that it depends on the ALM forwarding
  strategy.

- **Stretch:** The per-peer metric *stretch* describes the ratio between the length
  of an overlay path from the data source to a specific peer and the respective direct unicast path length. It therefore expresses the penalty regarding path lengths arising from using ALM instead of network-layer
  multicast.

- **Goodput:** An important metric is *goodput*, measuring which fraction of
  disseminated multicast packets is successfully received by a specific peer

in the overlay. In case of overlay refinement, recovery after errors, or peer fluctuations, data packets can be lost during the overlay-based forwarding process.

- **Join delay:** Peers have to become part of the overlay structure before they can start receiving multicast data. In order to do so, they often have to contact a so-called *Rendezvous Point (RP)* (being either a dedicated server or a peer) which provides information about how to enter the overlay. Furthermore, becoming part of the overlay often requires further protocol communication, like e. g. bargaining roles or gaining information about other peers to contact. All these factors increase the time it takes to enter an overlay multicast structure. Depending on the application case, this metric (*join delay*) can be important to evaluate the applicability of an ALM protocol for a specific group communication scenario.

- **Data Dissemination Delay:** Another common and relevant metric is the *dissemination delay* of the data packets to be multicasted in the overlay. It is subjective for every peer and is highly related to *stretch*, as it is defined as the delay any data packet experiences between being sent by a source peer and being received by a receiver peer. In general, this metric should be as low as possible or below a given delay bound.

- **Control Overhead:** Any ALM-based protocol inherently induces further communication overhead through the necessity of establishing and maintaining the overlay structure. As this implies further communication, it will increase the protocol's bandwidth consumption. The consideration of this additional consumption (referred to as *control overhead*) is of particular interest in order to use it as a cost metric. Furthermore, this bandwidth consumption will also affect other network-based services being concurrently used on the same end-system.

The first ALM protocols came up in the early 2000s and since then a multitude of protocols has been proposed [97]. They follow very different optimization goals and overlay building strategies. It is impossible to cover the myriad of proposed ALM protocols in its entirety in this chapter. Instead, a classification of ALM protocols is given in the following to provide an overview on the field and the major differences between the approaches. Furthermore, representative ALM protocols are described in the respective chapters of this thesis as far as they are related to the chapters' topics.

2.2.3.2 Classification of ALM Protocols

Hosseini et al. [97] proposed a set of important categories to consider for the classification on ALM protocols, partly derived from previous work by Diot et al. [60]. The categories can help to classify ALM protocols with regard to different group communication aspects:

- **Application Domain:** A first category to classify ALM protocols results from considering the application case. This includes the anticipated number of users, the data types to send and the optimization metrics. In [60] four representative classes of ALM application domains have been described, being *audio/video streaming* (usually sending multimedia data from one source peer to a possibly high number of receiver peers), *audio/video conferencing* (small to medium groups communicating via multipeer), *generic multicast* (supporting a variety of less constrained ALM cases), and *reliable data broadcast* (distribution of large files). These application domains have different requirements regarding data dissemination delays, bandwidth, and reliability, for instance.

- **Deployment Level:** Although ALM approaches typically target end-systems, protocols exist that focus on different deployment levels: Instead of limiting protocols to run on end-system peers exclusively (often referred to as *end-system ALM*), also dedicated systems in the network can be used to support an ALM service. With *proxy-based ALM*, proxy servers (*proxies*) are deployed in the Internet that self-organize into an own overlay structure and typically provide a generic ALM service. Peers send the data to be distributed to one of the proxies. Afterwards, the proxy distributes the data via the inter-proxy overlay, reaching all other peers being connected to one of the proxies. In proxy-based ALM, the available service bandwidth is—with help of the proxies—in most cases higher (compared to end-system ALM), and protocol complexity on end-systems can be reduced. On the other hand, proxies have to be deployed in advance and maintained, resulting in additional costs. Furthermore, proxy-based ALM solutions are less adaptable and in most cases less optimized compared to specialized end-system-based protocols [97]. Figure 2.5(a) shows an example for proxy-based ALM with two proxies (indicated through stars) being deployed in the network. Here, peer A sends data to the proxy $P1$ which forwards it to peer B and proxy $P2$. Finally, $P2$ passes the data to peers C and D.

- **Group Management:** To manage groups, different approaches are possible. Group management involves questions regarding joining and leaving groups or policies concerning data sending, for instance. Peers have to be able to find existing groups or multicast data sources. This can be accomplished by contacting a dedicated Rendezvous Point or by performing other mechanisms like e. g. flooding on an existing P2P overlay substrate. Furthermore, it has to be clarified whether sending data to a group is allowed even for non-group members, and whether participating peers are assumed to be rather transient and anonymous, or if they are assumed to be static and known.

- **Structure:** The question how peers are arranged in a group communication session has high influence on the protocol performance and behavior. It comprises decisions about how peers are arranged in the overlay structure, whether existing IP Multicast islands should be integrated, if and how the overlay should be refined, and how refinement mechanisms should behave, for instance. As has been pointed out by Banerjee et al. [12], ALM protocols in many cases employ two different topologies: The *control topology* and the *data topology*. The control topology helps maintaining and refining the overlay. It is often implemented as a richly connected graph (a so-called *mesh*). The data topology, in contrast, is used for the actual group data dissemination. ALM protocols can be differentiated by how they establish these topologies. Protocols first building the control topology are referred to as *mesh-first* approaches, while those establishing a data dissemination structure first (and refining on this structure) are called *tree-first* approaches. A third category is defined for protocols building a control topology and using it directly for data dissemination as well (referred to as *implicit* approaches). In mesh-first protocols, the control topology is established at the beginning and the data dissemination tree is embedded into the mesh. An example mesh structure with an embedded shared (and therefore bidirectional) tree is shown in Figure 2.5(b). Thus, the quality of the tree depends on the quality of the mesh, while the advantage lies in a higher robustness.

Tree-first approaches offer higher control over the tree, lower control overhead, and in most cases a less complex protocol design [97]. A simple example tree is shown in Figure 2.5(c). Tan et al. provided a performance comparison of tree-based protocols in [215]. Finally, Figure 2.5(d) gives an example for an implicit ALM approach where a synthetic coordinate space is used and partitioned into areas. Each peer is responsible for one area, and a peer sending data to the group (the black circle in the figure) always sends the data to all neighboring areas. The neighbor peers forward the data to their neighboring areas until all peers received the data. This example is very similar to the ALM protocol CAN Multicast [183], working on top of the structured P2P protocol CAN [180].

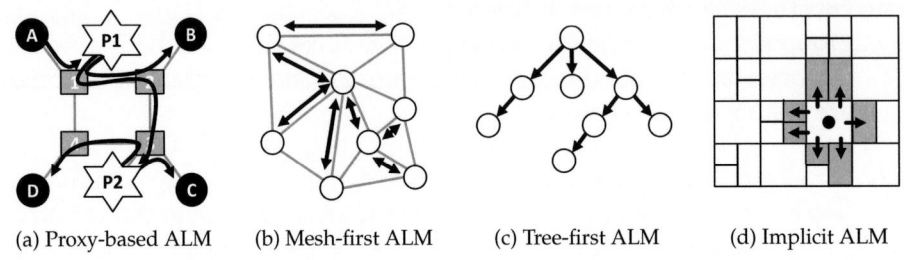

(a) Proxy-based ALM   (b) Mesh-first ALM   (c) Tree-first ALM   (d) Implicit ALM

Figure 2.5 Different Deployment Levels and ALM Structure Examples

- **Routing Mechanism:** How data is disseminated in the overlay structure is determined by the routing mechanism. The strategy behind the dissemination structure typically involves a (heuristic) solution to a graph theory problem [97]. The problem is to establish a structure connecting all participating peers that concurrently satisfies a given set of requirements, like e. g. delay minimization or degree constraints. Typical routing mechanisms are building a *Shortest Path Tree (SPT)* [47] (a shortest path dissemination tree with a single source peer) or establishing a *Minimum Spanning Tree (MST)* [47] (a single tree spanning all peers that can also be used for multipeer communication). Further routing mechanisms result from the implicit approaches where the routing is determined by the control topology. Also, approaches exist where given P2P topologies are enhanced by group communication capabilities by defining forwarding strategies on top of the topologies. These approaches have the advantage of using a structure that is already established, saving control overhead. However, they are less efficient compared to specialized solutions. A prominent example for enhancing existing P2P structures by group communication is Scribe [36], for instance.

2.3   Mobile Communications

Since several years the sector of mobile computing experiences rapid growth, as has already been pointed out in Chapter 1. Prominent communication technologies used in today's mobile computing are also considered in this thesis in the context of ALM. They can be divided into cellular-based wide area technologies and local area wireless technologies.

2.3.1   Cellular Wide Area Communication

For the provision of today's cellular wide area mobile communications, the spatial area to be supported is divided into *cells*, each cell attached to a specific cell antenna (Base Transceiver Station, BTS). Mobile user devices (Mobile Station, MS) connect to the BTS attached to the cell they currently reside in, and switching between cells (e. g. in case of mobility) is inherently supported by the system. Several cellular-based communication networks and standards exist and there are differences between distinct countries and continents. However, most cellular systems work in similar manner and the differences do not affect the general aspects of this work. Therefore, in the following the prominent cellular architectures GSM and UMTS are described, while alternative approaches like e. g. CDMA2000 or IS-136 are not covered.

2.3.1.1   GSM

The basis for highly established cellular systems deployed today has been *GSM (Global System for Mobile Communications)*. GSM (also referred to as *2G*) was the first fully digital mobile technology and the successor of the era of analogue mobile communications (*1G*). Figure 2.6(a) gives an overview on the GSM architecture[4]. A GSM system comprises a set of *Base Station Subsystems (BSS)*, each BSS managing a set of cells. In a BSS, a single *Base Station Controller (BSC)* administrates the different cells (represented by the BTSs). A BSC manages frequency reservations, handovers in a single BSS, and paging of MSs (searching for user end-devices) [197], for instance. A set of BSCs is managed by a *Mobile Services Switching Center (MSC)*, respectively. MSCs take the task of switching between BSCs and to other MSCs and thus can be seen as the backbone of a GSM system. Furthermore, *Gateway MSCs (GMSC)* accomplish the connection to other (fixed line network) communication systems like e. g. ISDN (Integrated Services Digital Network).

Besides the described GSM network components, the architecture also comprises several databases and maintenance components. The *Home Location Register (HLR)* holds information about all GSM users of a certain provider (e. g. telephone number or current location of a device) and also supports (itemized) billing, for instance. The *Visitor Location Register (VLR)* holds information for users attached to a specific MSC. As soon as a user device is attached to a MSC, the VLR copies the relevant information from the HLR. The *Authentication Center (AuC)* manages security aspects like encryption. Finally, the *Equipment Identity Register (EIR)* maintains a database comprising information about all end-user-devices of a specific provider. It can be used to blacklist stolen devices, for instance.

While GSM was originally based on circuit switching, with further development and extensions voice and data services became packet switched: Packet switching in mobile systems was first introduced with *GPRS (General Packet Radio Service)* as an enhancement to the GSM architecture. The extensions

---

[4]Figure 2.6 is limited to the most important parts of the architecture. More details can be found in [197].

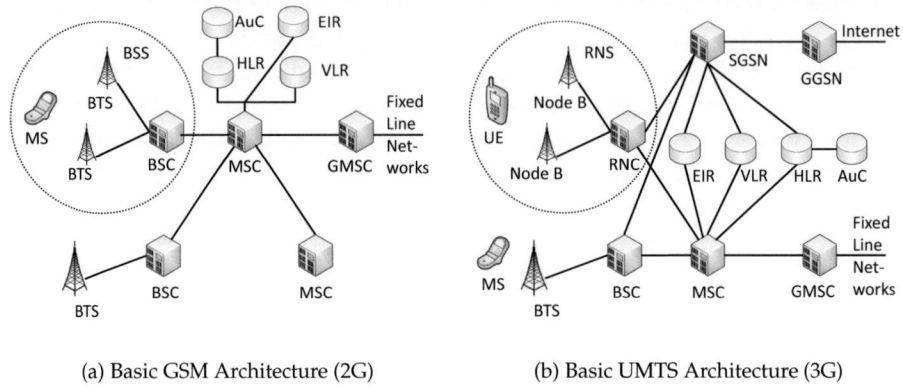

(a) Basic GSM Architecture (2G)   (b) Basic UMTS Architecture (3G)

Figure 2.6   GSM and UMTS Mobile Network Architectures

GPRS and HSCSD were replaced by *EDGE (Enhanced Data Rates for GSM Evolution, 2.75G)*, offering even higher data rates ($\approx$ 220 kbit/s) with comparably low startup costs for the providers [197]. EDGE was already a first step towards the next generation of mobile networks, UMTS.

2.3.1.2   UMTS

UMTS (Universal Mobile Telecommunications System) arose from the GSM architecture as a result of the incremental enhancements and is referred to as *3G* mobile communication networks. In contrast to the original idea behind GSM (voice communication) it clearly targets data services, reflected by considerably higher achievable data rates (2 mbit/s in theory, around 384 kbit/s in practice). Figure 2.6(b) shows the basic UMTS architecture. It comprises the components already used in GSM but also later enhancements related to packet switched communication: The *Gateway GPRS Support Node (GGSN)* provides connection to the Internet (similar to the GMSC regarding fixed line networks). The *Serving GPRS Support Node (SGSN)* works similar to the MSC in the packet switched network part. For packet switched services, the BSS is in UMTS replaced by a *Radio Network Subsystem (RNS)*. In a RNS the *Radio Network Controller (RNC)* corresponds to the BSC in a BSS. It manages a set of BTS antennas to which users are connected via their *User Equipments (UE)* (similar to the MS in GSM). The GGSN serves as an interface between a UE and the Internet. After the launch of UMTS data rate extensions for the downstream have been applied (*High Speed Downlink Packet Access, HSDPA*), shortly before also the upstream data rates were increased (*High Speed Uplink Packet Access, HSUPA*). Both extensions together are also known under the term *HSPA (3.5G)*. HSPA also allows for much smaller data dissemination de-

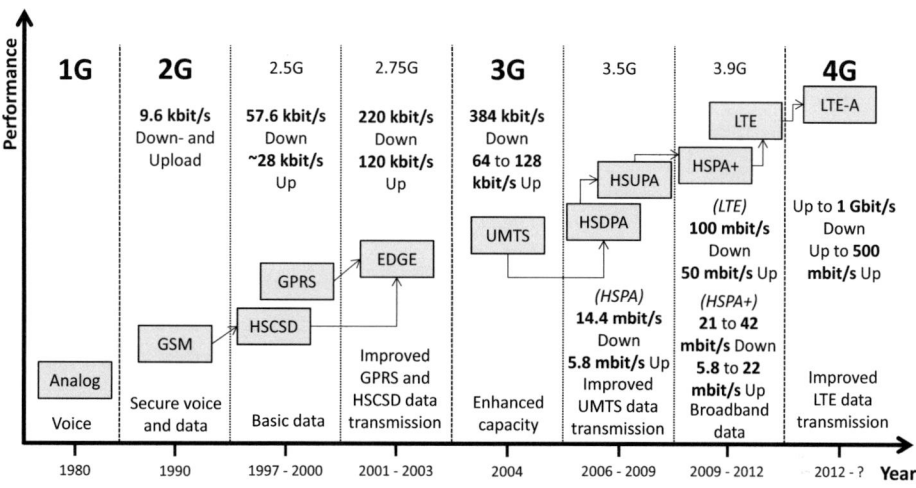

Figure 2.7 Cellular Mobile Technology Evolution (based on [17])

lays in UMTS networks (around 100 ms in contrast to approximately 300 ms without HSPA), reached through more efficient modulation techniques, reorganization of the packet switching, and optimized transmission power adaptation in a UMTS cell [197].

While HSPA is deployed in a high fraction of UMTS networks already, the next evolutionary step takes place by the time of writing this thesis. HSPA data rates are increased through an extension called HSPA+, and with *Long Term Evolution (LTE)* a different mobile technology is introduced, offering even higher communication performance (up to 100 mbit/s). Soon, the next step will be deployed with *LTE Advanced (LTE-A)*, also referred to as *4G* mobile networks. Figure 2.7 gives an overview on how cellular access technology has evolved, especially regarding the available access bandwidth.

In cellular networks the shared medium is accessed by end-systems using different multiplex techniques: GSM uses *SDMA (Space Devision Multiple Access)*, *FDMA (Frequency Devision Multiple Access)*, and *TDMA (Time Devision Multiple Access)*. SDMA is implemented by the cells, while FDMA and TDMA are jointly used to control the medium access among users. The frequency spectrum is divided into a set of channels which are assigned to the different end-systems. In UMTS, FDMA is used together with SDMA and *CDMA (Code Devision Multiple Access)*. Here, parts of the frequency spectrum are assigned to upstream and downstream direction, respectively. In both directions, all active end-systems send or receive data at the same time, using different codes. The codes allow signals to overlap and be decoded in the receiver stations.

In the context of this thesis cellular-based mobile access networks are considered as a wide-area Internet access technology, being always available. Part of the presented ALM protocols is assumed to be used on wirelessly connected end-systems which are equipped with 3G network devices. The cellular networks are used and analyzed especially with focus on the described capacity bottlenecks arising from heavy usage.

2.3.2   Wireless Local Area Communication

Mobile wireless local area technologies differ from wide area technologies to the effect that they offer higher flexibility and easier deployment at the cost of a smaller service coverage area. Wireless local area networks can be deployed by private persons, companies, or even governments to provide mobile data services to households, public places, or office buildings, for instance. Hence, inflexible cable installation can be avoided. Furthermore, wireless local area networks can also be employed without any dedicated (predeployed) support by connecting end-devices via *ad-hoc* communication. Different standards for wireless local communication have been developed, partly targeting different application domains. Bluetooth, for instance, focuses the near environment of users (up to several meters, often referred to as *Personal Area Networks, PAN*), while the IEEE 802.11 standards family is used to cover larger areas (approximately up to 100 m), also offering higher data rates compared to Bluetooth. Other standards have been proposed but have either not found equal importance or are not relevant to this work. Almost every mobile communication device sold today is equipped with IEEE 802.11 support and IEEE 802.11 networks are deployed all over the world, accordingly. Because this technology is also considered in parts of this thesis, the standard is briefly described in the following.

2.3.2.1   IEEE 802.11 (WiFi)

IEEE 802.11 [70]—often also called *WiFi*—belongs to the family of 802.x-standards. One main goal was providing a specification that allows operation anywhere in the world. Therefore, the initial WiFi standard operates in the license-free ISM frequency band around 2,4 GHz. Later enhancements and standards based on IEEE 802.11 also work in the license-free frequency band around 5 GHz.

WiFi networks can be used in two different operation modes, being *infrastructure-based* and *ad-hoc*. Figure 2.8(a) shows an exemplary infrastructure WiFi network architecture and its parts as defined in the standard. Mobile devices are connected wirelessly to Access Points (AP). The set of mobile devices attached to the same AP is called *Basic Service Set (BSS)* (including the AP). Different BSSs can be interconnected via a *Distribution System (DS)* which is

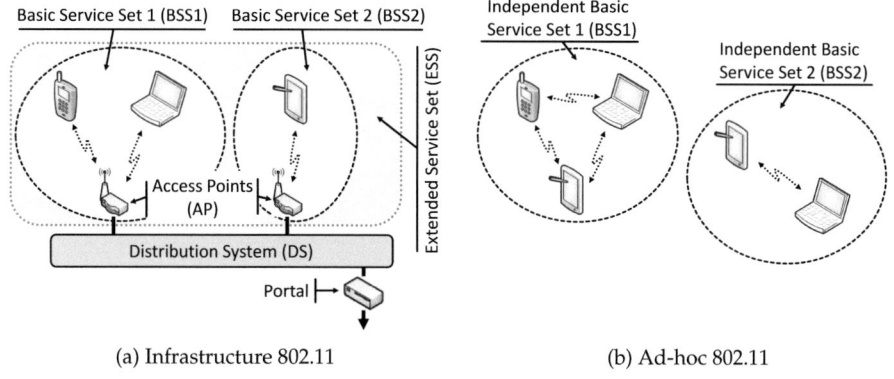

(a) Infrastructure 802.11   (b) Ad-hoc 802.11

Figure 2.8 IEEE 802.11 Wireless Local Area Network Operation Modes

not specified further in the original standard but provides bridging function-ality between the BSSs [197]. A set of BSSs being interconnected this way is called *Extended Service Set (ESS)*. Mobile devices may freely choose the AP to connect to and the APs support roaming between them. Furthermore, APs provide synchronization among all mobile devices in a BSS, power manage-ment functionality, and support for the medium access control, for instance. Finally, the *Portal* is defined as a rather logical than physical component, al-lowing interconnection to other networks (like e.g. fixed line local area net-works or the Internet). The Portal is commonly integrated in the AP directly.

Besides infrastructure-based local area networks, WiFi also allows to establish spontaneous wireless networks via ad-hoc WiFi. Here, a set of mobile devices residing in mutual wireless reachability and operating at the same frequency builds a so-called *Independent Service Set (IBSS)*, the term IBSS expressing the independence of an AP. Different ad-hoc IBSSs may overlap if they use differ-ent frequencies—otherwise they have to be spatially separated. Figure 2.8(b) shows two example IBSSs, each comprising a set of mobile devices commu-nicating directly.

To manage the access of the shared wireless medium among the mobile de-vices WiFi uses a mechanism called *Carrier Sense Multiple Access with Collision Avoidance (CSMA/CA)*. Because collisions on the medium (in case two or more mobile hosts send data at the same time) cannot be detected at the sender in semi-broadcast mediums, the intention of CSMA/CA is to decrease the prob-ability of collisions as far as possible. Three different mechanisms are defined for WiFi, being plain CSMA/CA, CSMA/CA with RTS/CTS, and Point Co-ordination Function (PCF). Only the first is mandatory for concrete WiFi im-plementations, the other two are optional. The RTS/CTS extension helps to cope with special situations like e. g. two mobile devices not hearing each other directly but intending to send data at the same time, possibly resulting in collisions (*Hidden Terminal Problem*). The PCF implements a centralized media access coordination and can only be used in infrastructure-based WiFi. In case a collision occurs and is detected during sending a data packet, the involved hosts choose a random backoff from a given backoff window before retransmitting the data with CSMA/CA. The backoff window is exponentially increased with each consecutive collision to further reduce collision probability.

Data in WiFi domains can either be sent by a host via unicast or broadcast. In infrastructure-based WiFis all data packets are first sent to the AP and are then forwarded to the destination host by the AP. Unicast transmissions are acknowledged by a dedicated mechanism and therefore provide reliability to some extent (though the number of retransmission attempts is limited), while broadcast transmissions remain unacknowledged. In the latter case, a host sends a data packet to be broadcasted in a WiFi domain to the AP via acknowledged unicast. Afterwards, the AP broadcasts the data packet to the WiFi domain. Table 2.1 provides an overview on important norms of the IEEE 802.11 family. It gives an impression how the standard developed and where it may be heading. WiFi networks experience rapid deployment all over the world, in private households as well as in public places and companies. They are configurable to be freely accessible or require credentials to join. Often, WiFi networks also provide Internet access through a gateway host (in infrastructure mode), while ad-hoc domains mostly provide local area wireless communication. In the context of this thesis WiFi networks are considered as network domains that can be integrated in ALM data dissemination in order to increase communication efficiency. In the different ALM protocols presented infrastructure-mode as well as ad-hoc WiFi communication is used. The focus is thereby put to application-level mechanisms for finding mutual WiFi reachabilities among peers and integrating them in the protocols.

Norm	Year	Frequency	Data Rates	Comment
802.11	1997	2.4–2.485 GHz	1/2 MBit/s	Original Standard
802.11a	1999	5 GHz	54 MBit/s	Extends Physical Layer
802.11b	1999	2.4–2.485 GHz	11 MBit/s	Incr. Rates in Lower Band
802.11g	2003	2.4–2.485 GHz	54 MBit/s	Succ. of 802.11b
802.11n	2009	2.4–2.485 GHz, 5 GHz	600 MBit/s	Multiple Antennas
802.11p	planned	5.85–5.925 GHz	27 MBit/s	Car-to-Car Comm.
802.11ac	planned	planned < 6 GHz	1 GBit/s	Succ. of 802.11n

Table 2.1 Selection from the IEEE 802.11 Norm Family

3. A Distributed Service Overlay Framework

For the provision of ALM-based group communication services different properties regarding the network and the involved end-systems are commonly assumed in many related proposals. This involves the establishment of direct underlay connections between arbitrary peers, given the peers are able to access the Internet. However, this assumption can not always be taken for granted. Developing distributed services for today's Internet is often complex and requires the consideration of many pitfalls and challenges. For instance, different protocol versions in different network domains may constrain direct connectivity, as well as the prevalent use of NAT-boxes. Furthermore, peer mobility may lead to link outages and the need to reestablish connections manually.

In this chapter a framework to support the development and deployment of overlay-based services is presented. It is designed to abstract from many underlay challenges and provide an easy-to-use interface for distributed services and applications. It's applicability is not limited to specific use cases, and various P2P protocols can be implemented with the architecture. In the context of this thesis it can especially be used to support the implementation of the presented ALM protocols and deploy them to heterogeneous network environments. The framework has been developed with colleagues in the context of the *Spontaneous Virtual Networks (SpoVNet)* project [203]. The general concepts of the framework are published in [26, 27, 226].

This chapter is structured as follows: In Section 3.1 the challenges for design and provision of Internet-wide distributed overlay-based communication services are pointed out. Section 3.2 describes related approaches in the field of overlay-based service frameworks. In Section 3.3 the SpoVNet framework's architecture is presented, focusing on the important parts and different abstraction layers. Furthermore, the implementation of the ALM protocols presented in this work in the SpoVNet architecture is described and how the protocols can benefit from the framework's features. As an example, a tree-based ALM data dissemination case is described and how the connected development complexity can considerably be decreased by the use of the SpoVNet architecture. Finally, in Section 3.4 a prototype implementation of the framework is described, together with demonstrators that have been presented at major international conferences. Section 3.5 concludes the chapter.

3.1   Distributed Service Provision in Today's Internet

P2P overlay systems have to be able to establish connections among the peers in order to work properly. In ALM dissemination structures, for instance, peers must be enabled to establish connections to arbitrary peers in the overlay in order to refine the dissemination structure with respect to the optimization goals. Although most existing P2P systems inherently require this possibility, different technologies, network constellations, and mechanisms used in today's Internet often hamper direct connectivity. Obstacles for the development of distributed services in the Internet are:

- **Middleboxes:** End-systems can be connected via different access networks and can potentially be located behind so-called NAT (Network Address Translation [63]) gateways, or firewalls. NAT gateways are common network components enabling to use single globally unique IP addresses as representatives for a range of local IP addresses. They can be found mainly in private home access networks. They often allow to initiate connections only from behind the NAT gateway to the outside. Likewise, firewalls hinder direct connections through filtering and constrained connectivity.

- **Protocol Heterogeneity:** With different protocol versions available (possibly facing a transition phase like e. g. in case of IPv4/IPv6) it can not be guaranteed that all peers participating in a distributed service use the same protocol versions, even if they communicate at the same Internet communication layer (cf. Figure 2.2). This is e. g. the case if peers are connected to different network domains which use different protocol versions to communicate.

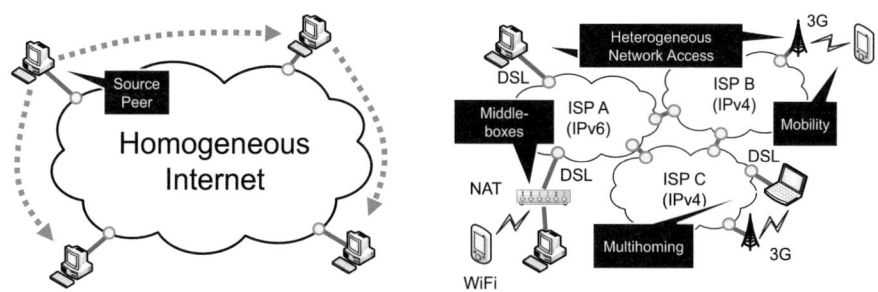

(a) Simplistic Network View from Overlay Devel- (b) Network View with Complexity Considera-
oper's Perspective   tions

Figure 3.1 Simplistic Network View versus Network Complexity Consideration for P2P-based Services (based on [27])

- **Different Communication Layers:** While protocol heterogeneity on the
  same communication layer can be difficult (e. g. IPv4/IPv6), also cases
  where layers in the communication stack are completely omitted on a
  peer can occur. One example is a peer being connected via Bluetooth
  RFCOMM [81], but using no network protocol at all to communicate.
  Such peers do not have the possibility to access the Internet without further mechanisms.

- **User Mobility:** The independence of wired connections enables users
  to change their locations (and therefore also their wireless connections)
  during an ongoing overlay communication session. As a result, devices
  can change their available access networks, loose communication possibilities in one moment, and gain new possibilities in another. The
  IP protocol does not provide transparent (transport connection preserving) mobility support without dedicated systems that must be deployed
  and maintained. Thus, distributed mobility support without central systems' support is challenging.

- **Multihoming:** Peers may have the possibility to connect to the Internet
  via more than one access network or communication device at the same
  time (*multihoming*). In such cases it has to be decided which access network or device to use for overlay communication, especially if different
  connections show different network characteristics (e. g. bandwidth or
  network latency).

Figure 3.1 provides different views on end-system-based services in the Internet from a service developer's point of view regarding the described aspects.

Figure 3.1(a) shows the simplistic network view from an overlay developer's perspective, assuming a homogeneous Internet. An exemplary ALM source peer disseminates data to a set of receivers using direct overlay connections. Figure 3.1(b), in contrast, differentiates the view by considering the different obstacles. Designing and developing distributed services requires the consideration of these issues. Furthermore, overlay developers have to consider them in every single overlay protocol to be implemented. In the following, requirements regarding a framework for distributed service development and deployment are derived from these challenges.

3.1.1   Functional Requirements

To provide a framework that supports the development of distributed overlay-based services and applications, the described obstacles have to be considered and hidden from the overlay developers. Furthermore, an easy-to-use interface has to be integrated to access the framework's functionality. The following functional requirements can be derived:

- **End-to-end Connectivity:** Peers have to be enabled to establish connections to other peers in the overlay, regardless of their access network technology, their used protocols, and their location.

- **Mobility Support:** The mobility of peers must not lead to interrupted connectivity between overlay peers. Connectivity has to be maintained transparently even in face of changing network access, if possible.

- **Multihoming Support:** The framework should be able to decide which access network to use for connectivity in case a peer has more than one possibility to access the overlay. For this decision service requirements provided by the application should be considered in order to choose the most appropriate connection. Furthermore, robustness should be increased by switching to available access network connections in case the formerly selected fails.

- **Service Quality Awareness:** The framework should maintain and handle connections between peers transparently to the service overlay. Nevertheless, overlay service developers benefit from connection awareness: Monitoring quality metrics like link latency or available bandwidth aids in establishing efficient service overlay structures, like e. g. ALM data dissemination structures. The framework has to provide generic mechanisms to obtain such information to service overlay developers.

3.1.2 Non-Functional Requirements

Besides functional requirements, also non-functional requirements should be provided by the framework in order to enable efficient and easy overlay service development:

- **Self-Configuration and Self-Maintenance:** No manual configuration or maintenance should be necessary when using the framework. This requirement follows the goal that service overlays should be completely self-organizing. The framework to be used should not require further manual actions, accordingly.

- **Scalability:** The framework should not constrain the number of participating peers in the service overlay. Therefore, scalability is an important non-functional requirement.

- **Usability:** The framework's benefit of abstraction should not require complicated usage. Rather, the framework should provide an easy-to-use yet powerful interface to access its functionality.

- **Extensibility:** The framework should allow the development of different overlay services, i. e. it should not be limited to multicast service development, for instance. Furthermore, the communication protocol selection process should be extensible, e. g. by allowing for the integration of new and upcoming protocols.

In the next section existing approaches for supporting overlay-based service development are described. Subsequently, a framework for the development and provision of distributed overlay-based services is presented.

3.2 Related Work

Coping with the described network difficulties can be a complex task. However, using service overlays to provide the development and deployment of new network services has been assumed a promising approach in recent years. The benefits of such approaches with respect to Internet Service Provider (ISP) independence, flexibility, and application complexity have been pointed out by Dave Clark [42], or Waldhorst et al. [227], for instance.

The requirements for distributed service development and deployment described in Section 3.1 have been partly assumed in various existing service overlay framework approaches. The views of these approaches differ: While e. g. JXTA [80] arose from a software development perspective, prominent other proposals have been developed in research projects (e. g. Hyper-Cast [139, 140], MACEDON [191], Overlay Weaver [199], FreePastry [76],

SATO [151, 206], or UIA [75]). The non-functional requirements described in Section 3.1.2 are provided in these works as they inherently avoid manual configuration and are scalable. Furthermore, their features are easily accessible and they abstract from the underlay network. SATO hides transport complexity by providing a dedicated *Ambient Service Interface*. Hypercast provides *Overlay Sockets*, enabling to accomplish neighbor discovery and overlay refinement while abstracting from network details. Overlay Weaver implements an interface similar to the Common API for Key-Based Routing (KBR) that has been proposed by Dabek et al. [50]. It enables the persistent addressing of peers by the use of unique identifiers. JXTA inter-connects peers by so-called *Pipes* and organizes them in logical groups.

The proposed approaches are extensible in different granularities: FreePastry supports the development of multicast structures relying on the basic connectivity the underlying overlay provides, based on Scribe [36]. Hypercast supports to add new overlay sockets in order to construct new overlay structures. In MACEDON, finite state machines are used to specify overlay protocols. Afterwards, they are automatically translated into running code. The KBR interface in Overlay Weaver allows to transparently exchange the underlying routing protocol, while basic mechanisms such as e. g. connection management are reused.

Regarding the functional requirements pointed out in Section 3.1.1, the existing proposals are limited to single aspects or a subset. End-to-end connectivity is provided, but is based on different assumptions concerning the underlay network: FreePastry provides NAT-traversal (allowing to establish connections in face of middleboxes). However, it assumes all devices to be located in a homogeneous (IPv4) network and does not consider heterogeneous protocols. The same applies to MACEDON and Overlay Weaver, as these approaches establish overlay connections based on TCP and UPD sockets and hence assume homogeneous network layer protocols. SATO supports heterogeneous protocols in the network layer, given it is implemented on top of the *NodeID Architecture* [7]. Likewise, Hypercast, UIA, and JXTA provide support for heterogeneous protocols. However, messages are always forwarded along the overlay, even if shorter underlay connections exist.

Peer mobility is supported in all related work approaches through the use of fixed unique identifiers in the overlay. They are mapped to potentially changing network addresses. Nevertheless, after a peer device has moved overlay connections are not maintained transparently but have to be reestablished explicitly. Multihoming is supported in most proposals by enabling to use either multiple access networks or multiple interfaces to a single access network. However, the transparent selection of an interface with respect to given service requirements of the service overlay is not considered (although SATO incorporates cross-layer information for access links).

Further existing overlay-based proposals that solve part of the described requirements are the Host Identity Protocol (HIP) [159], the Internet Indirection Infrastructure i^3 [209], and ROAM [244], the latter building on i^3. HIP integrates an ID/Locator split (differentiating between identifier and locator for a peer in order to support changing network addresses) and uses cryptographic identifiers. However, it depends on external mechanisms like e. g. DNS or a globally available DHT. i^3 and ROAM use peers inside an overlay structure to provide indirect data forwarding, seamless mobility support, and robustness. However, they do not cope with heterogeneity in the network layer.

None of the described approaches supports all functional and non-functional requirements that have been pointed out in Section 3.1. Maintaining direct connectivity among peers while transparently supporting mobility and multihoming are eligible features of a service overlay framework. They reduce the complexity in the development of distributed ALM protocols as those presented in later parts of this thesis. In the next section a service overlay framework for the easy development and deployment of overlay-based services is presented that fills this gap.

3.3 The SpoVNet Architecture

The SpoVNet architecture has been developed in the *Spontaneous Virtual Networks (SpoVNet)* project [226]. With the SpoVNet architecture, overlay networks can be established spontaneously in a per-application context.

3.3.1 Architecture Overview and SpoVNet Terms

Each overlay network established with the SpoVNet architecture is called *SpoVNet instance*. Two different application contexts (like e. g. two distributed game instances) result in two different SpoVNet instances. An end-system running the SpoVNet architecture is referred to as a *SpoVNet device*. SpoVNet devices can be PCs, laptops, smartphones, or tablets, for instance. A communication end-point within a SpoVNet instance is called a *SpoVNet node*. On a single SpoVNet device more than one SpoVNet node can run at the same time. SpoVNet nodes running at the same device can either be part of the same or different SpoVNet instances. The relations between the different parts are also shown in Figure 3.2. Here, four SpoVNet devices participate in two SpoVNet instances. Two of them run two SpoVNet nodes with one in each instance, respectively. The upper right SpoVNet device runs two nodes inside the same instance.

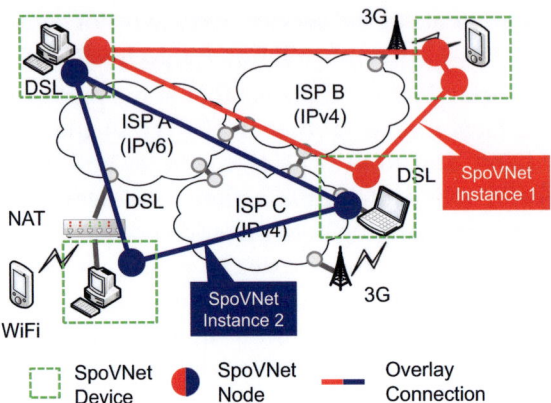

Figure 3.2   Relations between SpoVNet Instance, Node, and Device

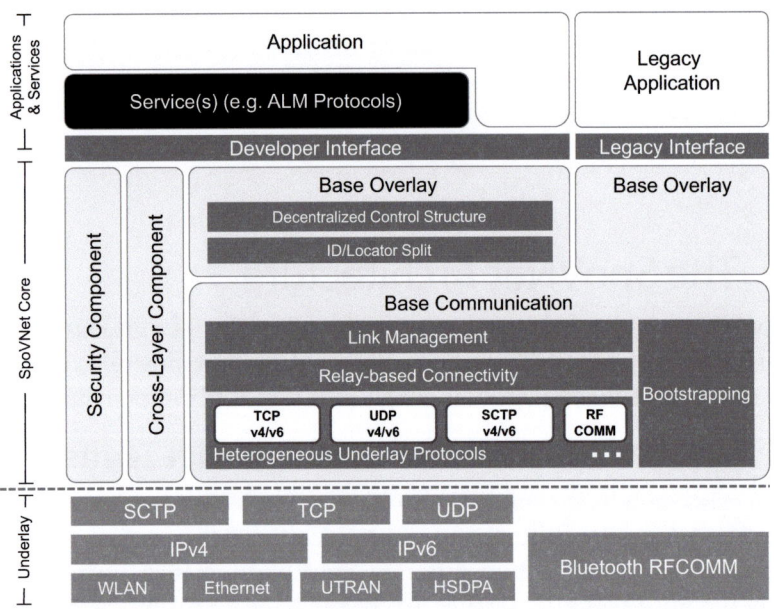

Figure 3.3   Overview of the SpoVNet Architecture (based on [27])

Figure 3.3 provides a schematic view of the SpoVNet architecture. The architecture resides in the application layer of the Internet model (cf. Figure 2.2(b)) and is roughly divided into the *Applications and Services* part (located above the interfaces) and the *SpoVNet Core* part, comprising *Base Overlay*, *Base Communication*, *Cross-layer Component*, and *Security Component*. In the following, the architecture's parts are described as well as how they work together to provide a framework for the development and deployment of overlay-based services.

3.3.2   Services and Applications

The SpoVNet architecture is either accessed by distributed applications (e. g. games, chat applications, or end-to-end file exchange) directly or by "higher" communication services that can be used by applications. Such services, called *SpoVNet services*, provide communication functionality like e. g. group communication, relieving applications from the need to implement the respective functionality. In a SpoVNet instance two layers reside above the framework's interface layer, one comprising the application and one comprising the SpoVNet services (the latter being highlighted as a black box in Figure 3.3). While there is exactly one application running in a SpoVNet instance per definition it can make use of an arbitrary number of SpoVNet services. Examples for services implemented in the SpoVNet architecture's service layer are the ALM protocols presented in this thesis. They provide multicast functionality to the application—e. g. a single-source video streaming application as described in Chapters 5 and 6—while relying on the lower SpoVNet functionality, accessible through the Developer Interface (described in Section 3.3.3).

An application does not necessarily need to use a SpoVNet service to work properly in the SpoVNet architecture (even SpoVNet-agnostic applications can be used as described below). SpoVNet services are freely designable and provide higher communication services, although the focus is put on group communication in this thesis. For example, an event notification service [126] has been developed in the SpoVNet architecture.

3.3.3   Interfaces

The development of applications using the SpoVNet architecture requires implementation against the *Developer Interface* and the SpoVNet services to be used. New applications have to be developed with consideration of the interface and the available SpoVNet services, while existing applications have to be modified in order to work with the SpoVNet architecture. To enable existing applications to use the architecture and benefit from the underlay abstraction without the need to modify them, a dedicated *Legacy Interface* has been integrated. Furthermore, also SpoVNet services (and therefore the ALM protocols presented in this work) have to be implemented against the Developer Interface in order to benefit from the framework's underlay abstraction. Both Developer Interface and Legacy Interface are described in the following.

Developer Interface

The Developer Interface offers access to the full functionality of the SpoVNet architecture and can be used by any application that has been developed against it. Table 3.1 gives an overview of its functions and callbacks. It is divided into two sub-interfaces, a *node-specific* interface and a *communication-specific* interface. The node-specific interface provides functionality for creating and joining SpoVNet instances as well as a set of callback functions to receive notifications for important events.

	Function	Description
Node-specific	`initiate`	Create an application-instance-specific SpoVNet
	`join`	Find other nodes in this SpoVNet instance and join
	`leave`	Leave the SpoVNet instance
	`onJoinCompleted`	Indicate join success
	`onJoinFailed`	Indicate join failure
	`onLeaveCompleted`	Indicate leave success
	`onLeaveFailed`	Indicate leave failure
Communication-specific	`bind`	Bind service with specific ID to SpoVNet instance
	`unbind`	Unbind a service from SpoVNet
	`establishLink`	Establish a virtual link to another NodeID
	`dropLink`	Drop a virtual link
	`sendMessage`	Send message over a link, if no link given built one up first
	`onLinkUp`	Indicate successful setup of virtual link
	`onLinkDown`	Indicate successful dropping of virtual link
	`onLinkChanged`	Indicate link mobility
	`onLinkFailed`	Indicate that the link has dropped
	`onLinkRequest`	Indicate incoming link request
	`onMessage`	Incoming messages on a virtual link

Table 3.1   Overview of the SpoVNet Developer Interface for Service and Application Development (based on [27])

The communication-specific interface is used to establish overlay connections between SpoVNet nodes and to send messages over these connections. An overlay connection between two SpoVNet nodes is represented by a *virtual link* in the SpoVNet architecture. Virtual links provide abstractions from underlay connections which can be either direct or indirect (in case intermediate overlay peers are involved). A virtual link appears as a transparent end-to-end overlay connection to services and applications, regardless of which protocols or intermediate systems are used in the underlay. Virtual links are described in more detail in the next section. Besides virtual link management the communication-specific interface also comprises callback functions for the notification of important link- and message-related events.

To allow more than one SpoVNet service to communicate with the architecture, each SpoVNet service is assigned a unique service-specific identifier

(*ServiceID*). SpoVNet services are bound to the architecture via this identifier, enabling multiplexing a set of SpoVNet services in a single SpoVNet instance.

With help of the Developer Interface ALM protocols developed in the SpoVNet architecture can be assigned a unique identifier and establish overlay connections to any other peer using the virtual link abstraction. Link changes are notified and underlay aspects are hidden. Hence, ALM overlay protocol developers can concentrate on the protocol's core group communication logic.

Legacy Interface

The usage of existing (legacy) applications with the SpoVNet architecture is enabled by a dedicated interface. It is designed to provide a common socket interface to legacy applications, avoiding modification of these applications. The Legacy Interface differs from the Developer Interface to the effect that it does not explicitly provide access to SpoVNet-specific functions. Rather, it hides the complete architecture from the application. Required communication functions (like e. g. the resolution of DNS names) is handled transparently by the core part of the architecture which is described in the following sections. Nevertheless, even without dedicated knowledge a legacy application can benefit from the underlay abstraction provided by the SpoVNet architecture.

3.3.4   Base Overlay

The Base Overlay is part of the SpoVNet architecture's core and provides a control structure used for signaling and basic connectivity between SpoVNet nodes. It preserves end-to-end connectivity between nodes during a SpoVNet session, even in face of e. g. user mobility. Furthermore, it offers a flat addressing scheme to SpoVNet services and applications (ID/Locator Split) and comprises a distributed storage component, e. g. usable for service bootstrapping (DHT).

ID/Locator Split

To provide persistent and flat addressing to SpoVNet services and applications, the Base Overlay uses identifiers for nodes (*NodeIDs*) and virtual links (*LinkIDs*), similar to the ServiceIDs. All IDs in the architecture are implemented by generated 160 bit hashes, either from static name strings, from cryptographic keys (described in Section 3.3.7), or randomly at start/runtime. From a SpoVNet service's or application's point of view nodes are always addressed using NodeIDs, being invariant against address changes in the underlying protocols. A NodeID is logically connected to a set of network locators which describes the SpoVNet node's physical network attachment, the

NodeID		
c07e00c4535f64a549fd15cf41439127b785710cfa029384		
Endpoint Descriptor		
Layer 4	TCP{31016};UDP{32020};
Layer 3	IP{192.168.178.23 ǀ 129.13.182.17 ǀ 2800:1450:8006::68};
Layer 2	RFCOMM{[00:26:5e:ab:f9:e7]:10};

Table 3.2 Example NodeID and logically attached Endpoint Descriptor (based on [27])

so-called *endpoint descriptor*. An example endpoint descriptor is shown in Table 3.2. The NodeID is logically connected to the node's reachable addresses (and ports) in different communication layers.

If a SpoVNet service or application requests the establishment of a virtual link to another node (e. g. for establishing a data forwarding link in an ALM structure), the participating nodes exchange their endpoint descriptors through the Base Overlay and test their mutual reachability. Transport connections from both directions are tried to be established with help of the Base Communication, described in Section 3.3.5. An established virtual link is persistently identified through a LinkID, being invariant to changes, similar to NodeIDs.

Decentralized Control Structure

The Base Overlay uses a dedicated overlay structure for signaling and control. It follows the concepts of Key-Based Routing (KBR) [50] based on NodeIDs, providing identifier-based addressing that comes with the non-functional requirements of scalability, self-configuration, and self-maintenance. If a virtual link between two nodes should be established the respective endpoint descriptors are exchanged via this overlay structure. Virtual links are set up on demand but are maintained transparently and autonomously, hence relieving developers from complex link maintenance between nodes. The SpoVNet architecture does not require a specific KBR protocol to be used as Base Overlay. Rather, any protocol providing key-based routing functionality can be used, like e. g. CAN [180, 181], Chord [210], Pastry [193], or Kademlia [153].

DHT

The decentralized control structure in the Base Overlay is also used to provide distributed storage functionality from which services and applications can benefit. The Base Overlay integrates Distributed Hash Table (DHT) [186, 187] functionality that can be used to store arbitrary information in the control structure distributedly. By use of this DHT nodes joining a SpoVNet instance can acquire information how to access a specific SpoVNet service by retrieving bootstrap information from the DHT, for instance. Nevertheless, joining a SpoVNet instance still requires dedicated bootstrap mechanisms, as described in the following section.

3.3.5 Base Communication

The Base Communication provides persistent connectivity between nodes even if this is complicated due to underlay challenges as described in Section 3.1. The underlay details are hidden from the Base Overlay, allowing to abstract from protocol heterogeneity, limited connectivity, or device mobility for all framework parts above the Base Communication. In contrast to the Base Overlay, the Base Communication does not use identifier-based addressing, but rather directly uses the underlay addresses of the involved protocols. Nevertheless, both components tightly work together to provide link establishment and maintenance.

Heterogeneous Underlay Protocols & Relay-based Connectivity

The SpoVNet framework resides above the transport layer. Hence, it is able to use different transport protocols (e. g. TCP, UDP, SCTP), network protocols (e. g. IPv4, IPv6), and link layer protocols (e. g. Ethernet, Bluetooth). The framework is able to choose the appropriate protocols needed for communication between two SpoVNet nodes, enabling connectivity in environments where different protocols are used. Furthermore, in cases where two nodes are not able to communicate directly (e. g. due to disjoint sets of supported protocols), so-called *relay nodes* can be found and used: Relay nodes are SpoVNet nodes used to maintain indirect end-to-end connections, bridging between two nodes not directly interconnectable. These relay nodes are found through self-organization mechanisms with help of the Base Overlay by exchanging endpoint descriptors as described in Section 3.3.4. The ability to use different protocols and locate and integrate relay nodes are key enablers for the transparent provision of end-to-end-connectivity in the SpoVNet framework.

Network domains in which any peer is able to connect to any other peer directly are called *Connectivity Domains*. In the SpoVNet architecture, Connectivity Domains are assumed to be dynamic, i. e. they potentially split or merge during the lifetime of a SpoVNet instance. Border peers of two Connectivity Domains, being able to connect to peers in both domains, comprise the set of relay nodes. Mies et al. proposed a dedicated Connectivity Domain Management Protocol (CDMP) [154–156] that has been developed in the SpoVNet project and is used to maintain Connectivity Domains and relay-based overlay paths in the SpoVNet architecture's Base Communication.

Link Management

Virtual links in the SpoVNet architecture can be established manually by SpoVNet services and applications (*manual links*), or they can be established automatically (*auto links*). Auto links are built if messages are sent to a SpoVNet node without specifying a dedicated LinkID. An auto link is used and maintained internally. After an idle period it is closed down automatically. While auto links do not require manual link establishment and therefore avoid sources of error for overlay service developers on the one hand, the direct control regarding link properties is limited, compared to manual links, on the other hand. Virtual links are built upon transport connections, potentially comprising more than one piecewise transport connection (in case relay nodes are part of a virtual link). A virtual link can comprise a chain of single TCP connections between SpoVNet nodes, for instance. To SpoVNet services and applications, a virtual link appears transparently as a single end-to-end connection between two SpoVNet nodes and thus offers a convenient abstraction from the underlay network. The Developer Interface described in Section 3.3.3 allows to establish requirement-oriented virtual links without knowledge about protocol selection or complex details. The specification of requirements thereby provides means to influence protocol selection to some extent. However, to specify requirements for virtual link establishment, SpoVNet services have to trigger the creation of manual links.

Bootstrapping

Bootstrapping is a general issue in distributed services, as means for entering a service are needed. Because nodes participating in the SpoVNet instance may change and no central entity is provided, a joining node needs to learn about nodes already present in the SpoVNet instance. For bootstrapping overlay services using the SpoVNet architecture the DHT can be used for storing addresses of entry nodes (cf. Section 3.3.4). This requires being part of the Base Overlay already. To bootstrap the Base Overlay itself (i. e. entering a SpoVNet instance) the framework provides a set of different mechanisms: Besides an IPv4/IPv6 broadcast protocol used to detect SpoVNet nodes in broadcast domains, also multicast-based DNS (mDNS) [37] as well as the Bluetooth Service Discovery Protocol (SDP) [81] are supported. Furthermore, bootstrap information can be specified manually out-of-band. The provided mechanisms are suitable for small and spontaneous networks in order to locate and find out underlay (network or link layer) addresses of SpoVNet nodes. To support large SpoVNet instances in the future random probing mechanisms and address caches [58] can be integrated, or novel bootstrap functionality (e. g. based on new features in IPv6 [28]) can be used.

3.3.6 Cross-Layer Information Component

The SpoVNet architecture offers a convenient abstraction from the underlay for overlay service developers by maintaining self-organized end-to-end-connectivity between nodes. This enables developers to concentrate on the overlay service functionality rather than having to cope with network complexity. However, this abstraction also hides link properties from developers, potentially leading to suboptimal overlay construction. In order to cope with the network challenges transparently but also allow developers to take own service-related decisions regarding overlay establishment, the SpoVNet framework offers the *Cross-Layer Information for Overlays* (CLIO) [88] component. CLIO provides an extensive set of information relevant for overlay building to developers. An overlay service node can request e. g. link latency, available bandwidth, or local communication possibilities from the component. Requests can either be registered as periodic (if the information is to be triggered periodically during the whole lifetime of the overlay), or they can be accomplished once. Information measured by CLIO is available for all running services in a SpoVNet instance, relieving developers from implementing own measurement functionality and avoiding measuring the same information twice if needed by two services, for instance.

CLIO accomplishes message-based network measurements among peers. One single CLIO instance is instantiated per SpoVNet device, hence measured network information can be gained once and then be shared among different SpoVNet nodes on the same SpoVNet device. Furthermore, through the use of *Remote Orders*, network information can also be requested for remote virtual links in order to support overlay building strategies that include the consideration of links not originated or ending at the local node. Finally, recently requested information is stored in a cache to avoid unnecessary measurements and network information measured distributedly and collected in the overlay is aggregated to increase efficiency. For developing ALM protocols as focused in this thesis CLIO can be used to request network information necessary to appropriately refine the overlay-based data dissemination structure. As many data dissemination cases are bound to given quality metrics, gaining knowledge about virtual link properties and changes in the network is crucial for adequate service provision. The concepts of CLIO are published in [86–93].

3.3.7 Security Component

Distributed high-scale overlay systems may be prone to attacks in order to compromise overlay communication. The SpoVNet architecture comprises a *security component* that provides concepts and mechanisms to increase communication security in SpoVNet instances. The security component can be

Mechanism / Feature	Mobility Support	Heterogeneous Characteristics	End-to-End Connectivity	Support for Multihoming	Scalability	Self-conf. & Maintenance	Extensibility	Usability
BC Heterogeneous Underlay Proto.	×	×	×	×				
BC Link Management	×		×	×			×	×
BC Relay-based Connectivity		×	×			×		
BC Bootstrapping						×		×
BO ID/Locator Split	×			×				
BO Decentralized Control Structure				×	×	×		
BO Distributed Hash Table						×		×
CL Cross-Layer Component		×		×	×	×	×	×
IF Developer Interface							×	×

Table 3.3 Overview of SpoVNet Components and Features relevant for this Thesis (based on [27])

used to generate NodeIDs and SpoVNetIDs[1] cryptographically. This allows proofing ownership of IDs as they are created from public/private key pairs. Cryptographically generated NodeIDs are used to establish integrity-protected, encrypted virtual links between SpoVNet nodes, providing resistance against spoofing attacks. Furthermore, SpoVNet instances can be created with validation of the instance creator by checking the ownership based on the public/private key pair. The private key is required to proof instance ownership. If instance ownership should be passed between nodes, it can be sent to a new owner node through a secured virtual link. Another concept in the security component is establishing so-called *hidden* SpoVNet instances. Hidden instances are not arbitrarily visible in the bootstrap phase, rather their visibility is limited to authorized nodes. Different authorization schemes can be used, like e. g. whitelists or pass phrases. The security component is conceptual part of the SpoVNet architecture to provide basic security if required in SpoVNet instances. However, it has minor relevance for the protocols presented in the remainder of this thesis.

---

[1] A SpoVNetID is a SpoVNet instance-specific unique identifier.

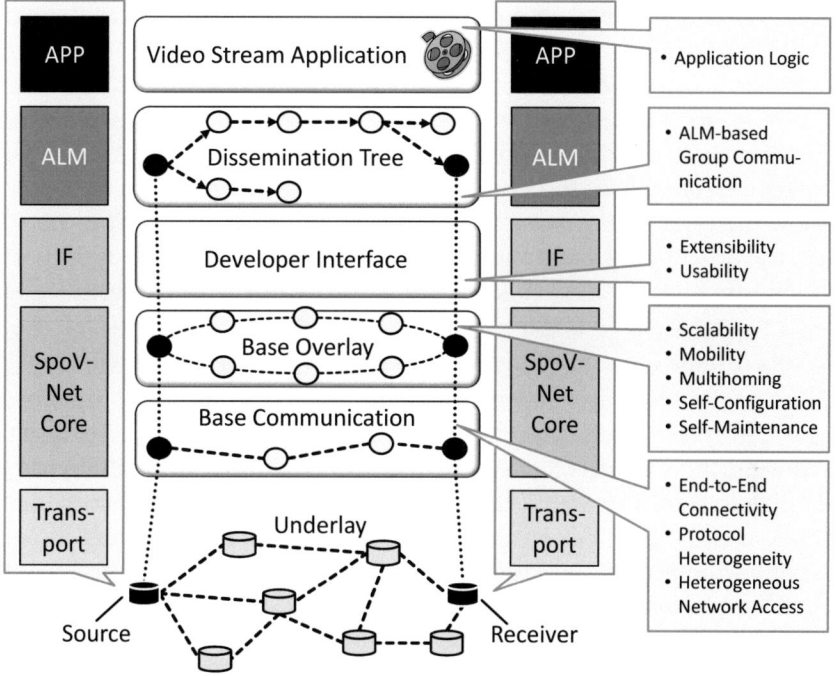

Figure 3.4 ALM as a Service in the SpoVNet Architecture (based on [27])

3.3.8 Developing Application-Layer Multicast Protocols with the SpoVNet Architecture

The SpoVNet architecture provides means to considerably reduce development and implementation complexity of overlay-based P2P services. Hence, it is also used as a basis for the ALM protocols presented in the remainder of this thesis. It relieves the protocol developer from coping with the underlay challenges described in Section 3.1 while still enabling him to maintain the overlay structure flexibly and concentrate on the overlay protocol's core functionality and behavior.

Table 3.3 summarizes the framework's features, divided into the architecture parts with relevance for the protocols in this work. It shows the Base Communication (BC), Base Overlay (BO), CLIO (CL), and the Developer Interface (IF). These parts are directly used by the developed ALM protocols, while the security component and the legacy interface are not further used. The table highlights the functional and non-functional aspects that the SpoVNet architecture offers for the ALM-based overlay services.

To give an example how the SpoVNet framework can be used in the context of this work's ALM approaches, Figure 3.4 provides a schematic view in which an exemplary single-source tree-based ALM protocol uses the SpoVNet architecture as abstraction platform. The use case here is the dissemination of a video stream to a group of receiver peers (similar to the CMA protocol described in Chapter 5). In the example eight nodes participate in the SpoVNet instance. In each layer, two of them are highlighted, one being the video source, the other being a common receiver. Additionally, in the right part the provided functionality of each layer is shown, using the terms from Table 3.3.

The tree-based ALM protocol is implemented as a SpoVNet service. Hence, it uses the framework's Developer Interface to access the SpoVNet core functionality. At the same time it provides its group communication functionality to the application which is implemented in the SpoVNet framework as well, also considering the Developer Interface and explicitly using the ALM protocol. The application sends the video stream to the ALM protocol at the sender's side and receives and displays the video at the receivers' sides. To establish and maintain the video dissemination tree the ALM protocol uses the SpoVNet framework to build manual virtual links between peers. With help of the CLIO component, the tree can be maintained and refined with respect to specified optimization goals (e. g. bandwidth and data dissemination delay considerations in the example). The CLIO component is not explicitly shown in the figure but resides in the SpoVNet core.

With the SpoVNet architecture the ALM protocol can be reduced to the overlay building/refinement strategies and the functionalities for data forwarding. Network and protocol heterogeneity as well as link outages and changing network locators are abstracted through the concept of virtual links behind the Developer Interface. Furthermore, the SpoVNet architecture fosters the development of distributed group communication services with the characteristics described in Chapter 1: It supports network independence through the transparent handling of different access technologies and protocols, flexibility through the generic SpoVNet service layer, and the integration of different access technologies through its multihoming consideration. Finally, it enables the provision of persistent end-to-end connectivity even in face of mobility and network dynamics, as basically assumed for the ALM protocols presented in this thesis.

3.4   Ariba - A SpoVNet Framework Implementation

Based on the concepts of the SpoVNet architecture a prototype implementation has been implemented: The *ariba* (abstraction base) framework [8, 102,

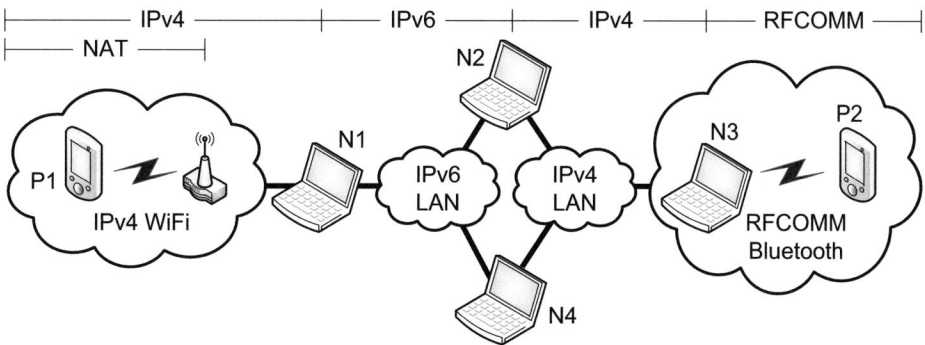

Figure 3.5 Ariba Demonstration Setup at ACM SIGCOMM 2009 (based on [101])

104, 105] comprises the Base Overlay, Base Communication, and both interfaces of the presented architecture. Besides the described functionality a set of tools and mechanisms for the easy development of overlay-based services, like e. g. timers, threads, and message serialization, have been integrated. Ariba has been developed in C++ [211] and uses different popular freely available C++ libraries (e. g. STL [205] and Boost [1]). This eases code migration to other platforms (the original implementation is Linux-based). The interfaces have been documented via Doxygen [62] and several tutorials on how to use it are provided. The ariba framework is completely open-source, has been released under the FreeBSD license, and is still under ongoing development. At the time of writing this thesis ariba is available for Linux, OpenWRT-based routers, and different smartphone systems (Open-Moko, Maemo, Android). A port to Windows systems is planned. Ariba is freely available on a dedicated web site [8].

Ariba has been presented on major conferences with demonstrators focusing on different parts and features of the architecture. At ACM SIGCOMM in 2009 [101, 104] the provision of end-to-end connectivity in heterogeneous networks has been demonstrated: A set of laptops and smartphones residing in different networks has been used to build a communication overlay which self-organizes and maintains connectivity even in face of link outages and manual reconfiguration of the network. Figure 3.5 shows a schematic view of the demonstration setup. Two IPv4 domains have been partitioned by an intermediate IPv6 domain. Laptops N2 and N4 were connected to both protocol domains via multiple multihomed devices. Additionally, a smartphone (P2) was connected via Bluetooth RFCOMM to a multihomed laptop (N3), and another smartphone (P1) was connected via WiFi behind NAT to laptop N1.

As reference application running on the architecture a distributed chat client has been used, allowing all nodes to exchange messages via ariba. As an exemplary communication service an ALM protocol closely related to NICE (cf. Chapter 4)) has been used to distribute chat messages among all SpoVNet nodes. Furthermore, the chat application comprised a network visualization GUI, allowing to get insight in how overlay connections are established and maintained.

In a demonstration presented at IEEE INFOCOM in 2010 [103] the easy usability and the provision of transparent end-to-end connectivity with ariba for unmodified (legacy) applications have been focused. The use of the Legacy Interface and the benefits for existing applications have been highlighted by using a web server as reference application, hosting an example website. On the other nodes unmodified browser application were used. By providing a special URI in the address field users could transparently access the website. The browser accessed ariba via a common communication socket, while DNS resolution has been accomplished in ariba.

3.5   Conclusion

In this chapter the SpoVNet architecture as a framework for easy development of overlay-based services and applications has been presented. The architecture is able to cope with different network challenges like e. g. peer mobility, access network and protocol heterogeneity, or middleboxes. The framework considerably reduces the overhead for the creation of overlay-based protocols. The provided abstraction hides the network complexity and offers persistent end-to-end-connectivity between peers. To allow for the optimization of developed overlay structures even in face of this abstraction a dedicated cross-layer component can be used to request information about overlay link properties. Parts of the SpoVNet architecture have been implemented as a prototype in the *ariba* framework as open-source, being freely available and still under active development. Ariba's features have been successfully demonstrated at several major international conferences.

In the context of this thesis the SpoVNet architecture can be used to ease the implementation of the ALM protocols presented in the next chapters. Each of the protocols can be implemented in the framework's service layer as a SpoVNet service providing group communication to applications while using the Developer Interface of the SpoVNet architecture to access the framework's underlay abstraction features.

Part II

Application-Layer Multicast Mechanisms

4. Cluster-based Scalable Application-Layer Multicast

As introduced in Chapter 2, Application-Layer Multicast (ALM) is a promising alternative to the non-available global IP Multicast service deployment. However, pushing multicast forwarding away from the network core towards the end-systems raises the question whether ALM protocols are able to offer enough performance to satisfy users.

Furthermore, as services implemented by ALM overlay networks typically provide worse service quality than native implementations in lower layers, careful parameterization and fine-tuning of the overlay protocol becomes essential. The large number of parameters and cross-dependencies between parameters make parameterization often complex and error-prone. Therefore, in-depth knowledge of an overlay protocol's internal working is necessary for rational selection of parameter values.

In this chapter the emphasis is put to one particular existing ALM proposal, being the NICE protocol [14]. NICE has been proposed in 2002 by Banerjee et al. and can be counted to one of the first but also one of the most prominent ALM proposals. In contrast to other ALM-related protocols that had been introduced before (like e.g. Narada [40, 98]), NICE was the first to aim at high scalability by limiting the number of direct overlay neighbors per peer. NICE is used in this thesis as a basis to analyze the impact of a prominent ALM protocol on multicast service performance. Furthermore, an extension to NICE is proposed that allows the runtime adaptation of a protocol parameter with high influence on performance. The results of the presented analysis are published in [106]. Besides evaluation of the peer-perceived performance NICE is enhanced by a mechanism to distributedly find and integrate wireless communication possibilities in the overlay later in this thesis in Chapter 6.

The chapter is structured as follows. In Section 4.1 related work is described. Then, the original NICE protocol proposal is presented as well as a description of the concrete implementation used for evaluations in this chapter. Afterwards, an in-depth review of NICE is provided with respect to peer-perceived protocol performance: The impact of significant protocol parameters is analyzed, before the scalability and the churn resilience of NICE are studied. In Section 4.2 a protocol extension to NICE is proposed. It aims at the runtime adaptation of one of the important protocol parameters in order to improve the protocol's flexibility and applicability to different and changing network conditions.

4.1   Peer-perceived Performance Evaluation of the NICE Protocol

In this section related work in the field of NICE protocol evaluation as well as approaches similar to the presented protocol enhancements are described. Furthermore, the term *peer-perceived* is clarified and how the focus of this chapter differs from other NICE-related studies. The assumed application scenarios for the evaluations are introduced, before the original NICE protocol is described, subsequently. Afterwards, the used NICE implementation is depicted. Finally, protocol evaluations are presented.

4.1.1   Related Work

The main work on NICE [13–16] focuses on underlay behavior in terms of link stretch and link stress. The authors state that both link stress and link stretch are bounded and can be easily handled by todays over-provisioned provider networks. Thus—following these insights—from a provider's point of view ALM is an attractive alternative to IP Multicast.

Tang et al. [217] focused on hop count behavior (i. e. end-to-end overlay forwarding steps from sender to receiver) in NICE, studying different clustering schemes. They showed that NICE outperforms comparable ALM approaches. However, their evaluations were limited to hop count as metric of interest. The behavior of NICE in face of network dynamics has been studied by Banerjee et al. [13]. They used a bulk churn model in which whole groups of peers leave the overlay structure at the same point of time. The evaluations showed good resilience properties of the NICE protocol in face of bulk churn.

In this chapter in-depth evaluation studies of the NICE ALM protocol are presented that enhance the results presented in related work. In particular, the focus is set to the *peer-perceived* performance of the protocol instead of performance from the network perspective which is mainly focused in related work. Peer-perceived performance focuses on the experienced metrics in the end-systems, indicating which performance properties peers (and hence indirectly users) have to expect in different network scenarios. Furthermore, the evaluations in this chapter use realistic—but aggressive—churn models to analyze NICE under real-world churn conditions. These churn models are based on recent work by Stutzbach et al. that analyzed churn behavior of real-world P2P systems [213]. Especially, this churn behavior is more realistic than the bulk churn model considered in [13].

Regarding overlay adaptation and optimization different approaches have been described in related work. Li et al. [136] presented Accordion, a DHT-based approach with self-adjustment capabilities for the routing-table size. Accordion focuses on trading off lookup latencies in the DHT against bandwidth consumption. Earlier work [137] by the same authors presented an analytical parameter-space evaluation that focuses on systems under churn. The authors identify the routing table size for DHT protocols as the most important parameter. Fan and Ammar [67] describe reconfiguration policies for adaptation of overlay topologies. The authors consider design problems for static and dynamic overlay networks, the dynamics being based on operation cost and reconfiguration cost. Their work provides insight into general reconfiguration and the question when to perform reconfiguration of overlay structures in dynamic environments. Jelasity and Babaoglu used a topology-space to develop a protocol for topology structure adaptation, called T-MAN [115, 117]. The T-MAN protocol allows for runtime variation of overlay topologies. Finally, Mao et al. presented the MOSAIC [150] system for dynamic overlay composition at runtime. The MOSAIC system can dynamically compose a set of overlay protocols to consider specific properties—like mobility or performance features—provided by the respective overlay.

While the overlay adaptation approaches in these works consider structured overlays or focus on general overlay adaptation aspects, the enhancements presented in this chapter focus on NICE. Like in Accordion, the cluster size is dynamically adapted, taking similar effects to the overlay as adapting the routing table size. However, the enhancement presented here is applied to the unstructured ALM protocol NICE exemplarily to study feasibility in the concrete case. Therefore, the enhancements are based on NICE's parameter space, optimizing protocol behavior inside this single overlay protocol.

4.1.2 Application Scenarios

The evaluations in this chapter target the following question: How long does it take until a user can start receiving multicast data after attempting to join

NICE? What is the transmission delay he or she has to expect? How much traffic is generated on a dial-up link? How do other users constantly joining and leaving the system affect the multicast service? For estimating these questions, the end-system-specific overlay performance metrics described in Chapter 2.2.3.1 are studied, being goodput, join delay, data dissemination delay, and control overhead.

ALM protocols should provide satisfactory performance properties in different application scenarios. While in the original NICE protocol no specific application context has been fixed (although newsticker-like behavior is given as an example), two exemplary cases are assumed in this chapter :

- **High-scale Broadcast:** One application case for group communication assumed is the broadcast of famous live events. Here, a single source peer disseminates stream-based data (e. g. video or voice) to all other peers participating in the NICE overlay structure. A common property of this scenario is that potentially a high number of peers joins the structure in order to receive the event stream, on the one hand. On the other hand, a comparably high stability in the structure is to be expected, since many people follow the transmission for the entire duration.

- **Short-lived Multicast Sessions:** The second application scenario assumed is the reception of a multicast transmission "along the way". Here, peers join and leave the dissemination structure to receive the data for a specific time, which is short compared to the broadcast case described above. This behavior naturally leads to fewer but rather instable users.

4.1.3   The NICE Protocol

NICE [14] belongs to the class of unstructured overlays, i. e. a peer's position in the overlay structure is not predetermined by an artificial identifier assigned to it (like e. g. being the case for other notable approaches like Chord [210]). Rather, the position depends on active network distance measurements between the peers. NICE explicitly aims at scalability by establishing a cluster hierarchy among participating peers.

NICE divides all participating peers into a set of *clusters*. In each cluster a so-called *Cluster Leader* is determined. A Cluster Leader is responsible for maintenance and refinement in the particular cluster it is the leader of. Furthermore, all Cluster Leaders themselves form a new set of logical clusters in the next higher layer. Cluster Leaders are determined in every hierarchy layer of the structure. This process is iteratively repeated from the bottom layer upwards until a single Cluster Leader in the topmost cluster is left, resulting in a layered hierarchy of clusters (cf. Figure 4.1). For hierarchy maintenance as well as application data forwarding peers only exchange messages with the direct neighbors in the clusters they reside in. This behavior results in limited peering overhead and finally enables the good scalability properties of NICE.

Each cluster holds between k and $(\vartheta k - 1)$ peers, ϑ and k being protocol parameters (typically implemented as low integer values). In case the number of peers in a cluster exceeds the upper bound $(\vartheta k - 1)$, the cluster is split into two clusters of equal size (or as near as possible to equal). If the lower bound k is undercut, in contrast, the cluster is merged with a nearby cluster.

Clusters are formed on the basis of periodic distance evaluations between peers, where distance is defined as network latency in the original protocol proposal. Cluster Leader election is accomplished by determining the graph-theoretic center of each cluster and choosing the peer closest to that point. Peers in the same cluster periodically exchange *Heartbeat Messages* to indicate their liveliness and report measurements of mutual distances to other peers in that cluster. Based on these information Cluster Leaders decide on possible splitting and merging of clusters as they are aware of the current cluster size and all distances between peers inside their cluster. The layers of the hierarchy are referred to as L_0 for the lowest layer and L_i for the layer of i hierarchy levels above L_0. The main purpose of NICE is to scalably maintain the hierarchy as new peers join and existing peers depart. Therefore, the following invariants are maintained at all times:

- At every layer peers are partitioned into clusters of size between k and $(\vartheta k - 1)$.
- Each peer belongs to exactly one cluster in hierarchy layer L_0.
- Each peer belongs to at most one cluster in every hierarchy layer.
- Cluster Leaders are the center of the respective clusters they are leaders of. All Cluster Leaders of layer L_i logically form the set of peers in layer L_{i+1}.

In case a peer intends to join the hierarchy (*Bootstrapping*) it queries an "oracle service" to determine the current network address of the Cluster Leader of the highest hierarchy layer. This oracle is called *Rendezvous Point (RP)*. The original NICE proposal leaves the realization of the RP open but it is common practice to assume the RP is directly implemented inside the highest Cluster Leader itself. The address of the RP is assumed to be known by any peer in advance.

The joining peer queries the RP for the set of peers residing in the highest cluster of the hierarchy. After having learned this set it determines its network distances to all of the peers in this cluster in order to learn which is nearest. Then, it also queries this nearest peer for the set of peers in the next lower

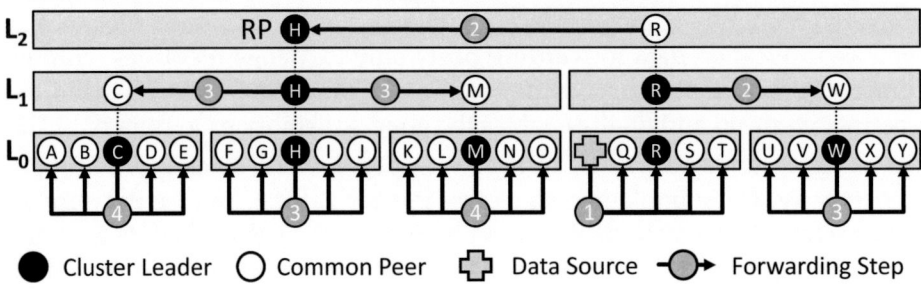

Figure 4.1 Layered hierarchical NICE Structure and Data Forwarding

layer cluster. This process is iteratively repeated by the joining peer until the lowest layer L_0 of the hierarchy is reached. As soon as this nearest L_0 cluster is determined the peer contacts the current L_0 Cluster Leader in order to join and finally become part of the L_0 cluster (and thus the hierarchy). Graceful or ungraceful leaving of peers (i. e. hierarchy departure on purpose or due to errors) is either detected by explicit protocol messages (in case of graceful leaving) or through missing Heartbeat Messages (in case of error).

NICE allows any peer in the hierarchy to send multicast data to the other peers in the structure. Doing so, it defines an implicit forwarding logic, meaning that the cluster hierarchy is used as a control structure as well as a forwarding structure concurrently. Accordingly, NICE belongs to the class of implicit ALM protocols (as described in Section 2.2.3.2). A peer intending to disseminate multicast data sends its multicast message to all neighbor peers in all clusters it currently resides in. A peer receiving a data message from inside its cluster forwards the message to all clusters it is currently part of except the cluster it received the data message from. This leads to each participating peer implicitly being root of a dissemination tree to all other peers in the overlay structure.

An exemplary NICE structure is shown in Figure 4.1. It consists of three hierarchical layers (L_0–L_2). The bottom layer L_0 holds five clusters, each cluster containing five member peers. Peer H is Cluster Leader in each layer and hence also takes the role as RP. In the figure one of the peers is assumed to send data to the structure. The implicit forwarding process is indicated by numbered arrows, showing how the data is disseminated through the different layers and clusters: First, the data source peer sends the data to all peers in the same L_0 cluster. The L_0 Cluster Leader (R in this case) forwards the data to its neighboring L_1 and L_2 peers, which subsequently forward the data to the respective hierarchy parts they belong to. After at most four forwarding steps all peers in the overlay have received the packet.

4.1.4 Design Decisions for Implementing NICE

The design decisions taken for this work's NICE implementation are stated in this section. These design decisions comprise aspects not fully described in the original protocol proposal but being necessary to implement a protocol that can finally be used for simulative evaluations as targeted here. These aspects are related to Heartbeat Messages, distance evaluation, bootstrapping, joining, refinement, and protocol recovery, in case of NICE. The design decisions do not conflict with the original proposal given in [14] but are essential for understanding the protocol's behavior. An overview on the different protocol message formats and contents is given in Appendix A.1.

4.1.4.1 Heartbeat Messages and Distance Evaluation

Heartbeat Messages are sent to direct cluster neighbors by all peers in all clusters periodically. The period for these messages is given by the *Heartbeat Interval (HBI)*. It is implemented as a timer (one for each peer), triggering periodic Heartbeat Message emission. Heartbeat Messages are used for the exchange of structure refinement information but simultaneously also for the evaluation of mutual distances between peers. Distances in the used NICE implementation are evaluated through *round-trip time (RTT)* measurements between Heartbeat Message-exchanging peers. Doing so, a peer A stores a timestamp value $t_{\mathrm{HB}}^{\mathrm{SEND}}(A)$ at the point of time it sends a Heartbeat Message to its cluster neighbors. In contrast, if a peer B receives such a Heartbeat Message of peer A, it stores the timestamp of arrival $t_{\mathrm{HB}}^{\mathrm{RECV}}(A)$, locally. Instead of answering with an own Heartbeat Message immediately, B waits for its own HBI to fire. As soon as the HBI fires B puts the time difference between the current time and $t_{\mathrm{HB}}^{\mathrm{RECV}}(A)$, being the time value $\Delta t_{\mathrm{HB}}(A)$, to its own Heartbeat Message to send. On reception of this message, peer A stores the time of arrival $t_{\mathrm{HB}}^{\mathrm{RECV}}(B)$ and can then calculate the round-trip time $\mathrm{RTT}(A, B)$ of the Heartbeat Messages to be

$$\mathrm{RTT}(A, B) = t_{\mathrm{HB}}^{\mathrm{RECV}}(B) - t_{\mathrm{HB}}^{\mathrm{SEND}}(A) - \Delta t_{\mathrm{HB}}(A).$$

The distance evaluation method is shown schematically in Figure 4.2(a). As those distance evaluations may be prone to variance in real network environments, an exponentially weighted moving average method (EWMA) as proposed by Brown [31] is used in order to smooth distance values over time:

$$\mathrm{EWMA}_t(A, B) = \begin{cases} \varphi \cdot \mathrm{RTT}_{t-1}(A, B) + (1 - \varphi) \cdot \mathrm{EWMA}_{t-1}(A, B), & \text{if } t > 1 \\ \mathrm{RTT}_t(A, B), & \text{else} \end{cases}$$

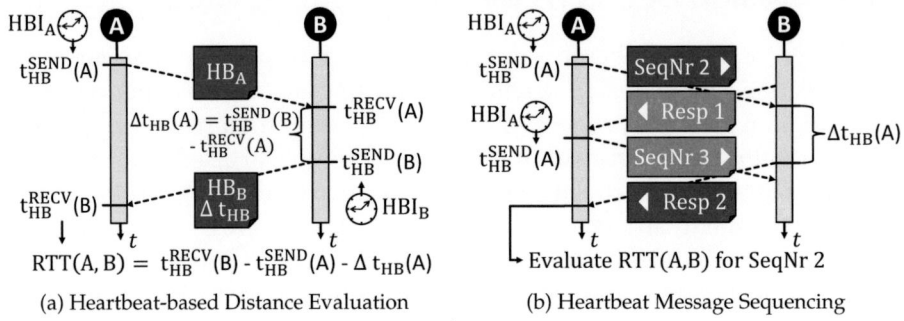

(a) Heartbeat-based Distance Evaluation   (b) Heartbeat Message Sequencing

Figure 4.2 Using Heartbeat Messaging to evaluate Peer Distances in NICE

Here, $\varphi \in [0,1]$ is the smoothing factor of the EWMA and t is the HBI period in which the estimation is accomplished.

As Heartbeat Message sending is based on the local peers' HBI timers, intersecting Heartbeat Messages interfere with distance measurements in case they overlap in time. To avoid such effects a dedicated Heartbeat Message sequencing method is used in the implementation. Each Heartbeat Message holds an incrementally increased sequence number. Additionally, a peer sending a Heartbeat Message always includes the information which sequence number it has received prior from that particular peer it is sending the Heartbeat Message to. This helps to assign Heartbeat Messages to the correct distance estimations and to avoid error-prone distance evaluations even if out-of-order message receptions occur.

The Heartbeat messaging method is exemplarily shown in Figure 4.2(b). Here, peer A sends a Heartbeat Message with sequence number 2 to peer B. Next, it receives a Heartbeat Message from B which is in this case assigned to a predecessing message with sequence number 1. Without sequencing peer A would calculate the distance based on this (too early) received Heartbeat Message. Finally, peer A waits for the corresponding Heartbeat Message from B to be received before evaluating the correct distance for the estimation with sequence number 2.

4.1.4.2 Bootstrap and Join Phase

For bootstrapping NICE an out-of-band oracle service is used. It can be queried for the network address of the current RP. The role of the RP is always assigned to the Cluster Leader residing in the highest hierarchy cluster. To join the NICE overlay structure a peer first contacts the oracle and afterwards queries the RP for the set of peers residing in the highest cluster. Then, the iterative process of stepping down in the structure to find an appropriate L_0 cluster, as described in Section 4.1.3, is initiated.

4.1.4.3   Maintenance and Refinement

After having successfully joined the hierarchy peers start maintaining the overlay structure with respect to their individual network view. For verifying cluster neighbor peers' liveliness and ensuring the protocol invariants described in Section 4.1.3 at all times the Heartbeat Messages play the most influential role. As they are used for propagation of mutual distances, peers are able to take decisions autonomously and distributedly. In this thesis different types of Heartbeat Messages are introduced and used to account for the different peer roles of Cluster Leader and common peers.

A peer being Cluster Leader in cluster C_j in layer L_i periodically emits a distinct *Leader Heartbeat Message (LHB)* in this cluster. A LHB holds the contents of a normal Heartbeat Message but in addition it provides information about members in the direct supercluster (SC) C_s in layer L_{i+1}. This information is used by neighbor peers in C_j to check whether a L_i cluster in proximity potentially exists to which they should change their membership due to lower distances. Therefore, peers evaluate their distances to all supercluster peers they learned from the Leader Heartbeat Message. A peer from that supercluster is considered "better" if the specific peer's distance to that supercluster peer is at least min_{RTT}^{SC} percent smaller than towards the Cluster Leader the peer is currently attached to (min_{RTT}^{SC} being a protocol parameter).

Should a closer Cluster Leader B in C_s be found for a querying peer A, the latter will change its cluster membership to the cluster in layer L_i that B is Cluster Leader of. The effects of the parameter min_{RTT}^{SC} will be examined again in Section 4.1.6.2. Furthermore, neighbor peers in C_j use the neighbor information in the Leader Heartbeat Messages to update their current view of the cluster peer memberships immediately, i.e. they add new peers or delete peers that are no longer part of the cluster in their local views.

If a Cluster Leader detects a violation of the cluster size upper bound ($\vartheta k - 1$) it has to establish a cluster split. Doing so, it determines the resulting two new clusters by calculating all possible combinations and evaluating the resulting cluster distances. The cluster split algorithm used is shown in Algorithm 1. For each disjunct possible partitioning of the original cluster the Cluster Leader calculates the maximum resulting distance from any of the clusters' peers to their respective new potential Cluster Leader (lines 4–6). $\delta(A, B)$ is the network distance between peer A and peer B. Finally, a set of new clusters with minimal maximum distance is evaluated which determines the new cluster set (lines 7–9).

Algorithm 1: Splitting Clusters in the NICE Implementation

---

1 C_i: /*Cluster to split*/
2 C_j, C_k: /*Resulting new Sub Clusters*/
3 $RTT_{MAX} = \infty$ /*Known maximum Distance*/
4 **for** $\{\{C_l, C_m\} | (C_l \subseteq C_i \backslash C_m) \wedge (C_m \subseteq C_i \backslash C_l)\}$ **do**
         /*Check all possible Combinations for C_l and C_m*/
5 | $MaxDistance(C_l) = max(\delta(ClusterLeader(C_l), X), X \in C_l)$;
6 | $MaxDistance(C_m) = max(\delta(ClusterLeader(C_m), X), X \in C_m)$;
7 | **if** $\{min(MaxDistance(C_l), MaxDistance(C_m)) < RTT_{MAX}\}$ **then**
       | /*Found new Split Solution with minimal maximum
       | Cluster Sizes*/
8 | | $RTT_{MAX} \leftarrow max(MaxDistance(C_l), MaxDistance(C_m))$;
9 | | $C_j \leftarrow C_l; C_k \leftarrow C_m$;

The number of combinations to be evaluated is bounded by the cluster size parameter k. If the original cluster to be split C_i holds n peers, $n \leq (\vartheta k - 1)$, a total of

$$\frac{n!}{2 \left(\frac{n}{2}!\right)^2}$$

combinations has to be observed. As soon as an appropriate cluster split set has been determined the Cluster Leader signals the change information throughout the specific cluster and all involved higher layer clusters by integrating it in its Leader Heartbeat Messages.

Should the size of any cluster fall below k peers (as a result of peers changing positions or peer fluctuation) the cluster is merged with one of its neighboring clusters on the same layer. The Cluster Leader of the specific cluster C_j in layer L_i is also part of the next higher cluster C_k in layer L_{i+1}. Therefore, it knows its estimated distances to the remaining peers residing in C_k. With this information the Cluster Leader is able to determine the nearest peer of C_k, being the candidate to merge cluster C_i with. It initiates the cluster merge operation by actively triggering a merge request to that candidate peer.

As part of the periodic refinement process all peers in a cluster distributedly decide if the current Cluster Leader remains optimal. This is accomplished by finding the peer with the smallest maximum distance to all other peers in this cluster, based on each peer's local distance knowledge. To avoid fluctuations in refinement a lower bound backoff value min_{RTT}^{CL} is used. It has always to be exceeded in order to initiate a Cluster Leader change.

4.1.4.4 Protocol Recovery

Changes in the network or the NICE cluster hierarchy may lead to temporary soft-state inconsistencies between peers. In case of severe hierarchy inconsistencies (like e. g. partitioning of hierarchy parts or peer failure) peers can decide to reconnect to the structure from scratch. If the inconsistencies are temporary and non-crucial the protocol attempts to fix these issues by protocol signaling as described in the following.

In some cases it occurs that more than one Cluster Leader feels responsible for the same set of peers. This can happen due to temporary duplicate leaderships in clusters, packet loss during leader transfers, or similar other inaccurate negotiation procedures. In the used implementation duplicate leaderships are detected by Leader Heartbeat messaging. If a peer A, after reception of a Leader Heartbeat Message LHB_1 at time t_1 from Cluster Leader B, receives a second Leader Heartbeat LHB_2 from a distinct Cluster Leader C at time t_2 with $(t_2 - t_1) <$ HBI, it assumes a possible duplicate leadership. If so, it further checks if the predecessing Leader Heartbeat message (the one before LHB_1) was also sent from Cluster Leader B. This indicates a child relationship to both B and C with high probability. In this case peer A resolves the situation by proactively indicating a cluster leave request to Cluster Leader C.

In addition to duplicate Cluster Leader detection through common peers also Cluster Leaders themselves have to be able to detect mutual duplicate leaderships inside a specific cluster. Duplicate cluster leaderships appear if one peer decides to become new Cluster Leader while the old Cluster Leader did not yet take this decision—or in some cases never will due to different distance knowledge. Such situations are detected if a Cluster Leader receives a Leader Heartbeat Message in the same cluster it is Cluster Leader of. Both Cluster Leader candidates then actively rebargain their roles and announce the decision to the cluster peers.

4.1.5 Simulation Environment

In this section the simulation environment used for NICE protocol evaluation is described as well as the specific setup and parameterizations. Furthermore, the consideration of the performance metrics as introduced in Section 2.2.3.1 is described in the context of NICE.

4.1.5.1 OverSim

The NICE experiments have been conducted using the P2P simulation framework *OverSim* [19]. OverSim provides a flexible framework for simulation of structured and unstructured overlay networks. It has been designed with a focus on scalability of the simulation models with respect to the number of simulated peers as well as reuse of modules implementing overlay functionality. It allows for large-scale simulations and use of different churn models.

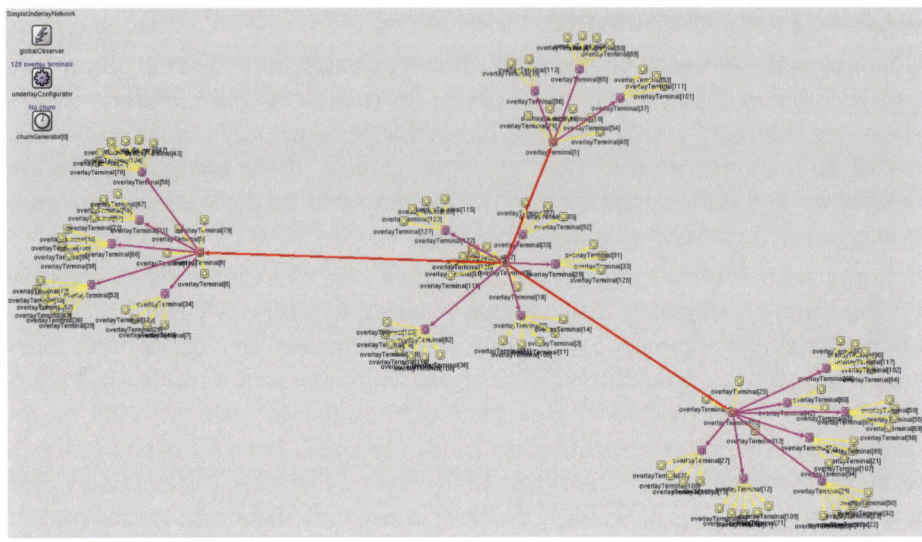

Figure 4.3 Visualization of the NICE Dissemination Structure in OverSim

The core part of OverSim comprises various network models, each modeling the underlying network with a different level of detail, and thus, complexity of the simulation model and simulation runtime. The network model of choice in this work is OverSim's *SimpleUnderlay*, being frequently used for performance evaluation from the end-system perspective. This network model abstracts from the network and transport mechanisms and arranges peers in an n-dimensional euclidean space. The euclidean distance of two peers determines the basic data propagation delay between them. The positions of the peers are chosen to match the Internet latency measurements from the CAIDA/Skitter project [201], providing more realistic delay properties between peers than in case of e. g. random placement. The SimpleUnderlay offers low computational overhead with high accuracy. Hence, it is an opportune model for simulating large overlay networks running NICE.

The NICE protocol has been implemented as an overlay module in OverSim based on the technical descriptions given in [15] and using the assumptions and decisions described in Section 4.1.4. Figure 4.3 shows a screenshot from the protocol evaluations. The visualization clearly draws the cluster hierarchy, using different colored arrows to indicate the relations between Cluster Leaders in different hierarchy layers and the respective non-leader peers. In the following, details on the setup of the OverSim-based evaluations are provided.

4.1.5.2 Parameterization

For evaluating NICE different numbers of peers are analyzed, ranging from 500 up to 8 000 peers concurrently residing in the simulation. The number of peers differs among the experiments. The peers are arranged in a two-dimensional field of size [150, 150], i. e. the maximum artificial network delay experienced for a transmission between two peers is ≈ 212 ms, according to euclidean distances. The network model is configured to generate no packet losses, i. e. every packet that is sent is received by the destination peer. This assumption follows the original design of NICE aiming at landline Internet-wide communication and is consistent with the behavior in other ALM simulation studies, e. g. [14].

The simulation experiments consider three different aspects of NICE, being the influence of protocol parameterization (Section 4.1.6), NICE scalability (Section 4.1.7), and resilience under churn (i. e. peer fluctuation, Section 4.1.8).

Each simulation is subdivided into two phases. In the *Initiation Phase* after the start of the simulation the NICE hierarchy is incrementally constructed. That is, one new peer joins the network approximately every second until the anticipated number of peers is reached. This method is chosen in order to avoid confusing effects that could arise in the initial stage and that are not subject to the targeted evaluations.

After the last peer has joined the simulation a backoff time of 60 seconds is used to stabilize the hierarchy. The Initiation Phase is then followed by the *Data Exchange Phase*. In this phase a given peer—fixed but chosen uniformly at random from the set of all peers—sends a multicast packet every 5 seconds for evaluation of scalability and every 1 second for evaluation of churn, respectively. Although the resulting data rate appears to be low it is sufficient

Table 4.1 Protocol and Simulation Parameters used in NICE and OverSim

NICE-specific		Simulation-specific	
Parameter	Value	Parameter	Value
ϑ	3	Number of Peers	500 − 8 000
HBI	$\{1, 5, 10\}$ s	Offset After Last Join	60 s
Maintenance Interval	3.3 s	Measurement Phase	600 s
Peer Timeout	2 HBI	Peer Joins	∼every 1 s
Query Timeout	2 s	Data Interval (Churn)	1 s
Structure Timeout	3 HBI	Data Interval (Scalability)	5 s
min_{RTT}^{CL}	30%	Field Size	[150, 150]
min_{RTT}^{SC}	30%	Simulation Time	920 s − 8420 s
k	3		

to quantify the performance metrics of interest as described in Section 4.1.5.4. After 10 minutes of data exchange another backoff of 60 seconds is used before finishing the simulation run.

Table 4.1 lists the used simulation parameters. It is divided into NICE-specific parameters and simulation-specific parameters. The *Peer Timeout* parameter determines after what time interval a peer is assumed to be gone (either from a cluster or from the whole overlay structure). The *Structure Timeout* parameter indicates after what time interval a peer itself assumes to be partitioned from the overlay. Both parameters are defined relatively to the HBI because the timeouts have to be correlated to Heartbeat messaging. The *Maintenance Interval* determines the period in which a peer initiates refinement procedures like e.g. checking locally for the protocol invariants. Finally, the *Query Timeout* parameter determines how long a peer waits for response after having queried a remote peer for protocol-related information. After this timeout, the peer resends the query.

Depending on the considered application scenario peers are either stable during the Data Exchange Phase or they join and leave the NICE cluster hierarchy at arbitrary times due to churn. For the latter case, the employed model for dynamic peer fluctuation behavior is described in the following section.

4.1.5.3   Churn Model

Churn is the process of peers joining and leaving the overlay structure. As joins and leaves trigger adaptation and therewith reconstruction of the overlay they can cause packet loss due to inconsistencies or partitioning. Overlay resilience against churn is conventionally achieved through redundant links in the overlay structure, resulting in higher cost [137]. Furthermore, dedicated mechanisms for overlay robustness have been developed to cope with high churn [185].

To review the performance of NICE under heavy churn appropriate churn models for the simulations have to be defined. Several churn models have been described in literature which use either Poisson, Random, Exponential,

Table 4.2   Weibull Parameters and Properties used for Churn Simulation

Parameter	Values Used in this Work						
μ	0.50						
λ	0.83	2.50	5.00	7.50	10.00	12.5	15
Mean [minutes]	1.66	5	10	15	20	25	30
Mean [seconds]	100	300	600	900	1 200	1 500	1 800
Variance [minutes]	14	125	500	1 125	2 000	3 125	4 500

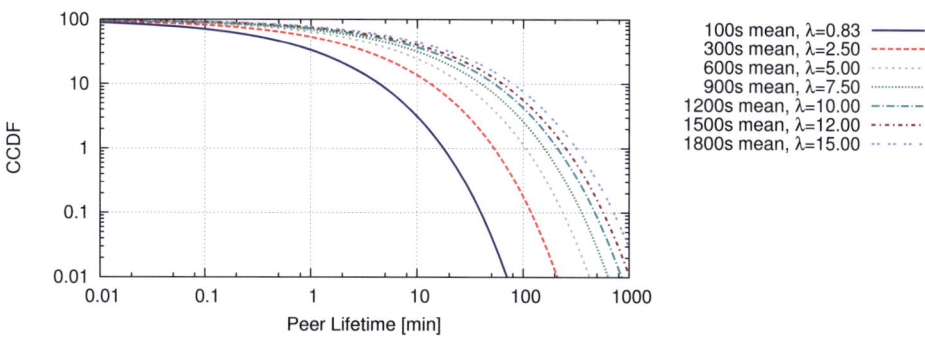

Figure 4.4 Peer Lifetime Behavior with High Churn using Weibull Modeling

or Weibull distributions to model a peer's session length, i.e. its dwell time in the cluster hierarchy. Stutzbach et al. [213] analyzed different real-world networks (Gnutella [79], KAD[1], Bittorrent [25]) and identified that (1) the session length distribution is quite similar over different networks and (2) the session length distribution is best modeled through a Weibull distribution. Prior work on NICE evaluated the protocol under bulk churn where groups of peers collectively join and leave the overlay simultaneously [14]. Opposed to [14], individual churn following the Weibull distribution is used in this chapter's simulations. Therefore, churn is employed in accordance to the Weibull Probability Distribution Function (PDF) which is defined as

$$ f(x, \lambda, \mu) = \begin{cases} \frac{\mu}{\lambda} \left(\frac{x}{\lambda}\right)^{\mu-1} e^{-(x/\lambda)^{\mu}}, & x \geq 0 \\ 0, & x < 0 \end{cases}. $$

Table 4.3 Weibull Parameters and Properties: Real-world Observations from Stutzbach et al. [213]

Parameter	Stutzbach et al.		
μ	0.34	0.38	0.59
λ	21.30	42.40	41.90
Mean [minutes]	117.25	163.38	64.46
Mean [seconds]	7035	9802	3867
Variance [minutes]	241 986	313 390	13 395

---

[1]KAD is a protocol implementation based on Kademlia [153].

As a compromise of shape values identified in the work of Stutzbach a shape parameter $\mu = 0.5$ is used. As the scale parameter λ varies significantly depending on the observed system the simulations are accomplished with different λ values to achieve different mean lifetimes of the peers, i.e. different degrees of churn. All parameter values of the churn model together with the corresponding mean (in minutes and seconds) and variance of the session length are shown in Table 4.2. Furthermore, the churn behavior is graphically illustrated in Figure 4.4. It shows the Complementary Cumulative Distribution Function (CCDF, y-axis) for different peer lifetimes in minutes (x-axis). The figure indicates which probability is to be expected for a peer to be still running after a given time.

As one dedicated goal is to find the limits of robustness for the NICE protocol, the used scaling of values results in much smaller mean lifetimes than the values presented by Stutzbach et al. For ease of comparison the latter are also provided in Table 4.3.

For churn simulations a mean of 128 peers is used, together with single-source multicast data dissemination. The simulation time is 3 600 s, subdivided as follows: Again, an *Initiation Phase* is used where 128 peers are added to the simulation in the first 128 s, one peer per second. The churn model, together with the Data Exchange Phase, start at simulation time 200 s and end at simulation time 3 540 s. The source peer of the transmission is selected as described above and is not subject to churn. Finally, the simulation ends at 3600 s. Different churn rates as detailed in Table 4.2 are evaluated.

4.1.5.4   Performance Metrics

In this section the metrics of interest are briefly revisited and put in the the context of the NICE protocol. Furthermore, it is clarified how the metrics are obtained during the simulations.

Join Delay

In the NICE protocol the join delay is the time it takes for a joining peer to be fully integrated into the cluster hierarchy. Since this is the time a user has to wait until he or she can receive a multicast transmission, this measure is considered to be of particular interest from the user's perspective. For a given peer the join delay is measured as the time between first contacting the RP and finally becoming a member in a cluster at layer L_0, following the iterative procedure described in Section 4.1.3.

Data Dissemination Delay

The data dissemination delay in NICE is the time required by data packets to reach a peer in the cluster hierarchy following the overlay-based dissemination. It is calculated as the time difference between when the packet has been emitted by the data source and the time it arrives at a specific peer. This delay is of particular interest for users following e. g. real-time transmissions. In the simulations it is measured by setting timestamps when sending and receiving a specific multicast message, respectively. Furthermore, the *hop count* (i. e. the number of application-layer overlay hops in the NICE hierarchy that must be traversed to deliver a multicast message) can be computed using a dedicated field in the message header. This field is incremented in every forwarding step. The hop count is considered here since it is a factor that directly influences dissemination delays and is also considered an important metric in related studies, e. g. in [217].

Finally, the evaluations show that the data dissemination delays naturally depend on intra-cluster forwarding delays. Thus, also Heartbeat Message delays are measured, being the network delay experienced by Heartbeat Messages between peers as described in Section 4.1.4. They indicate (1-hop) intra-cluster forwarding delays.

Control Overhead

Maintaining the NICE cluster hierarchy comes at a cost which is quantified by the bandwidth consumption for sending control messages. Throughout the rest of this chapter this cost is simply referred to as *overhead*. Overhead is relevant from the user's perspective since it must be transmitted over the user's access link. The overhead for a given peer is measured by summing up the sizes of all control messages it generates according to the protocol descriptions for a given time slot. Peer addresses are assumed to have a size of 32 bit. Furthermore, maintenance messages like e. g. Leader Heartbeat Messages hold all known cluster member peers together with their related distance evaluations, each stored also in a 32 bit numerical value.

Goodput

Although the used SimpleUnderlay configuration does not consider packet losses in the network, multicast data messages may be lost due to structural changes in the NICE hierarchy, in particular when being exposed to heavy churn. Since data message losses directly affect the transmission quality they are considered to be of particular interest from the user's perspective. Computing the fraction of successfully delivered packets (denoted as *goodput*) in the simulation is non-trivial since it is unclear how to count a peer that is part of the cluster hierarchy when a data message is sent by the source peer, but leaves the hierarchy before the message is able to reach it. Hence, successfully delivered messages are only measured for those peers which are a part of the hierarchy when a message is sent and do not leave the hierarchy until transmission of the next message.

In the following section it is analyzed how influential protocol parameters affect NICE protocol behavior and performance in general. These insights help to get a deeper understanding of reciprocal effects in the protocol parameterization. Afterwards, NICE's behavior with respect to both scalability and churn is analyzed.

4.1.6 Important Protocol Parameters and their Impact on Performance

The protocol behavior of NICE is adjustable by a variety of parameters (cf. Section 4.1.4). For completeness, all parameters are briefly rementioned here in order to focus on the most relevant, subsequently:

In the implementation of NICE used in this thesis ϑ, k, HBI, min_{RTT}^{CL}, and min_{RTT}^{SC} are the parameters with high relevance for protocol performance. They trigger cluster size bounds, interval length between Heartbeat Messages, and decision bounds for Cluster Leader estimations, respectively. Furthermore, the protocol employs several timers to detect failures in communication or structure. The *Maintenance Interval* determines the interval in which a peer checks the protocol invariants defined in Section 4.1.3. *Peer Timeout* is defined to be the period of time after which a peer assumes another peer has failed or left the overlay. It is implemented as a configurable multiplicity of HBI. *Structure Timeout* is the period of time after which a peer assumes to be partitioned from the structure and attempts to reconnect. The *Query Timeout* detects lost queries in NICE for initiation of retransmissions.

The evaluations of NICE have shown that three of the parameters have major impact on protocol behavior and performance. Hence, the following studies focus on these three, being

- the cluster size parameter k,
- the agility of peers to change their cluster memberships during refinement, especially expressed through the change bound value min_{RTT}^{SC}. This parameter and its protocol-related refinement procedure is in the following also referred to as *inter-cluster refinement*, and
- the rate of protocol Heartbeat Messages, expressed through the interval value HBI.

The first two parameters (k and min_{RTT}^{SC}) and their influence on protocol performance and robustness are discussed in the following sections. The impact of HBI is part of the churn analysis provided in Section 4.1.8.

4.1.6.1 Cluster Size Parameter k

The cluster size parameter k determines the thresholds of cluster sizes that trigger splitting and merging of clusters. As all peers in a cluster directly exchange protocol messages, increasing k will intuitively increase per-peer

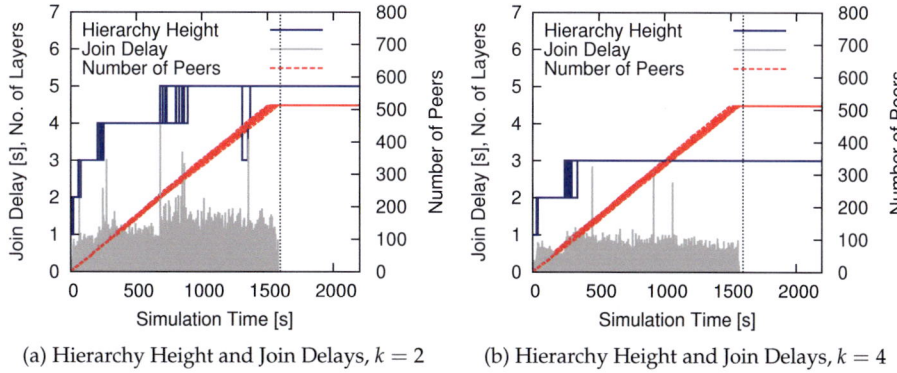

(a) Hierarchy Height and Join Delays, $k = 2$ (b) Hierarchy Height and Join Delays, $k = 4$

Figure 4.5 Influence of the Cluster Size Parameter k on the NICE Hierarchy

overhead. In contrast, larger cluster sizes also lead to fewer layers in the hierarchy. Therefore, data packets have to traverse less overlay hops, leading to lower overall data dissemination delays. Hence, adjustment of k trades off protocol overhead against data dissemination delays.

Figure 4.5 gives an overview on the impact of two different choices for k. The cluster size parameter k is chosen to be 2 (Figure 4.5(a)) and 4 (Figure 4.5(b)), respectively. In both figures, three aspects are shown: (1) The resulting height of the cluster hierarchy, (2) the number of peers currently part of the overlay, and (3) the delay it took a joining peer to become part of the overlay structure. Hierarchy height and join delay are attached to the left y-axis, the number of peers to the right y-axis. The x-axis shows simulation time. A total of 512 peers joins the hierarchy here, one being started every 3 seconds. Both figures provide data for 10 different simulation runs. These runs are not shown as average values but explicitly and jointly in the same figure. For insights into the behavior of the overlay structure distinct simulation runs offer more detail that would be lost in the calculation of average values.

In Figure 4.5(a) the cluster hierarchy incrementally reaches a height of 5 with more peers joining[2]. Clearly to see, the point in time when the 6th layer (layer 5 in the figure) is established differs between the 10 runs because it depends on the placement of peers in the field. In one of the simulation runs the height is decreased to 3 between 1 000 and 1 500 seconds for a short time which happened due to structure maintenance. After approximately 1 500 seconds the

---

[2]Height 0 here means the cluster layer L_0, therefore, for the actual hierarchy height a value of 1 has to be added.

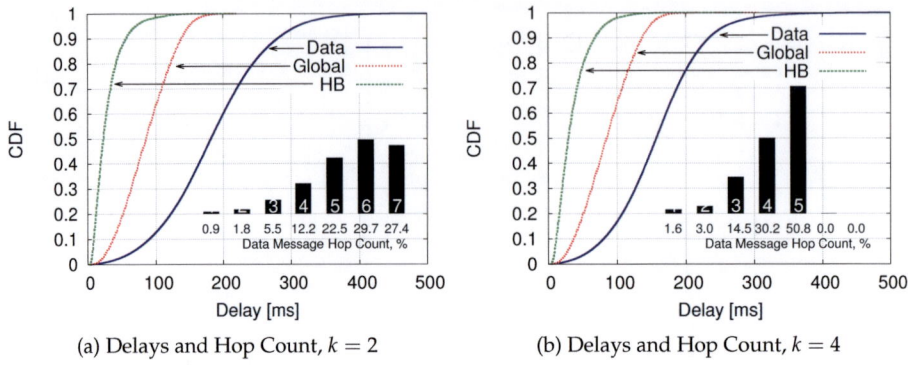

(a) Delays and Hop Count, $k = 2$ (b) Delays and Hop Count, $k = 4$

Figure 4.6 Influence of the Cluster Size Parameter k on Delays

structure is stable and does not change anymore in all cases since no more peers join and the overlay converges into a stable state.

The join delays of peers increase with growing hierarchy height. This is due to the fact that the join delay reflects the time that has passed between first contacting the RP and finally joining a cluster in layer L_0. With more layers to query the join delay increases because more steps result from the iterative join procedure. Some of the join attempts obviously show a comparably high join delay. This behavior results from overlay refinement in which packets involved in the iterative join procedure have been lost. Then, the *Query Timeout* (cf. Section 4.1.5.2) fires, and the respective peer resends the query packet.

Figure 4.5(b) shows the same evaluation metrics for 10 simulation runs with k being set to 4. In accordance with the original NICE proposal ϑ has been set to 3, resulting in a maximum cluster size of $(\vartheta k) - 1 = 11$. As a result, the final hierarchy height decreases by 2 layers. Concurrently, the join delays for the peers decrease due to less iterative hierarchy layer queries. Again, scattered join delays exceed the average due to structure refinement. In general it can be observed how incrementing k leads to a decrementing of the hierarchy height already with small changes of k.

The properties of the hierarchy also determine the overall data dissemination performance. Figure 4.6 shows how k influences data dissemination delays and number of overlay hops any data message traverses in the overlay structure. The metrics are acquired after the cluster hierarchy has converged to a stable state in each case.

The figures show three types of delays in NICE:

- Global network delays between all peers as they have been placed in the simulation field according to the CAIDA/Skitter data (referred to as *Global* in the figures). They reflect the direct network distance between any two peers in the simulation and gives an impression of peer placement's influence on 1-hop-delays in the field.
- Intra-cluster delays, acquired by evaluating the delays experiences by all Heartbeat Messages inside clusters (referred to as *HB*).
- The data dissemination delays that the data messages experience when being forwarded through the overlay (referred to as *Data*).

For each of these types the CDF is shown, measured for all peers during the whole simulation time. Furthermore, the distributions of hop counts for the data messages are provided. They indicate how many overlay hops any message has passed before it reaches a specific receiver peer in the NICE hierarchy.

The difference between direct network delay (*Global*) and the data dissemination delay (*Data*) constitutes the effects of *path stretch* as experienced by the user. It is directly related to the number of overlay hops a data packet traverses in NICE (hop count). The hop count distributions for both parameterizations are embedded in Figure 4.6. In case of k being set to 2 the hop count distribution shows the biggest fraction in the area of $5 - 7$ hops (Figure 4.6(a)). The influence of increasing k to 4 is visible in Figure 4.6(b) where the highest fraction of data messages has been forwarded over 5 overlay hops, while no message experienced a higher hop count than 5 at all. Also, the data dissemination delays decrease substantially as a result of less overlay hops.

Regarding intra-cluster delays (*HB*) it is clearly visible how NICE combines peers to clusters considering their mutual network distances bases on network delay measurements. In both figures the delays experienced in Heartbeat Message exchange are considerably lower than the global mutual network delays (*Global*), showing how network proximity is directly transferred to logical overlay cluster proximity to some extent. How this in turn influences the data dissemination delays will be revisited in Section 4.1.7.

As k determines the cluster size it also determines with how many other peers a given peer has to exchange Heartbeat Messages with, periodically. Therefore, k has a major influence on how much overhead (in the context of NICE as introduced in Section 4.1.5.4) is generated locally on a peer (and therefore on a peer's access link). Figures 4.7(a) and 4.7(b) compare the resulting mean overhead per peer for $k = 2$ and $k = 4$, respectively. In both figures the mean overhead is shown in the granularity of 1 second. As overhead in NICE shows high variance at small time scale due to refinement procedures being executed periodically, also the average overhead is shown in the granularity of 10 seconds. With $k = 2$ the mean overhead per peer can be expected to remain at constant 0.5 kbit/s while it grows beyond 1.5 kbit/s with $k = 4$. The difference arises from the need to exchange protocol messages with more peers in case of higher k because the clusters also hold more neighbor peers in that case.

Overall, it can be concluded from this section that adjusting the cluster size parameter k enables trading off data dissemination delay and join delay against control overhead in NICE. Adjusting k also influences the impact on the underlay network by trading off between resulting *path stress* and *path stretch*, as has been further investigated in [14].

4.1.6.2   Inter-Cluster Refinement

The second parameter with considerable influence is related to NICE's agility concerning structural refinements. The parameter min_{RTT}^{SC} indicates a percentage threshold which has to be exceeded for deciding whether a peer changes its cluster membership. Should the network distance between the peer and a potential new Cluster Leader underrun the distance to the current Cluster Leader (minus the threshold), the new Cluster Leader is assumed to be nearer (in the network) and therefore a better choice as Cluster Leader.

The decision is based on explicit periodic distance measurements to all supercluster peers in order to find the nearest. While a small value for min_{RTT}^{SC} results in a change even with little difference, a higher value leads to a less reactive change mechanism. Additionally, as percentage values in some cases (e. g. clusters of very small dimension with distance measurement fluctua-

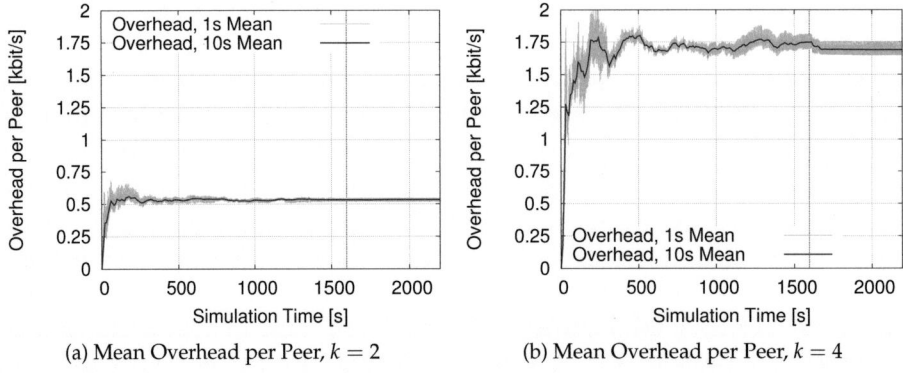

(a) Mean Overhead per Peer, $k = 2$ (b) Mean Overhead per Peer, $k = 4$

Figure 4.7   Influence of the Cluster Size Parameter k on Peer Overhead

Table 4.4 Relevant NICE Protocol Events and State Transitions

Event / State Transition	Description
QueryTimeout	A query for cluster memberships has been lost during joining
StructurePartition	The NICE structure is partitioned
QueryContent	The contents of a query do not match the requested information
QueryDestination	The destination of a query packet is wrong
JoinToWrongPeer	A join to a wrong peer is initiated
JoinWrongContent	A join packet holds wrong contents
LTAlreadyLeader	A leader gets indication to become the Cluster Leader although it already is
DoubleLeaderConflict	A peer receives Leader Heartbeat Messages in the same cluster from two Cluster Leaders concurrently
HBForeignCluster	A peer received a Heartbeat Message from a foreign cluster
MutualLeaderConflict	Two or more Cluster Leaders in the same cluster
ClusterLeaderChange	Cluster leadership in a cluster changed
SCLeaderChange	Peer elected new Cluster Leader and changed cluster

tions) lead to alternating decisions, an absolute minimum backoff value min_{BO}^{SC} is introduced which has to be exceeded at least in order to take the change decision. In contrast to min_{RTT}^{SC}, it is defined absolutely as network distance in milliseconds rather than a percentage value. Algorithm 2 shows the decision process for Cluster Leader changes in NICE. From all peers in the direct supercluster potential change candidates are collected (lines 7–11). The one with minimum network distance is checked against the defined bounds and is only chosen as new Cluster Leader if both conditions are fulfilled (lines 12–14).

While NICE's periodic protocol refinement procedures assure maintaining invariants and efficiency of the cluster hierarchy they also come with the drawback of possibly generating inconsistencies in the peers' local views. These inconsistencies may lead to packet loss or induce further need for restructuring the overlay. Therefore, the refinement agility of the protocol forms a trade-off between inconsistencies and optimality of the overlay structure. Table 4.4 lists all relevant inconsistencies, protocol refinement events, and state

---

Algorithm 2: Inter-Cluster Refinement: Changing Cluster Memberships

---

1 ClusterLeader$_{\text{CURR}}$ /*Current Cluster Leader*/
2 ClusterLeader$_{\text{CAND}}$ /*Candidate Cluster Leader*/
3 ClusterLeader$_{\text{NEW}}$ /*New Cluster Leader*/
4 v_i /*Peer measuring against Cluster Leader*/
5 RTT$_{\text{MIN}} = \delta(\text{ClusterLeader}_{\text{CURR}})$ /*Known mimimum Distance*/
6 C_k /*Direct Supercluster*/
7 **for** $(v_j \in C_k)$ **do**
8   ClusterLeader$_{\text{CAND}} \leftarrow v_j$;
9   **if** $(\delta(v_i, \text{ClusterLeader}_{\text{CAND}}) < \delta(v_i, \text{ClusterLeader}_{\text{CURR}}))$ **then**
10   RTT$_{\text{MIN}} \leftarrow \delta(v_i, \text{ClusterLeader}_{\text{CAND}})$;
11   ClusterLeader$_{\text{NEW}} \leftarrow v_j$;

12 **if** $(RTT_{MIN} < \left\lceil \delta(v_i, \text{ClusterLeader}_{\text{CURR}}) - min_{RTT}^{SCC} \right\rceil)$ **then**
13   **if** $(\left\lceil \delta(v_i, \text{ClusterLeader}_{\text{CURR}}) - min_{RTT}^{SCC} \right\rceil > min_{BO}^{SC})$ **then**
14   Initiate Change to ClusterLeader$_{\text{NEW}}$;

---

transitions that have been identified in this work's evaluation of the NICE protocol.

Fig. 4.8 shows an exemplary study of the influence of the parameters min_{RTT}^{SC} and min_{BO}^{SC}. Here, the number of peers is set to 512. Different gradually increased percentage offset values $min_{RTT}^{SC} = \{0\%, 10\%, 20\%, ..., 100\%\}$ are used. Furthermore, in the left part of the figure, min_{RTT}^{SC} is fixed to 10% while the

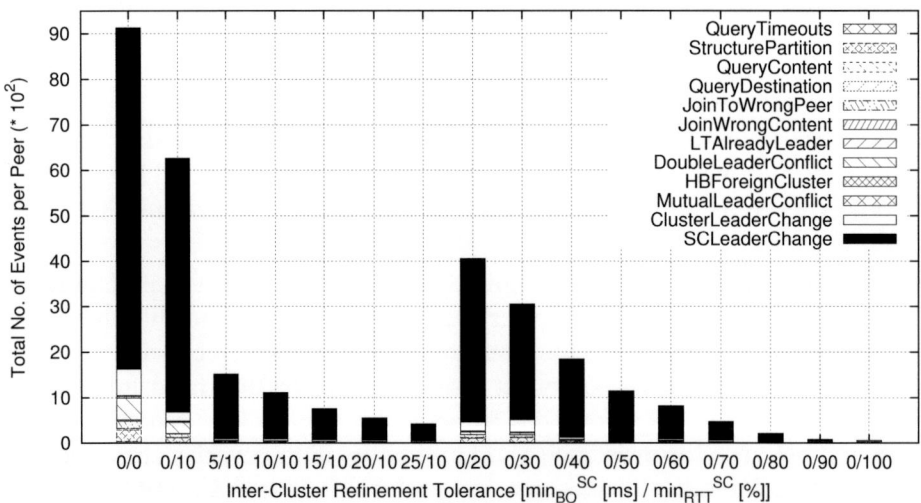

Figure 4.8 Influence of Inter-Cluster Refinement Tolerance in NICE

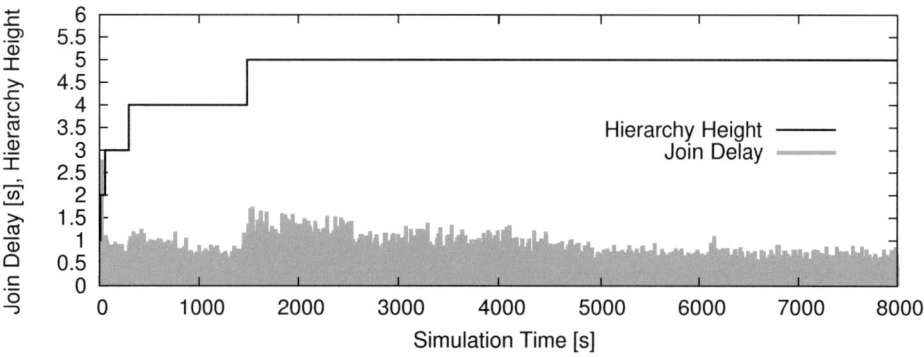

Figure 4.9 Hierarchy Height and Join Delays in NICE, 8 000 Peers

backoff parameter min_{BO}^{SC} is increased ($min_{BO}^{SC} = \{0, 5, 10, ..., 25\}$). All state transitions and inconsistencies per peer are summed up over a complete run, classified following the list given in Table 4.4. Mean values over 30 runs are provided.

As expected, lower decision bounds lead to comparably high numbers of cluster changes per peer in order to refine the structure with respect to optimal clustering. The *SCLeaderChange* constitute the larges fraction of protocol events in all cases, shown as the highest blocks in the figure's bars. What becomes clear from the figure is that with many Supercluster Leader changes there is also a tendency to induce more other inconsistencies that will in turn lead to further need for refinement or (in the worst case) data outages. In the experiments the parameter min_{BO}^{SC} had high influence with small values already while the effects of min_{RTT}^{SC} followed rather gradual behavior. Thus, the parameter choice should depend on the actual network case and reflect the target scenario as well as the implicit needs for either robustness or structural requirements, as parametrization forms a trade-off here.

4.1.7 NICE Protocol Scalability

This section analyzes peer-perceived performance of the NICE protocol from a scalability perspective. Consistent with [14], it focuses on the performance during initial construction and during stable operation of the overlay multicast structure, while the performance under churn will be considered in Section 4.1.8. Opposed to [14], especially large scenarios (i. e., up to 8 000 peers) are analyzed.

4.1.7.1 Join Delay and Hierarchy Height

Figure 4.9 exemplarily shows the join delays of all peers in a session with 8 000 peers. The join delays are plotted as a function of time in the first 8 000 seconds of simulation to indicate how they evolve with more peers joining the hierarchy. One peer per second joins and the join delay it experienced is drawn as a vertical bar. Join delays depend on the number of layers in the hierarchy since a peer starts to join at the RP in the highest layer L_k and descends through the hierarchy. In order to relate join delay and hierarchy height the figure also depicts the current number of layers in the structure.

The figure shows that for below 1500 peers the resulting hierarchy has a height of 4 layers, while it has 5 layers for larger group sizes. Again, the join delay—as expected—is influenced by the current number of layers. With each new hierarchy layer established also the average join delays increase notably. As an interesting fact the figure indicates that for a hierarchy with Layers $L_0, \ldots, L_k$, the join delay is highest directly after Layer L_k has been established. Subsequently, the average join delays decrease until Layer L_{k+1} is added to the hierarchy. This is due to the fact that a newly established layer leads to small numbers of peers in the higher layer clusters. For understanding the decrease in join delays depicted in Figure 4.9 recall that a peer must perform a distance estimation for one cluster on each layer $L_k, \ldots, L_1$ until it reaches the lowest layer L_0. Since peers in higher layers may have comparably high mutual network distances, querying information from these peers takes more time. This effect is mitigated over time by optimizing the clusters, grouping peers in proximity.

The development of cluster sizes over time in different layers of the hierarchy can also be observed in Figure 4.10. This figure plots the mean number of peers in clusters for each layer, computed once a second. The figure makes clear that the cluster size in the lower layers stays quite constant over time. In contrast, higher layer clusters are incrementally filled with peers much slower, confirming the claim made above.

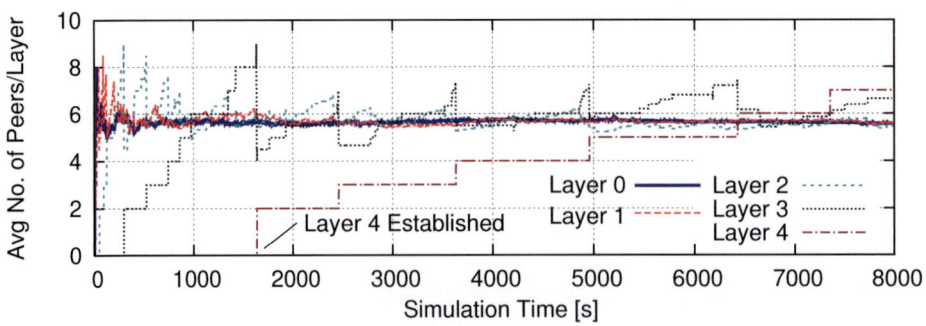

Figure 4.10 Average Cluster Sizes per Layer, 8 000 Peers

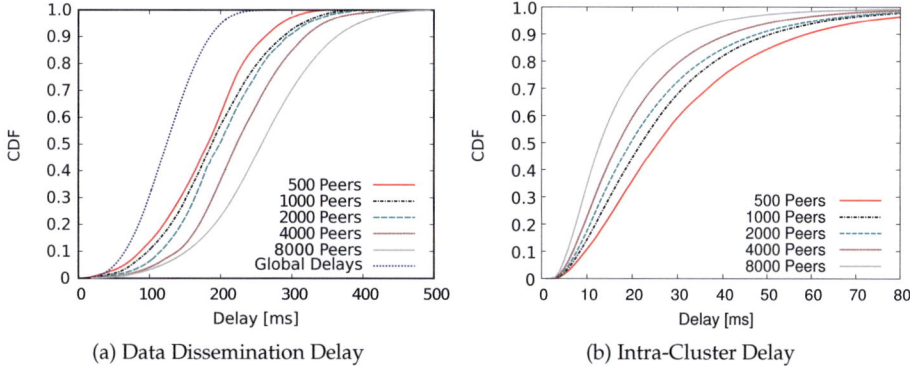

(a) Data Dissemination Delay   (b) Intra-Cluster Delay

Figure 4.11 Observed Dissemination Delays and Intra-Cluster Delays in NICE

Although join delays increase after a new layer has been established and show tendency to decrease afterwards, they also show a distinct variation even between peers joining shortly one after another. This variation results from the different "paths" that joining peers step down during the iterative join process in the overlay structure. Since different clusters can have different dimensions (in terms of network distance), querying them can take different time. These differences sum up, resulting in varying join delays. However, the join delays are significantly below 2 seconds with an average of 0.51 seconds in the shown example. Thus, it can be concluded from Figures 4.9 and 4.10 that even for large multicast groups NICE is able to provide a reasonable join delay for the users.

4.1.7.2 Data Dissemination Delay and Intra-Cluster Delay

Now, the focus is put to data dissemination delay as defined in Section 4.1.5.4. The observations are restricted to the data dissemination delays experienced after the cluster hierarchy has stabilized.

Figure 4.11(a) shows the CDF of the data dissemination delays. One would expect delays to heavily increase with an increasing size of the multicast group. However, the data dissemination delays acquired through the experiments behave relatively stable regardless of group size, e.g. a growth in number of peers from 500 to 4000 increases mean data dissemination delays by only 31 % (from 173.6 ms to 228 ms).

To gain deeper insight into this behavior the CDF of intra-cluster Heartbeat Message delays measured inside each cluster as well as the hop count distributions for multicast packets are provided in Figures 4.11(b) and 4.12, respectively. Confirming the claim made earlier, Figure 4.11(b) indicates that intra-cluster delay decreases significantly with an increasing number of peers in the overlay since the chances for clustering nearby peers increase. Hence, every hop a data message has to traverse for delivery takes less time. This fact compensates the moderate increase in path length that results from increasing the height of the hierarchy to some extent. The hop count distributions are illustrated in Figure 4.12.

This behavior overall attests NICE's main goal of providing good scalability properties with respect to data dissemination delays. Its generated protocol communication overhead per peer is observed in the following.

4.1.7.3 Overhead

In this section control overhead as defined in Section 4.1.5.4 is considered. It is shown as a function of time in a simulation with 8 000 peers in Figure 4.13. Since control overhead depends on the position of a peer in the cluster hierarchy the overhead is subdivided by the layers in the figure. Therefore, the overhead for each layer is averaged over all peers residing in the same hierarchy layer. The control overhead (i. e. the bandwidth consumption of each peer) is both aggregated by 1 s and 10 s, respectively.

As expected, the figure shows that the overhead for peers in the highest layer cluster and especially for the RP (layer 4) is significantly higher than for peers being only members of lower layer clusters since Heartbeat Messages have to be sent to each neighbor peer in each cluster a peer resides in. The fact that each additional cluster membership (i. e. each additional layer a peer resides in) adds additional overhead for cluster maintenance leads to a similar average overhead increase with the number of clusters. However, it has to be noted that the control overhead per second can reach high peaks in phases

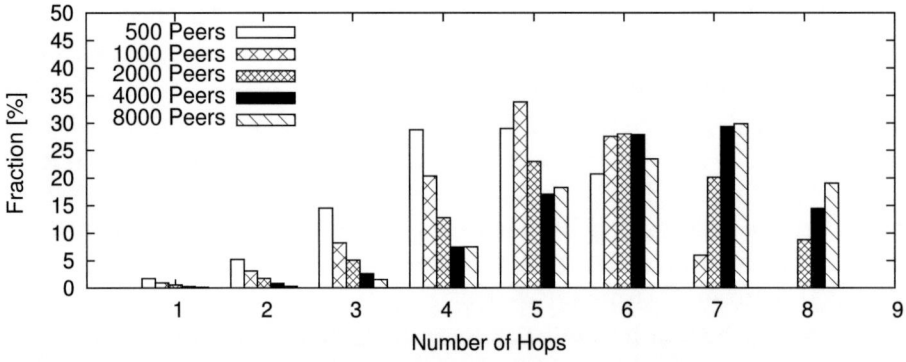

Figure 4.12 Hop Count Distributions for delivering Multicast Packets

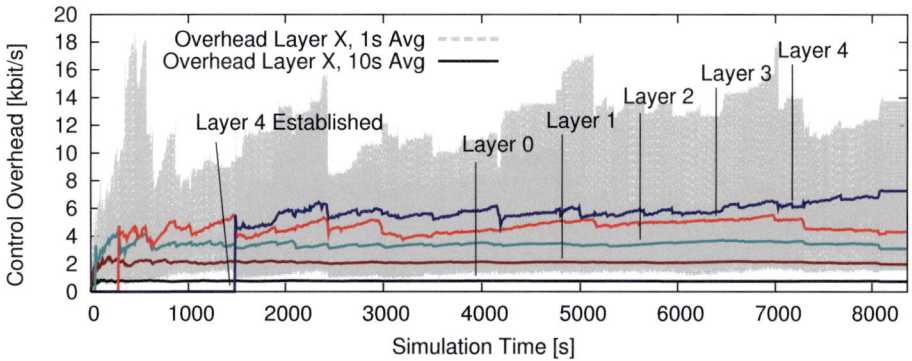

Figure 4.13 Average Overhead per Peer in different Hierarchy Layers, 8 000 Peers

where protocol refinement procedures are agile, like e. g. after the establishment of a new hierarchy layer or when merging or splitting clusters. Here, the control overhead reaches dimensions of up to approximately 18 kbit/s, also visible in Figure 4.13. As the control overhead per hierarchy layer only depends on the hierarchy height (which grows sub-linearly with the number of peers), the cluster size parameter k, and the Heartbeat Message interval HBI, NICE can be considered a scalable ALM protocol regarding growing numbers of peers. However, Cluster Leaders experience higher control traffic load due to their membership in more clusters.

In summary, analyzing NICE with respect to its scalability properties indicates that the NICE protocol from a peer's perspective performs well for high numbers of peers. However, depending on the application scenario, coping with large group sizes might be less important than providing stability of the multicast structure under high peer churn. These aspects are examined for NICE in the following.

4.1.8 Churn

In this section the peer-perceived performance of the NICE protocol under the realistic churn model introduced in Section 4.1.5.3 is evaluated. Recall that—as the goal is to find the limits of robustness for NICE—the scaling values of the churn model result in considerably smaller mean lifetimes than the values presented by Stutzbach et al. Furthermore, an average number of 128 peers is considered in this scenario, being rather instable as a result of churn. This peer number is sufficient to get an idea of NICE's ability to manage fluctuations during multicast transmissions.

In a first consideration the impact of churn on the structure of the NICE hierarchy is analyzed. Similar to Figure 4.9, both the join delay and the hierarchy

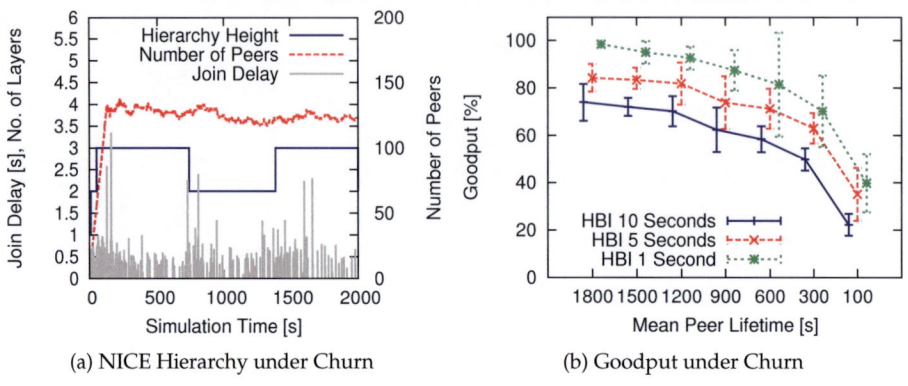

(a) NICE Hierarchy under Churn   (b) Goodput under Churn

Figure 4.14 NICE Hierarchy and Goodput under Churn

height are shown as a function of time in Figure 4.14(a). The figure further shows the number of group members changing over simulation time. As can be observed from the figure, the hierarchy height alternates between 2 and 3 layers during the Data Exchange Phase due to churn. However, adding or removing layers does only affect the join delay experienced by a few peers. In fact, the join delay of most peers is almost unaffected by churn (with an average of 470 ms in the shown experiment), although some scattered peers may experience higher join delays. This behavior results from the fact that joining the overlay structure takes little time in general and is only affected by churn if peers join or leave in the same time window and inflict inconsistencies to the structure (or are target of information queries in the join process). Further experiments have shown that data dissemination delay is also not affected by churn, although multicast packets may be lost on the overlay path. Therefore, it can be concluded that NICE performs well under churn from the perspective of peer-perceived data dissemination and join delays.

Since packet loss certainly affects peer-perceived performance, the proportion of successfully delivered multicast packets (*goodput*) as defined in Section 4.1.5.4 is analyzed in the following. Using variations in Heartbeat Intervals (HBI, as defined in Section 4.1.3) and using the churn rates given in Section 4.1.5.3, the protocol goodput is analyzed to find the robustness limits of the NICE hierarchy. Figure 4.14(b) plots the probability for successful delivery of a multicast packet as a function of mean peer lifetime together with the involved standard deviations. The Heartbeat Interval HBI is set to values of 1 s, 5 s, and 10 s, respectively. Note that without churn (not shown in the figure) NICE delivers close to 100 % of the multicast messages successfully since the NICE hierarchy is stable and packet losses on lower layers are not considered in the employed underlay model. However, even under moderate churn a HBI value larger than 1 s implies significant packet loss to the effect that 10 % and more of the packets are not delivered. Only an aggressive HBI value of 1 s is able to compensate the churn up to a certain extent at the cost of higher overhead. Nevertheless, for peer lifetimes smaller that 900 s even such aggressive parametrization of NICE fails to successfully deliver more than 90 % of the packets.

In summary it can be observed from Figure 4.14(b) that high churn requires aggressive efforts to maintain the NICE hierarchy in the original protocol proposal. Alternatively, further resilience mechanisms to increase the goodput in dynamic environments can be integrated in NICE, for instance like proposed by Birrer and Bustamante [24]. However, these approaches are based on redundancy in data dissemination and therefore induce additional communication overhead. The usage of such mechanisms depends on the dynamics of the network environment. The NICE analysis shows that the original protocol is able to cope with peer fluctuations to some extent already, if configured accordingly.

4.2 NICE Runtime Parameter Adaptation

In the predecessing sections the NICE protocol as it has originally been proposed has been analyzed from a peer perspective. While it could be observed from the evaluations that NICE provides promising scalability, robustness, and dissemination delay properties, these properties of course highly depend on the parameterization and the current network and peer state. NICE is employable in various application scenarios although its parameterization and behavior is predetermined and does not adapt to a changing network situation. To further extend the protocol's applicability to ALM group communication scenarios a mechanism for the runtime adaptation of protocol parameters in NICE is presented in the following.

In Section 4.1 the applicability of NICE to large scenarios as well as the interdependencies of protocol parameters have been observed. It has been shown that NICE is able to provide good performance properties, depending on the predetermined protocol parameterization. Unfortunately, runtime changes of network conditions as well as application and user requirements can make a good parameterization turn worse during the lifetime of an overlay. This requires readjustment of overlay parameters during runtime to prevent degradation of service quality—at best without any service downtime. In Section 4.1.6 the size of the peer clusters maintained by NICE, the thresholds for cluster refinement, and the interval of the Heartbeat Messages exchanged by members of a cluster have been identified as relevant parameters for tuning the service quality. Now, a scheme is proposed to dynamically set the cluster size parameter k during runtime as an example for adaptive parameterization in NICE.

In the following an algorithm for dynamically choosing the cluster size parameter k is proposed. Furthermore, its impact on the service quality metrics is shown. In Section 4.1.6 it has been stated how k implicitly trades off overhead against data dissemination delay in NICE. Assuming the protocol has knowledge about the desired delay constraints, on the one hand, and the tolerable resulting overhead bound, on the other hand, it may adaptively readjust k during runtime to provide desired data dissemination delays without exceeding its overhead bounds. As data messages in NICE traverse the whole structure through the hierarchy layers, delays increase with the height of the hierarchy.

Given a NICE structure of height d (d being the number of hierarchy layers). To decrease the overall hierarchy height by one k has to be chosen such that all peers in layer L_{d-1} become part of one bigger cluster. In that case there will be only one Cluster Leader left on layer L_d, i.e., this cluster is eliminated. To determine an appropriate k under a worst case assumption the Cluster Leader of the highest cluster in layer L_d must assume that every cluster in layer L_{d-1} holds its maximum peer number of $\vartheta k - 1$ peers. As the highest Cluster Leader knows the number x of peers in layer L_d (i.e. its direct neighbors in the single highest cluster), it may determine the maximum possible number of peers in layer L_{d-1} to be $x(\vartheta k - 1)$. Based on this information, the Cluster Leader calculates a new value k_{new} as follows:

$$k_{new} = (x * (\vartheta * k_{old} - 1) + 1)/\vartheta.$$

This ensures that all peers in layer L_{d-1} fit into a single cluster, resulting in a decrease of one layer in the hierarchy structure. After calculating k_{new} the Cluster Leader instructs all peers in layer L_d to merge their $L_{(d-1)}$-clusters with it so that it stays the last peer in layer L_d which is equivalent to eliminating the highest layer cluster. Furthermore, it propagates k_{new} to its new cluster members by including the new value in its periodic Leader Heartbeat Messages. A peer receiving a changed value k updates its own cluster it is the leader of, but with a randomized bounded backoff to prevent all peers from refining their structural part at the same time.

Note that the given estimation may raise k to a value that potentially induces much more overhead to the participating peers than necessary (because a worst case assumption regarding the number of peers in layer L_{d-1} is made). To mitigate this effect the protocol can be optimized by the following addition: If the highest Cluster Leader knows the exact number of peers in layer L_{d-1}

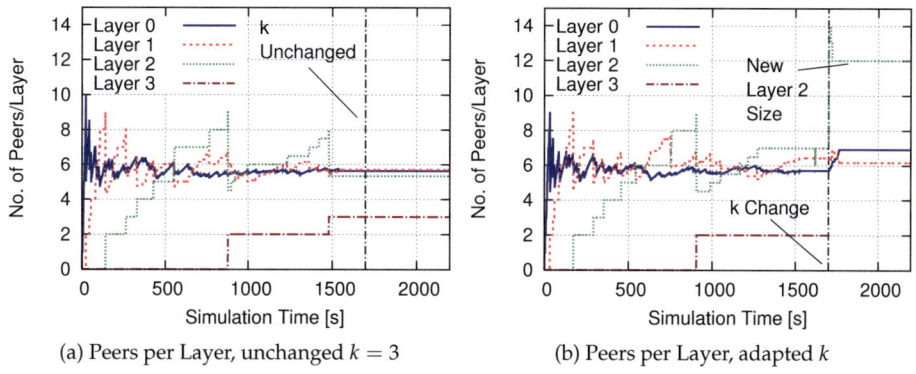

(a) Peers per Layer, unchanged $k = 3$ (b) Peers per Layer, adapted k

Figure 4.15 Cluster Sizes in different Layers depending on k

(instead of taking the worst case assumption) it can choose k to be just large enough to hold all such peers in one cluster. To gain this knowledge all peers in cluster layer L_d tell their specific current number of L_{d-1} cluster peers to the Cluster Leader of the highest cluster by including this information in their periodic Heartbeat Messages. At the time of changing k the highest Cluster Leader sums up these numbers to the value n_{d-1}. Then, it determines a value k_{new} that satisfies the following:

$$k_{new} \leq n_{d-1} \leq x * (\vartheta * k_{new} - 1).$$

In general this value is more appropriate than the one computed using the worst case assumption, leading to a smaller choice for k_{new}.

To demonstrate the feasibility of the extension runtime adaptation of k has been implemented and simulated in OverSim. Two cases have been compared, being (1) no runtime adaptation of k at all, and (2) optimized adaptation of k to decrease the hierarchy height as described above. In case (2) the adjustment of k is triggered actively 300 seconds after the structure has stabilized, i.e., the new value of k is propagated and the merge of all clusters in layer L_{d-1} is triggered. This point of time is indicated through a vertical line in Figure 4.15(b).

Figures 4.15(a) and 4.15(b) compare the development of the average numbers of peers in the different hierarchy layers for the two cases (1) and (2), respectively. Fig. 4.15(a) shows that with a static value of k the clusters in each layer show a similar size, with more layers being created with growing number of

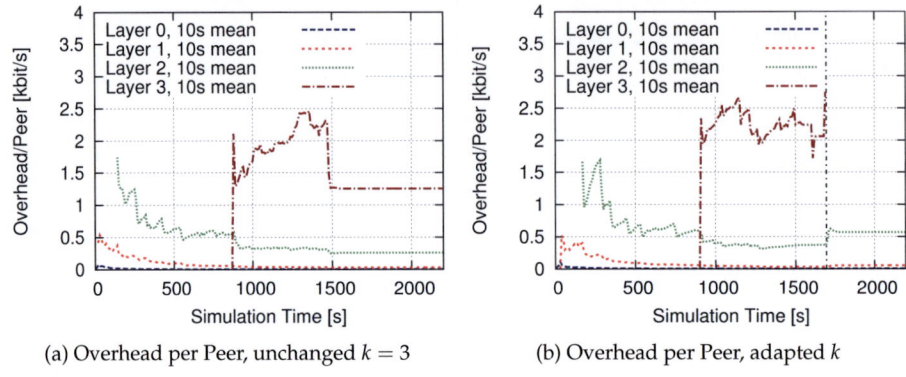

(a) Overhead per Peer, unchanged $k = 3$ (b) Overhead per Peer, adapted k

Figure 4.16 Overhead per Peer in different Layers

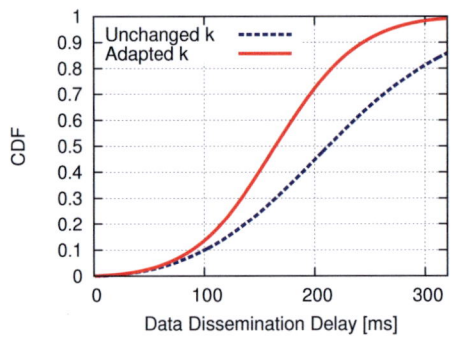

Figure 4.17 Data Dissemination Delays with Unchanged and Adapted k

participants. When adapting k at runtime (Fig. 4.15(b)), the highest layer is eliminated, while the next lower layer grows notably.

Looking at the overhead per peer, Fig. 4.16(a) and Fig. 4.16(b) show that the overhead per peer naturally grows with the highest layer the peer resides in. In case of adapting k, all peers in the highest layer after the adaptation have higher overhead due to the higher number of cluster participants they have to exchange protocol messages with. While the overhead slightly increases, it still remains viable.

Comparing data dissemination delays it can be observed that delay can be significantly reduced by adapting k, as shown in Fig. 4.17. To illustrate the gain of the adaptation more clearly the figure compares the dissemination delays before and after the runtime adaptation of k. The figure shows the CDF of the data dissemination delays for both cases. Regarding mean delays a decrease by approximately 25 % for the observed evaluated example case can be observed. Overall, the proposed scheme allows the cluster size parameter k to be adapted at runtime in order to dynamically change the delay and overhead properties of NICE.

4.3 Conclusion

In this chapter NICE as a prominent ALM protocol has been analyzed with respect to its peer-perceived performance properties. Since ALM protocols are prone to decreased performance compared to solutions integrated in the network, this performance remains as a critical and limiting factor for the deployment of ALM. Thus, the peer-perceived performance of NICE has been observed, especially in large and highly dynamic networks. To this end, NICE has been studied with high numbers of participants as well as aggressive churn to give an idea of expected performance experience to the user and reliability in difficult environments. The evaluations showed that NICE has good scalability properties due to limited per-peer overhead while it provides dissemination delays that grow sub-linearly. Also, join delays get optimized over runtime and in environments with heavy churn high data success rates can still be achieved if aggressive refinement intervals are employed. Furthermore, to increase NICE's applicability an exemplary scheme for the runtime adaptation of the cluster size parameter k has been presented. In Chapter 6 NICE will be revisited and used as an exemplary ALM protocol for the integration of wireless communication domains in the P2P overlay.

5. Capacity Matching in Tree-based Application-Layer Multicast

The highest fraction of Internet traffic is generated by video streaming applications [41], as has already been pointed out in Chapter 1. With more users consuming bandwidth-intense contents the load on content servers is naturally increasing, on the one hand. Since a growing fraction of video streaming applications runs on mobile devices like smartphones, laptops, oder tablets, the data traffic load is additionally increasingly shifted from common home networks to mobile access networks, on the other hand. As a result service providers struggle with effects from the growing bandwidth demands [9].

Most solutions to the access network capacity problem as well as constrained server capacities are connected to high costs and the need for modifications in the network. Also, especially access network technology has inherent capacity limits, e. g. concerning wireless modulation and spatial partitioning. As a different approach P2P approaches could be used to offload servers and also actively consider the network traffic load state: The provision of end-system-based forwarding enables to flexibly react to network changes and adapt the overlay dissemination structure to the current access network traffic load situation. At the same time, costly network infrastructure development from provider's side could be limited.

In Chapter 4 NICE as an approach for scalable ALM has been described and extended. However, this approach has limits in the direct controllability of important properties: While it offers means to adapt the ALM structure with respect to global optimization goals, runtime changes that affect e. g. individual access network capacities are hard to accomplish. Therefore, in this chapter the focus is put to the class of tree-based ALM protocols. These protocols are able to more flexibly adapt to the current network situation and hence offer higher control over important service metrics from a user's and a network provider's point of view.

An approach to use P2P overlays and adapt the ALM tree to access network capacity limits in the context of live video streaming is presented and studied in this chapter. The proposed ALM protocol is called *CMA* (Capacity Matching ALM). It is used to analyze the trade-off between flexibilization and higher traffic load and to answer how well the latter can be controlled. *Flexibilization* here means the freedom of end-system-based forwarding decisions (on which further mechanisms concerning traffic load balancing will developed in Chapter 6). The concepts and evaluation results of CMA are published in [100, 108, 110].

The remainder of the chapter is structured as follows. First, the application scenario targeted in this chapter is defined in Section 5.1, together with a description of the design goals for a tree-based ALM solution. Section 5.2 describes related work in the context of this chapter. Section 5.3 introduces the concept of *Capacity Matching*, which enhances the common approach of Topology Matching in P2P overlays and defines the strategy behind the developed ALM solution. Section 5.4 introduces a system model that helps to better understand what parts of the network scenario are involved, how they relate, and how they finally influence the behavior of the used ALM protocol. Also, the mappings of this system model to the real world network scenario are described. In Section 5.5 the functionality and the parts of the ALM protocol used for the focused application case are described in detail. In Section 5.6 the protocol's ability to cope with the access network traffic load is evaluated with respect to various cases.

5.1   Application Scenario & Goals

Since video streaming services create the highest fraction of current and most probably also future Internet traffic a near-live video streaming scenario is chosen for this chapter's observations.

5.1.1   Scenario

A video stream is disseminated from a video source to a group of receiver peers. Thereby, the following aspects are assumed for the scenario:

- The source peer can either be a dedicated server or one of the end-systems, e. g. in case a live video is recorded and sent to the overlay from a popular sports event which the source peer's user attends.

- "Near-live" dissemination basically means the reception of the video stream by every participating receiver peer in comparably short bounded time, where the target bound can be specified and typically is below a couple of seconds.
- The end-systems reside in cellular 3G access networks, being interconnected by an ALM overlay tree structure that is used to forward the video stream.
- Although end-systems are assumed to be mobile devices the users are assumed to reside in fixed locations in this chapter (e. g. receiving the video stream at a park bench or in a coffeehouse).
- The video stream to be disseminated is not changed or adapted during the overlay-based dissemination process. Rather, it is assumed to be a constant stream of unchanged fix data rate during the lifetime of the overlay in order to provide the same video quality to all peers.
- For the explicit consideration of access network capacities a dedicated information service to request the current load status of a 3G cell is assumed to be available. Proposals exist to serve this purpose and will be described in Section 5.3. While this assumption contradicts the original assumption of depending only on the basic routing service of the underlay such an information service is crucial for congestion avoidance in access networks. Hence, the benefits of such a service are studied in this chapter's evaluations.

5.1.2 Goals

The goals to be accomplished by using P2P in the described scenario are:

- The video source has to be relieved from data forwarding overhead that exceeds its capacities. This goal is inherently reached by using an overlay tree that considers the forwarding capacities of the source peer and shifts part of the load to the overlay structure.
- The involved cellular access networks should not experience congestion due to the data traffic forwarding load. Hence, the access networks' forwarding capacities have to be explicitly considered in overlay tree construction and refinement.
- The ALM dissemination tree has to be established with respect to the defined upper dissemination delay bound to ensure the requirement of near-live video stream dissemination.
- The proposed ALM solution should provide a flexible distributed system that is able to establish and refine a tree autonomously. Furthermore, it should be configurable in order to fit different trade-off priorities between congestion avoidance and dissemination delays.

- The ALM solution should be extensible with respect to the integration of further mechanisms that support the goal of congestion avoidance. Hence, the mechanisms to be integrated should fit into the protocol design without major modifications.

In the following related work in the field of P2P-based video streaming and underlay consideration is described, before a new overlay building strategy as basis for CMA is presented subsequently in Section 5.3.

5.2   Related Work

Finding a dissemination tree among a group of peers that fits given optimization goals is highly related to the well-known class of Steiner tree problems [176]. While these problems are typically solved in a centralized manner under the assumption of complete graph knowledge, establishing a P2P tree requires distributed approaches.

Several P2P-based video streaming protocols have been proposed for use at Internet scale in recent years. Already deployed and actively used systems can be divided into commercial products (e. g. PPS.tv [174], Joost [121], or Zattoo [240]) and protocols originally proposed in the scientific community (e. g. PPLive [173]). In this section P2P-based video streaming systems are classified regarding the streaming service and the established overlay structure. Furthermore, P2P protocols which consider the underlay network topology and forwarding capacities in overlay establishment are described, as they are directly related to the presented CMA protocol. With respect to the application scenario described in Section 5.1 only single-source approaches are considered.

5.2.1   Classification of P2P Video Streaming Systems

Regarding the video streaming service, P2P streaming systems either provide *live video streaming* or *video-on-demand (VoD)* streaming services. In live streaming systems the same video content is disseminated to a group of receiver peers at the same time synchronously, at best with minimal dissemination delay. In VoD systems, in contrast, peers request different videos at different times and watch the contents asynchronously, or they request the same contents, but the playback is not synchronized among the peers. Furthermore, P2P video streaming systems follow different approaches regarding the established overlay structure: They can be divided into *tree-based* and *mesh-based* approaches. Surveys are presented by Liu et al. [143] or Yiu et al. [238], for instance.

Tree-based streaming protocols use either a single tree (*single-tree ALM*) or establish multiple trees at the same time in the same protocol instance (*multi-tree*

ALM). The latter approaches have been introduced as a solution to the lack of traffic load fairness in single-tree protocols, since a high fraction of peers (the leaf peers) does not experience any forwarding load here but only consumes the video contents. Early single-tree live streaming protocol proposals have been introduced as a replacement to IP Multicast: Jannotti et al. [114] focused on bandwidth maximization for all peers, while Chu et al. [40, 98] designed ESM, a protocol for rather small groups of receiver peers. As a first multi-tree protocol, SplitStream [34, 35] establishes multiple dissemination trees where any peer is a forwarding peer in exactly one tree, while being pure consumer (leaf peer) in the remaining trees. This approach enhances fairness regarding content forwarding. Multi-tree approaches have also been studied regarding robustness against attacks. Strufe [212] proposed a trade-off between efficiency and robustness, while Grau et al. [82] described different attacker models for live streaming cases.

In mesh-based protocols no (rather static) tree-based overlay is established. Instead, peers maintain connections to multiple neighboring peers. This approach increases protocol robustness but in turn increases maintenance overhead and complexity. Furthermore, with mesh-based protocols it is difficult to manage seamless data reception of live video streams, as typically the connections in the mesh are frequently dropped and reestablished. The video stream in mesh-based protocols is therefore often partitioned into *chunks*. Then, different chunks can be received from different neighbors and recombined locally. Bullet [129, 130] is a mesh-based protocol that is able to receive data chunks from multiple peers in the mesh concurrently, aiming at increased bandwidth in content reception. However, the maintenance of multiple overlay structures inside a single protocol instance is comparably costly. GridMedia [241] is a gossip-based approach that works similar to Bullet. While its push-pull mechanism is simple and robust, providing low delay bounds for video reception is hard to accomplish. Besides pure tree-based or mesh-based protocols also hybrid approaches have been proposed to gain benefits from both paradigms: mTreebone [228] builds a tree among peers considered stable and then establishes a mesh used for high-bandwidth data dissemination, for instance.

Adapting the overlay structure to the optimization goals is a common approach, but others exist. In recent years efforts have been put into studying how streaming contents can be adapted distributedly at runtime to fit varying peer demands. For instance, Ouyang et al. [165] propose a layered coding scheme to provide adapted multimedia streams to peers with different access capacities. A similar approach is taken by Iqbal and Shirmohammadi [112, 113] who propose to shift the computation load for adapting video contents to the intermediate peers in the overlay. Under the term *Scalable*

Video Coding (SVC) [164] a whole area of research is concerned with video stream adaptation.

The aforementioned P2P-based live streaming approaches in related work use different overlay structures for stream dissemination and follow different design goals. For the application case focused in this chapter VoD protocols are not applicable due to their "cache-and-relay" functionality, precluding live video dissemination. Content-adaptation is neither focused, as remaining access network capacities should not influence the experienced service quality of the peers. Furthermore, most current P2P streaming designs are not ISP friendly, i. e. they do not consider the network state and the generated traffic volume. As a result, the video content distribution cost is shifted to ISP networks (especially today's mobile access networks as described in Chapter 1) without any profit for the ISPs [143]. Related proposals considering the network are described in the following.

5.2.2   Underlay Network Considerations in P2P Protocols

Building overlay structures without consideration of the underlying network topology often leads to the problem of sending data via long overlay paths that do not match possible short underlay path, resulting in inefficient data dissemination. This issue is known as *zigzag routing*. This inefficiency comes with increased traffic load in the network as well as unnecessary long overlay paths. To avoid it, approaches exist that try to build P2P overlays with connections being established preferably between peers that are close to each other in the real underlay network.

The strategy of peering with physically close peers in the overlay is known as *Topology Matching*. The *Location-aware Topology Matching (LTM)* protocol [144] builds an overlay mesh and refines it with respect to the underlay mismatching by dropping inefficient links and actively looking for shorter links during the lifetime of the overlay. The *Adaptive Overlay Topology Optimization (AOTO)* [145] approach uses enhanced flooding techniques and changing peer roles to accomplish multicast communication with underlay topology consideration. The *PROP* [177] approach adapts overlay networks to the underlay topology by switching peers' roles in the overlay. Qui et al. [178] take a similar approach for peer identifiers in structured P2P networks. Further classes of Topology Matching protocols employ either so-called *landmarks* as persistent network components used to determine peers' relative network distances or they establish artificial coordinate spaces to estimate physical network distances. A prominent landmark-based approach has been proposed by Ratnasamy et al. [182], while example coordinate-based protocols include *GNP* [162], *Vivaldi* [48, 49], or *HTRAE* [3, 4]. The *SAT-MATCH* protocol [184] avoids the use of landmarks by using iterative local optimizations, reducing lookup latencies in structured P2P networks.

Besides pure Topology Matching also protocols have been proposed that explicitly consider shared links in the underlay (i. e. links being used by more than one overlay connection). *LCC* [242, 243] models an overlay using linear capacity constraints in order to build maximum-bandwidth multicast trees with help of a distributed heuristic. Kim et al. [125] propose a distributed algorithm that is able to construct an overlay-based multicast tree which provides the source rate of a multimedia dissemination to all receiver peers.

Topology Matching enables to build overlays that induce less communication overhead to the network in general and increase communication performance. However, these approaches are not applicable regarding local network congestions like they occur e. g. in cellular mobile access networks. The explicit consideration of shared links in the underlay (e. g. LCC) is similar to the protocol presented in this chapter. However, most existing protocols following this idea target throughput maximization from a receiver's point of view, not congestion avoidance in the access networks.

In the following section a different approach for building tree-based ALM protocols is described that—in contrast to e. g. Topology Matching—explicitly considers the current traffic load status of access networks in order to find a balance between peer-perceived performance and the access network traffic load.

5.3   Capacity Matching for P2P Protocols

Wireless access networks—regardless which concrete access technology is used—have in common that their data forwarding capacities are shared among all peers residing inside the same access network.

In this thesis the term *Shared Access Medium Domain (SAM)* is introduced and used for all shared access networks in order to abstract from the concrete communication technology. SAMs are used to point out the property of shared capacities from a conceptual point of view but abstract from network access details. However, SAMs can still have different properties, depending on the modeled access technology: *Bidirectional SAMs* model wireless network domains in which incoming and outgoing data affects the shared capacities in similar manner. Hence, one single wireless medium is occupied when data is sent or received. An example for a bidirectional SAM can be a WiFi network domain, for instance. In contrast, *unidirectional SAMs* differentiate medium occupancy in sending and receiving direction. In 3G, for instance, the medium is partitioned into disjunct frequencies and parts of the frequency spectrum are assigned to upstream and downstream direction, re-

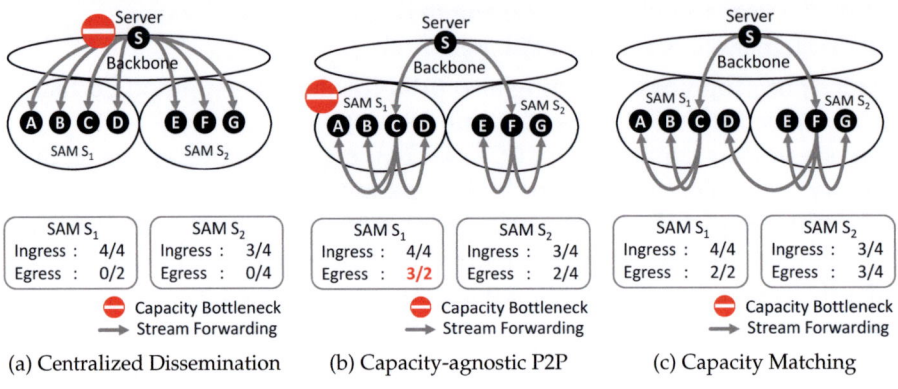

SAM S_1		SAM S_2	
Ingress :	4/4	Ingress :	3/4
Egress :	0/2	Egress :	0/4

SAM S_1		SAM S_2	
Ingress :	4/4	Ingress :	3/4
Egress :	3/2	Egress :	2/4

SAM S_1		SAM S_2	
Ingress :	4/4	Ingress :	3/4
Egress :	2/2	Egress :	3/4

⊖ Capacity Bottleneck
→ Stream Forwarding

⊖ Capacity Bottleneck
→ Stream Forwarding

⊖ Capacity Bottleneck
→ Stream Forwarding

(a) Centralized Dissemination   (b) Capacity-agnostic P2P   (c) Capacity Matching

Figure 5.1 Capacity-agnostic and Capacity-aware Video Dissemination Strategies

spectively (cf. Chapter 2). Hence, different capacities are available in each direction and a dedicated medium occupancy affects only one direction at a time. In this chapter data traffic being sent inside a given SAM is called *ingress traffic*, while traffic being sent from inside a SAM to the outside is called *egress traffic*.

Figure 5.1 shows three example video dissemination strategies in this context. Here, a server acting as the video source is located somewhere in or near to the Internet backbone. Two (unidirectional) SAMs (S_1 and S_2) hold seven receiver peers that receive the video stream. In Figure 5.1(a) a common centralized dissemination approach is shown where the server sends single video streams to each peer. The streams traverse the backbone and enter the SAM domains, inducing ingress traffic. The boxes below the pictures show the exemplary capacities of each SAM domain, expressed linearly in terms of number of streams in ingress and egress direction. These capacities may differ between two SAMs due to different technologies, a different traffic load situations, or different build-out stages inside one access network technology. In the centralized approach the server may run into forwarding congestions due to high numbers of peers requesting the video stream, as indicated in the figure. Also, the limited ingress capacities of the SAMs may run short (like in SAM S_1 in the figure). Data traffic congestions are indicated as red warning signs in the figure denoted as "Capacity Bottleneck".

To unburden the server from its traffic load P2P protocols can be used, shifting the forwarding load to the involved peers. Figure 5.1(b) shows an exemplary implementation. Here, one peer in each SAM (C and F) takes the task of receiving the video stream from the server and forwarding it to its SAM neighbor peers. To avoid zigzag routing and inefficient overlay paths Topology Matching P2P approaches like described in Section 5.2 can be used in order to keep data traffic local. However, while Topology Matching may increase the similarity between overlay and underlay with respect to network distances, local congestion is not avoided (if not even worsen). In Figure 5.1(b) this becomes obvious in case of SAM S_1's egress capacities which are exceeded in the local data forwarding process.

A new P2P building strategy, called *Capacity Matching*, is introduced and used in this chapter to mitigate the problem of local data traffic congestions in wireless access networks. Topology Matching keeps P2P traffic local, which is desirable as long as involved wireless access networks are not congested due to the P2P-induced additional data traffic. In case too many peers' traffic influences a specific access network severely the overlay should be rearranged by leaving the locality goal of Topology Matching in favor of traffic load balancing. Figure 5.1(c) exemplarily shows how the egress traffic can be balanced among different SAM domains in the example, shifting forwarding load from congested SAMs to domains which have capacities left (if existent). The Capacity Matching idea is the basis for the ALM protocol CMA used in the remainder of this chapter.

A general question to be answered is how the ALM protocol is able to acquire the needed information for taking structural decisions. Measurement-based values can be acquired through active probing, as will be described in the following sections. Underlay-specific information like traffic load in the involved wireless access networks is a more severe (and general) problem but is highly required for building the ALM tree. In literature and the scientific community several proposals unanimously argue that providers should share underlay information actively with P2P networks in order to gain benefits for both sides. The *Provider-aided Distance Information System (PaDIS)* [172] ranks any client-host pair in a network based on distance information such as delay, bandwidth, or number of hops. Aggarwal et al. [5, 6] study the effects of different ISP/P2P topologies and show that ISP-aided P2P locality benefits both P2P users and ISPs. Xie et al. [234, 235] propose an architecture called *P4P* to allow for more effective cooperative traffic control between applications and network providers. Dan et al. [51] provide an overview on different approaches regarding ISP and P2P interworking. Furthermore, they develop a classification and insights into the challenges and the benefits. Finally, they state that mutual cooperation between both parties is highly promising but still lacks a good standardization.

As knowledge about the traffic load in the involved access networks is crucial for avoiding congestions, in this chapter's scenario it is assumed that such a mechanism exists and is available to every peer in the overlay at any time.

Hence, the focus of the studies lies on the question if the data traffic load can be efficiently balanced to cope with the P2P drawback of higher traffic load. Also, the implications on other service metrics like dissemination delays have to be studied.

The observed scenario focuses on cellular access networks in which network reachability between all peers is assumed in order to enable the used algorithms to work properly. In the following, a formal system model is introduced to model the network parts and end-systems involved in the target scenario. Afterwards, the ALM protocol CMA is described and evaluated with respect to the goal of congestion avoidance through Capacity Matching.

5.4   System Model

The given scenario focuses on a case in which a live video stream has to be disseminated to a group of wirelessly attached peers. In this section a system model is developed that helps to better understand which parts of the network are involved, how they relate, and how they finally influence the behavior of the ALM protocol. First, the system model parts are introduced as abstract entities. Then, the relations to real physical network parts are clarified. Finally, the constraints that an ALM solution has to fulfill are defined. These constraints also directly determine the ALM protocol configuration which is described subsequently.

In general, most networks can be modeled by a graph $\mathcal{G} = (\mathcal{V},\mathcal{E})$, $\mathcal{V}$ being the graph vertices and $\mathcal{E}$ being the graph edges. For the target scenario in this chapter an enhanced directed multigraph

$$\mathcal{G} = (\mathcal{V},\mathcal{E},\mathcal{C},\mathcal{S})$$

is used, where $\mathcal{V} = \{v_1,...,v_n\}$ denotes the set of *vertices* (peers) and $\mathcal{E} \subseteq \{(u,v)|u,v \in \mathcal{V}, u \neq v\}$ denotes the set of *edges*. Each edge connects exactly two vertices in the dedicated direction from u to v. No reflexive edges are allowed in the graph. Additionally, the model comprises *channels* $\mathcal{C}$, each being mappable to a subset of $\mathcal{E}$ as well as SAMs $\mathcal{S}$, each being mappable to a subset of $\mathcal{C}$. The following sections detail on these model parts.

Vertices

The graph vertices $\mathcal{V}$ represent all participating peers (i.e. end-systems) in the target application scenario (cf. Section 5.1). Each vertice $v \in \mathcal{V}$ holds a specific internal capacity value

$$cap^{(io)}(v) : \mathcal{V} \rightarrow \mathbb{R}_0^+.$$

Figure 5.2(a) exemplarily shows a simple graph with four participating peers labeled A to D and eight edges.

Edges

The edges $\mathcal{E}$ express how the participating peers are able to communicate with each other. An edge from peer u to peer v indicates that v is directly reachable for u. A multicast dissemination tree among all vertices comprises a subset $\overline{\mathcal{E}} \subseteq \mathcal{E}$ of edges (cf. Figure 5.2(b)). Sender and receiver of an edge e are determined by the mappings $snd(e) : \mathcal{E} \rightarrow \mathcal{V}$ and $rcv(e) : \mathcal{E} \rightarrow \mathcal{V}$.

Each edge $e \in \mathcal{E}$ is associated to two cost metrics (cf. Figure 5.2(b)), being

$$\delta(e) : \mathcal{E} \rightarrow \mathbb{R}_0^+$$

and

$$\beta(e) : \mathcal{E} \rightarrow \mathbb{R}_0^+.$$

Channels

The number of incoming or outgoing edges per vertice is bounded in the graph model. This bound is individual per vertice and is modeled through the graph's *channels*. One or more channels are attached to each vertice and each channel comprises a subset of the specific vertice's incoming or outgoing edges.

Hence, a channel $c \in \mathcal{C}$ can be mapped to its contained edges via two mapping functions

$$out(c) : \mathcal{C} \rightarrow \{\{e_1, ..., e_m\} | e_i \in \mathcal{E}\}$$

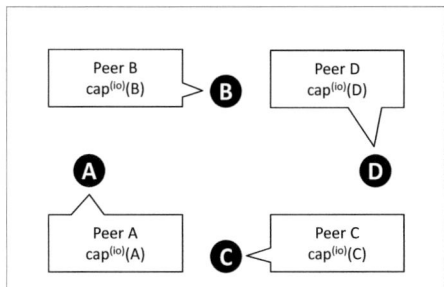

(a) Four Vertices with internal Capacity Values

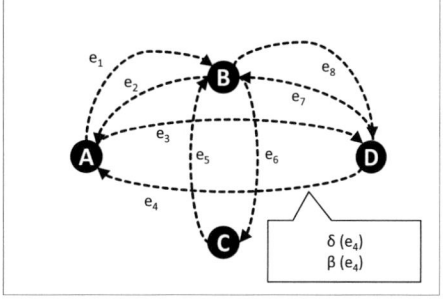

(b) Edges model Communication Possibilities

Figure 5.2 Example Graph

and

$$in(c) : C \rightarrow \{\{e_1, ..., e_n\}|e_i \in \mathcal{E}\}.$$

Likewise, for a given edge $e \in \mathcal{E}$, the mappings

$$chan^{(snd)}(e) : \mathcal{E} \rightarrow C$$

and

$$chan^{(rcv)}(e) : \mathcal{E} \rightarrow C$$

return the involved channels for that edge. Fig. 5.3(a) shows a set of channels in the example (c_1 to c_5), visualized through colored circles around the respective vertices a channel is attached to. The example model comprises five channels, two of them are attached to vertice B, while all other vertices comprise exactly one channel.

Like vertices, also channels hold specific capacity values. In case of channels, they are differentiated between incoming (ingress) and outgoing (egress) edges:

$$cap^{(egress)}(c) : C \rightarrow \mathbb{R}_0^+$$

and

$$cap^{(ingress)}(c) : C \rightarrow \mathbb{R}_0^+.$$

A special property of channels is that their capacity values are potentially connected, meaning that they describe a shared value. In this case incoming and outgoing edges consume the same (shared) capacity of the channel and no differentiation by the direction of sending is necessary. This property models the difference between bidirectional and unidirectional capacity con-

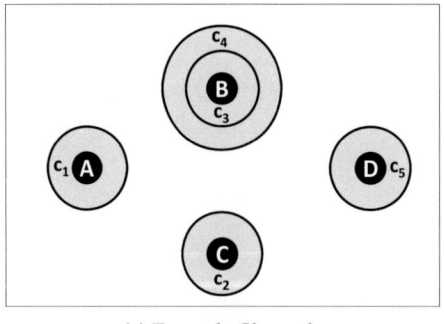

(a) Example Channels

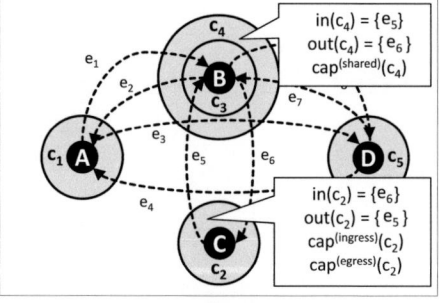

(b) Channel Attributes

Figure 5.3   Channels and Channel Attributes in the Graph Model

straints (cf. Section 5.3). In case of bidirectional capacities a channel holds one single capacity value

$$cap^{(shared)}(c) : C \rightarrow \mathbb{R}_0^+.$$

Fig. 5.3(b) exemplarily shows the complete attribute sets connected to two of the channels, one located at peer B and one at peer C. The capacity values at peer B's channel (c_4) are bidirectional.

SAM Domains

A SAM $s \in \mathcal{S}$ is defined as a set of channels. A SAM can be mapped to its contained channels:

$$channels(s) : \mathcal{S} \rightarrow \{\{c_1, ..., c_p\}|c_i \in \mathcal{C}\}.$$

Fig. 5.4(a) shows three SAM domains in the example graph model. Again, the channels are labeled c_1 to c_5 and SAMs are visualized through dotted ellipses (labeled s_1 to s_3). Similar to channels, SAMs have attached capacity values. Therefore, two distinct capacity values correspond to a SAM domain $s \in \mathcal{S}$, being

$$cap^{(egress)}(s) : \mathcal{S} \rightarrow \mathbb{R}_0^+$$

and

$$cap^{(ingress)}(s) : \mathcal{S} \rightarrow \mathbb{R}_0^+.$$

Furthermore, these capacities may just as well be either unidirectional or bidirectional in SAMs. In the latter case a SAM only holds one single capacity value

$$cap^{(shared)}(s) : \mathcal{S} \rightarrow \mathbb{R}_0^+.$$

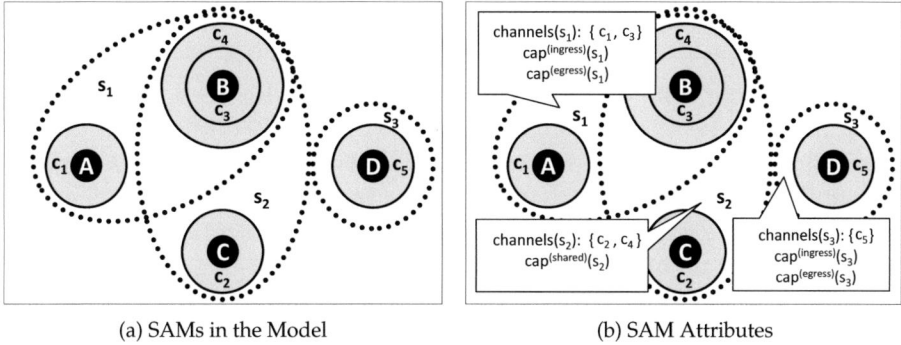

(a) SAMs in the Model   (b) SAM Attributes

Figure 5.4 SAMs and SAM Attributes in the System Model

Fig. 5.4(b) shows the complete attribute sets for the three example SAMs. Furthermore, s_2 holds the property of bidirectional capacities.

Graph Model Constraints

In a valid graph model, the following constraints have to be met:

- Each vertice has at least one channel being attached to it at all times.
- For every SAM in the model a given vertice may have either none or exactly one channel being attached to this SAM.
- No two distinct edges may have the same channel in incoming and outgoing direction concurrently, i. e.

$$\forall e_i, e_j \in \mathcal{E}, i \neq j : (chan^{(snd)}(e_i) = chan^{(snd)}(e_j))$$
$$\Rightarrow (chan^{(rcv)}(e_i) \neq chan^{(rcv)}(e_j))$$

and

$$\forall e_i, e_j \in \mathcal{E}, i \neq j : (chan^{(rcv)}(e_i) = chan^{(rcv)}(e_j))$$
$$\Rightarrow (chan^{(snd)}(e_i) \neq chan^{(snd)}(e_j)).$$

Model Relations to the "Real World"

In this section the relations between the introduced system model and the real world are explained to ease the understanding of the model. Since communication in today's Internet—especially in wireless environments—cannot be assumed to have the same properties in both directions between two participants, the model uses a directed multigraph. Here, each edge can be used to model a specific direction of communication with its specific properties. The model further abstracts from intermediate systems that may be part of a real underlay (like e. g. routers) and only models end-to-end communication relations. Despite this abstraction it still sufficiently considers important properties (like e. g. network bottlenecks) of involved underlay systems.

A vertice's value $cap^{(io)}$ reflects the amount of data this vertice is able to actively forward to other vertices. Kristiansen et al. [131–133] point out that especially in small mobile end-systems the forwarding capacity is often not only limited by the wireless device, but also by the internal processing capabilities of the end-system. They argue that these effects must not be ignored when modeling mobile end-systems that are involved in peer-assisted data forwarding. Wireless end-systems in a P2P scenario potentially take high forwarding responsibility. Hence, the value $cap^{(io)}$ implements a limiting factor for communication, besides the wireless device capacity. In scenarios with high-bandwidth video, for instance, situations may occur when a peer's number of outgoing edges will be bounded by its internal capabilities even if its wireless network device capacities would allow for more.

Edges do not necessarily indicate active data transmissions nor active connections, but rather show all possibilities the peers may have to directly communicate via the underlying network path that connects them (end-to-end connectivity). Each data transmission via one of the edges is in a real communication scenario always connected to some network transmission delay which is accommodated in the model by the non-negative distance value $\delta(e)$. Finally, communication between peers will always consume a specific amount of network bandwidth per time—which also applies to edges in the model. This capacity consumption is accommodated by applying the dedicated bandwidth consumption value $\beta(e)$.

A peer has a specific data capacity it may send or receive via a specific wireless communication technology. This capacity is shared by all incoming or outgoing edges via this technology on this specific peer. The edges influence each other with respect to the remaining local capacities which are reflected in the model by the concept of *channels*. To reflect the mentioned local capacity constraints channels occupy their specific capacity values $cap^{(egress)}$ and $cap^{(ingress)}$. These capacities may be bidirectional, i. e. both egress and ingress traffic consume part of it. Examples are WiFi domains (bidirectional) or 3G (unidirectional), respectively. The model has the ability to reflect this issue by connecting the values logically, providing a single capacity value $cap^{(shared)}$. To put it simple, all channels attached to a vertice model this peer's network devices with their specific capacity constraints.

SAMs reflect whole shared access network domains like 3G cells or public WiFi domains, for instance. SAM capacities $cap^{(egress)}$ and $cap^{(ingress)}$ model overall capacities (i. e. constraints of the network access technology), being shared by all channels (and therefore vertices) that belong to a specific SAM domain. Just like in case of channels, these capacities may as well be bidirectional in SAMs. As SAMs are intended to model real communication domains, in the real world there is potential of mutual affection and disruption between two such domains in the same local area. One example is operation in the same frequency spectrum, e. g. in case of WiFi and Bluetooth. These effects are not part of the model.

Constraints for an ALM Solution in the System Model

The problem statement with respect to the graph model can be formulated as finding a multicast dissemination tree that connects all peers and considers the described constraints. Hence, the goal is finding a subset of edges $\overline{\mathcal{E}} \subseteq \mathcal{E}$, forming a tree with the source peer as root and providing the following properties: Each peer's internal capacities $cap^{(io)}$ may not be exceeded. The same holds for all involved channels and SAMs concerning their egress and ingress capacity constraints. These constraints define the solution space in which the ALM protocol instance operates to find a dissemination solution that is close to optimal. They are defined in the following:

- The involved vertices' internal processing capacities restrict communication in the solution. Thus, a vertice $v \in V$ may never forward more data through its outgoing edges than its internal capacity $cap^{(io)}$ allows. Hence, it must hold that

$$\forall v \in V, e \in \mathcal{E}: \sum_{snd(e)=v} \beta(e) \leq cap^{(io)}(v).$$

- Channels occupy capacity bounds in incoming and outgoing direction. The sum of bandwidth consumption through edges may not exceed these bounds. Therefore, it must hold that

$$\forall c \in \mathcal{C}: \sum_{e \in in(c)} \beta(e) \leq cap^{(ingress)}(c),$$

and analogously

$$\forall c \in \mathcal{C}: \sum_{e \in out(c)} \beta(e) \leq cap^{(egress)}(c).$$

In case of $\mathcal{C}$ being all channels that have bidirectional capacity properties, meaning that the capacity is shared in both incoming and outgoing direction, it must hold that

$$\forall c \in \mathcal{C}: \sum_{e \in \{in(c) \cup out(c)\}} \beta(e) \leq cap^{(shared)}(c).$$

- For each SAM in the model the sum of ingress bandwidth consumptions may not exceed the respective ingress capacity constraints $cap^{(ingress)}$ of this SAM, similar to capacities in channels. Then, the following must hold at all times:

$$\forall s \in \mathcal{S}, c \in \mathcal{C}, e \in \mathcal{E}: \sum_{c \in channels(s)} \sum_{e \in in(c)} \beta(e) \leq cap^{(ingress)}(s).$$

Likewise, as a SAM's upstream capacity is also bounded by $cap^{(egress)}$, it has to hold that

$$\forall s \in \mathcal{S}, c \in \mathcal{C}, e \in \mathcal{E} : \sum_{c \in channels(s)} \sum_{e \in out(c)} \beta(e) \leq cap^{(egress)}(s).$$

Finally, in case of S being the set of all SAMs that have bidirectional capacity properties, meaning that the capacity is shared in both incoming and outgoing direction, it must hold that

$$\forall s \in \mathcal{S}, c \in \mathcal{C}, e \in \mathcal{E} : \sum_{c \in channels(s)} \sum_{e \in \{out(c) \cup in(c)\}} \beta(e) \leq cap^{(shared)}(s).$$

In the following a tree-based ALM solution that holds the described constraints is presented. Its overall goal is the provision of a live video stream dissemination with consideration of limited access network capacities and the resulting video dissemination delays. The specific design goals are formulated in the next section. The protocol is further used to analyze how capacity considerations impair dissemination delays in tree-based ALM and how well the P2P-inherent additional traffic load can be balanced among the wireless access networks.

5.5 Capacity Matching ALM Protocol

In this section the tree-based ALM protocol *CMA* (Capacity Matching ALM) is described. It aims at considering the traffic load status in wireless access networks in its dissemination tree establishment while at the same time taking the resulting dissemination delays in the tree into account. The protocol is used for evaluation and to analyze the trade-off effects between traffic load and data dissemination delay in the described application scenario (cf. Section 5.1). First, the general design goals of the protocol are revisited with respect to the scenario and the graph model. Then, the parts of the protocol and the functionality of each part are described in detail.

5.5.1 CMA Design Goals

The P2P protocol CMA aims at the following design goals:

- It has to consider the data traffic load situation of the wireless access networks involved in the data dissemination process. Hence, CMA has to build and maintain its tree with respect to the cellular access networks the peers reside in. Accordingly, CMA follows the Capacity Matching approach described in Section 5.3.
- Besides Capacity Matching, the protocol has to provide sufficient service quality with respect to the application case of near-live video streaming.

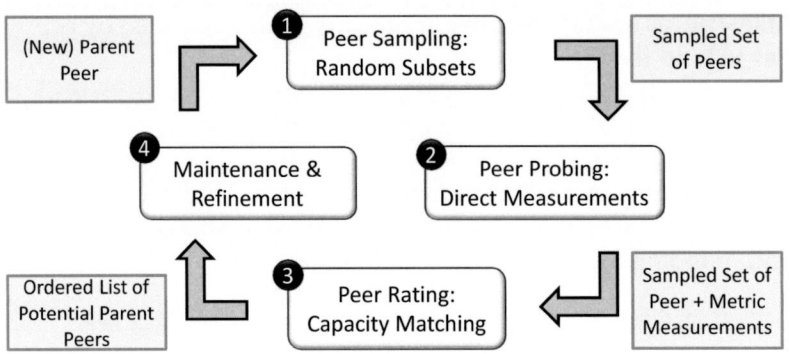

Figure 5.5 Chain of functional Mechanisms in the CMA Protocol

Therefore, it has to allow for the specification of an upper delay bound to be considered in the tree-building process.

- The constraints for a solution stated in Section 5.4 have to be fulfilled at all times in order to avoid exceeding capacity constraints of end-systems and wireless access networks.

To accomplish these design goals CMA comprises a set of functional protocol parts, described in the following.

5.5.2   CMA Protocol Parts

As a pure P2P approach CMA has to take its decisions completely distributedly and without any central entity. Therefore, each peer has to execute the protocol and acquire the information needed for building and maintaining the tree and forwarding the stream autonomously. Doing so, each peer executes a chain of functional mechanisms. The mechanisms implement the typical steps a distributed tree-based protocol has to accomplish and aims at finding potential better parent peers to refine the tree. The chain is executed periodically, each period is called *epoch*.

First, knowledge about other peers in the tree has to be acquired (*Peer Sampling*). Second, measurements against these other peers have to be initiated to determine the involved metrics to be considered (*Peer Probing*). Third, the peers have to be rated according to a certain quality function (*Peer Rating*), and last, further refinement steps and robustness mechanisms should be executed (*Maintenance & Refinement*). The latter includes the decision if and how a peer should initiate a position change in the dissemination tree.

Figure 5.5 gives an overview on the functional mechanisms and the information being shared between them. The mechanisms and their inner workings in CMA will be described in the next sections. Furthermore, Appendix C gives an outlook on a possible generalization of the concepts used in this chapter in order to provide means for more generic tree-based ALM protocols with respect to flexibility and extensibility. CMA itself is a concrete implementation which focuses on design goals relevant to the near-live video streaming scenario as described in Section 5.5.1.

5.5.2.1 Peer Sampling: Random Subsets (RanSub)

Since the number of peers in the overlay tree may be high, a peer sampling mechanism is needed that preferably provides the following properties:

- It has to scale with the number of peers, i.e. required per-peer state and network communication overhead should grow sub-linearly with the number of peers in the overlay.
- Each subset received by a peer should consist of peers uniformly distributed across the global set of peers such that each remote peer appears with equal probability.
- Different subsets should be available for each peer, periodically. Thereby, no correlations should exist between the contents of two consecutive subsets received by a peer.
- Peers that leave the overlay or fail should be excluded from the sampling process and should not be considered in future subsets.

To provide a peer sampling mechanism that fulfills these requirements the *RanSub* [128] protocol is used, being proposed by Kostic et al. and being specifically designed to operate on tree-based structures. Alternative approaches with similar functionality are e.g. *RandPeer* [138] or *SwapLinks*[222]. As RanSub allows to work on the dissemination tree directly without requiring further components, structures, or mechanisms that add complexity, it is chosen as peer sampling mechanism here.

The Peer Sampling functional mechanism—and therefore also RanSub—is executed once per epoch. Internally, RanSub comprises two phases: The first phase (*Collect Phase*) is used to learn about peers in the tree, while the second phase (*Distribute Phase*) propagates random subsets of these peers down the tree. Figure 5.6(a) exemplarily visualizes both phases in case of eight tree participants. In the following, the phases are described in more detail.

Collect Phase

In the Collect Phase peers send *Collect Messages* up the tree, starting from the leave peers. Once a peer received Collect Messages for one epoch from all of its children in the tree, it further propagates an own aggregated Collect Message to its parent peer. Collect Messages contain peer addresses from subtree peers (Collect Sets, CS). The number of peer addresses contained in a Collect Set is configurable in RanSub. In CMA a size of $log_e(n)$ is used, n being the total number of peers. Furthermore, the addresses in the Collect Messages are chosen probabilistically and uniformly distributed from all subtree peers. To ensure that a Collect Message contains probabilistic and uniformly representatives of all peers in a subtree RanSub uses a special *Compact* operation. *Compact* incrementally builds new Collect Messages by choosing peers based on the number of subtree members that a given Collect Message represents. An example is shown in Figure 5.6(b) where peer A executes *Compact* based on two Collect Messages it received from peer B and D, respectively. Here, the Collect Message from peer B represents 30 peers in its subtree, while the message from peer D represents only 10 subtree peers. Both Collect Sets hold $|CS| = 8$ peers, and the target output size is also set to be 8. Based on this information a new aggregated Collect Message is built by choosing 6 peers from peer B's Collect Message and 2 peers from D's Collect Message, accounting for the fraction of peers both messages represent. This procedure ensures a uniform distribution of chosen peers considering the sizes of the involved subtrees.

Distribute Phase

After the *Collect Phase* RanSub starts the *Distribute Phase*. The goal of the Distribute Phase is to provide every peer in the tree with random subsets based on the information learned in the Collect Phase. Starting from the root peer of the tree each peer sends *Distribute Messages* to all of its children. A Distribute Message contains addresses from a subset of all peers that have been collected in the Collect Phase. RanSub basically offers three choices of how to built Distribute Messages in its original proposal, differing in complexity and target scenario. The protocol instance employed in this chapter is configured to use the mechanism called *RanSub-ordered* (for details on the other mechanisms see [128]).

RanSub-ordered imposes a total ordering among all collected peers. In the process of building a Distribute Message for a child only peers are consid-

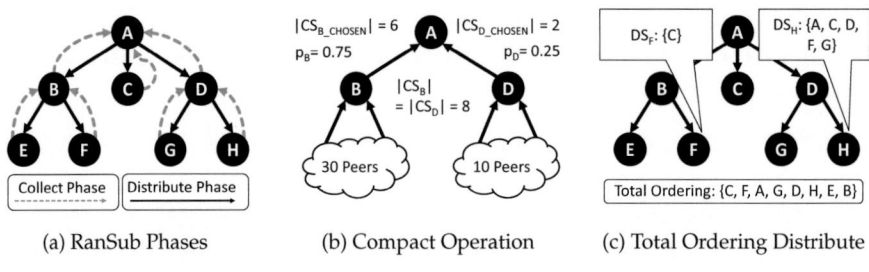

(a) RanSub Phases   (b) Compact Operation   (c) Total Ordering Distribute

Figure 5.6 Distributed In-tree Peer Sampling with RanSub

ered to be chosen if they are predecessors of this child with respect to the total ordering. The total ordering ensures that simultaneous tree transformations based on the Distribute Messages will not introduce loops. Figure 5.6(c) shows an example how RanSub-ordered chooses Distribute Message contents and provides Distribute Sets (DS) to the peers, accordingly. Two peers (F and H) are chosen as example receivers of random subsets in one epoch. Here, a total ordering is determined at root peer A that leads to peer F receiving only one peer address, since it is among the first peers in the total ordering, being successor of peer C only. Peer H, in contrast, receives more peer addresses in its random subset due to its position in the total ordering. This drawback from F's point of view will be relativized in the next epochs when a new total ordering is determined. This procedure ensures that, with growing number of epochs, all peers have similar chances of receiving appropriate randomized peer subsets.

5.5.2.2 Peer Probing: Direct Measurements

In the CMA protocol peers in the sampled set are directly probed to determine the required metrics for tree refinement. A peer v_0 receiving a set $\mathcal{R} = \{v_1, ..., v_n\} \subseteq \mathcal{V}$ through the mechanisms described in Peer Sampling starts a dedicated measurement to each peer in the set $\mathcal{R}$ as soon as the Peer Sampling mechanism has finished. Additionally, peer v_0 measures against its current direct parent peer p_0 in the tree. The measurements are used to gain knowledge about properties of the network paths between v_0 and the probed peers, on the one hand. On the other hand, also local information from each peer (e. g. remaining capacities or network distance to the root peer) are requested.

Information	Description
$\delta(v_0, p_0)$	Network distance betw. peer v_0 and peer p_0
$\Delta(p_0)$	Root-to-peer network distance (overlay hops) of parent peer p_0
$\Delta(v_i)$	Root-to-peer network distance (overlay hops) of peer v_i
$\kappa(v_i)$	Current internal processing load on peer v_i
$cap^{(io)}(v_i)$	Overall internal capacity of peer v_i
$\sum_{e \in out(c_i)} \beta(e)$	Current egress bandwidth usage in channel c_i
$cap^{(egress)}(c_i)$	Overall egress bandwidth capacity of channel c_i
$\sum_{c \in channels(s_i)} \sum_{e \in in(c)} \beta(e)$	Current egress bandwidth usage in SAM s_i
$cap^{(egress)}(s_i)$	Overall egress bandwidth capacity of SAM s_i

Table 5.1 Acquired Peer Probing Information in CMA

Table 5.1 provides an overview on the information that is acquired by Peer Probing in CMA. In each epoch v_0 learns about its network distance (i.e. transmission delay) to its direct parent peer p_0, denoted as $\delta(v_0, p_0)$. Also, it learns about p_0's current network distance to the root peer of the tree, denoted as $\Delta(p_0)$. This value is acquired by incrementally summing up all values $\delta(v_i, p_i)$, v_i being all peers upwards in the tree with their respective parents p_i. Thus, $\Delta(p_0)$ reflects the sum of overlay-hop distances between p_0 and the root peer. Likewise, v_0 learns about its network distance to every peer $v_i \in R$ ($\delta(v_0, v_i)$) as well as their respective distances to the root peer ($\Delta(v_i)$). The distances to the root peer directly reflect the respective current video stream dissemination delays, being a crucial metric for the targeted multicast service.

Furthermore, v_0 learns about the current internal processing load (denoted as $\kappa(v_i)$) as well as the overall internal processing capacity $cap^{(io)}(v_i)$ of each probed peer v_i. Similarly, the current bandwidth usage for a probed peer's channel is learned, denoted as $\sum_{e \in out(c_i)} \beta(e)$, together with the overall capacity of the latter, denoted as $cap^{(egress)}(c_i)$.

To consider the traffic load status in the access networks v_0 queries the current consumed outgoing bandwidth of each SAM domain s_i in which the probed peer v_i currently resides. A dedicated component, for instance P4P [234, 235], is assumed to be available here (cf. Section 5.3). The current consumed outgoing bandwidth of a SAM s_i is denoted as $\sum_{c \in channels(s_i)} \sum_{e \in in(c)} \beta(e)$. Additionally, v_0 learns the respective overall outgoing capacity $cap^{(egress)}(s_i)$ of SAM s_i. This information is crucial for balancing the induced egress load in the access networks. The information learned in Peer Probing is directly used in Peer Rating as described in the following. Peer Rating thereby directly follows the idea of the Capacity Matching approach.

5.5.2.3 Peer Rating: Capacity Matching

In the Peer Rating functional part the quality of probed peers regarding their role as potential tree parents is determined. The part thereby follows the Capacity Matching idea. It has to accomplish two steps:

- First, it has to sort out those peers in R that will miss the constraints defined in the graph model in Section 5.4.
- Second, it has to sort the remaining candidate peers (according to its used quality measures) to determine the best.

The quality measure in CMA is based on a weighted sum heuristic. It is employed to transform multiple tree optimization objectives into a scalar value in order to reach comparability. In multi-objective problems the weighted sum approach is a traditional technique to achieve optimization [141]. It preserves decidability even in face of a set of very different (and contrary) optimization objectives. In the case observed here the weighted sum takes information acquired through Peer Probing as input.

The weighted sum heuristic is designed to provide the possibility to trade off between traffic load consideration and resulting dissemination delay, reflecting the two main dimensions of optimization in CMA. It is a trade-off since disregarding dissemination delay optimization creates higher probability for load balancing opportunities and vice versa, as will be shown in evaluations. Furthermore, the design constraints have to be considered and met in the weighted sum. The formal description of the used weighted sum heuristic is introduced in the following before the mapping of the given constraints and optimization goals for CMA in the concrete scenario is discussed.

Objectives & Weighted Sum

To express optimization goals CMA uses a set of *Objectives*. Furthermore, these Objectives are assigned to different classes, influencing how Objectives are evaluated in CMA. The different classes indicate whether an Objective defines *strict discrete bounds* that must not be exceeded or *non-strict optimization goals* that aim at metric minimization. For evaluating the weighted sum in CMA's Peer Rating part the collected sampling set $\mathcal{R}$ is used, together with the measured metric values gained in Peer Probing.

Given n (measurable[1]) metrics $(m^{(1)}, ..., m^{(n)})$, n weight factors $(\alpha^{(1)}, ..., \alpha^{(n)})$, $\alpha^{(i)} \in [0,1]$, n normalization values $(\mathcal{T}^{(m^{(1)})}, ..., \mathcal{T}^{m^{(n)}})$, and n value domains $(\mathcal{D}^{(1)}, ..., \mathcal{D}^{(n)})$. For each tuple $(m^{(i)}, \mathcal{T}^{(m^{(i)})})$, $m^{(i)}$ and $\mathcal{T}^{(m^{(i)})}$ belong to the same value domain $\mathcal{D}^{(i)}$, like e. g. $\mathcal{D}^{(i)} = \mathbb{R}_0^+$ in case of the network distance $\delta(v_i)$. This restriction is important in order to ensure comparability between the values. An Objective $\mathcal{O}^{(i)}$ is always evaluated for a candidate peer v_{cand} and is of the form

$$\mathcal{O}^{(i)}(v_{cand}) = \alpha^{(i)} \cdot \left[\frac{m^{(i)}(v_{cand})}{\mathcal{T}^{(m^{(i)})}} \right].$$

$m^{(i)}(v_{cand})$ holds the estimated metric value for metric $m^{(i)}$ regarding peer v_{cand}. In CMA the set of Objectives $\mathcal{X} = \{\mathcal{O}^{(1)}, ..., \mathcal{O}^{(n)}\}$ defines the overall optimization goal for this CMA tree.

---

[1]"Measurable" means the metric can either be gained via active network measurements or by requesting the specific metric value from the probed peer directly.

The Objectives $O^{(i)} \in \mathcal{X}$ can be transformed into a scalar value $\Psi(v_{cand})$ via a weighted sum heuristic Ψ:

$$
\begin{aligned}
\Psi(v_{cand}) &= \sum_{i=1}^{n} \mathcal{O}^{(i)}(v_{cand}) \\
&= \mathcal{O}^{(1)}(v_{cand}) + \mathcal{O}^{(2)}(v_{cand}) + \cdots + \mathcal{O}^{(n)}(v_{cand}) \\
&= \alpha^{(1)} \cdot \left[\frac{m^{(1)}(v_{cand})}{\mathcal{T}^{(m^{(1)})}} \right] + \alpha^{(2)} \cdot \left[\frac{m^{(2)}(v_{cand})}{\mathcal{T}^{(m^{(2)})}} \right] + \cdots \\
&\quad + \alpha^{(n)} \cdot \left[\frac{m^{(n)}(v_{cand})}{\mathcal{T}^{(m^{(n)})}} \right].
\end{aligned}
$$

Each value $m^{(i)}(v_{cand})$ represents a metric value of interest (acquired in Peer Probing), while each $\mathcal{T}^{(m^{(i)})}$ represents an upper bound value in the same value domain $\mathcal{D}^{(i)}$. Hence, $\frac{m^{(i)}(v_{cand})}{\mathcal{T}^{(m^{(i)})}}$ expresses a quality measure, reflecting how the quality of peer v_{cand} regarding Objective $\mathcal{O}^{(i)}$ is. The weight factors $\alpha^{(i)}$ are used to express a relative importance for each Objective $\mathcal{O}^{(i)}$. It must hold that $\sum_{i=1}^{n} \alpha^{(i)} = 1$, conforming to common practice in weighted sum heuristic approaches. If no such relative importance is specified it is implicitly assumed that $\alpha^{(i)} = \frac{1}{n}$.

Objective Classification

Two classes of Objectives are differentiated in CMA: *Constrained Objectives* ($\mathcal{CO}$) and *Optimization Objectives* ($\mathcal{OO}$). An Objective $\mathcal{O}^{(i)}$ belongs to at least one class but can also belong to both classes, concurrently. Objectives can therefore be of one of three types. The Objective classes directly influence how Ψ is further evaluated in CMA's Peer Rating.

- **Optimization Objectives** ($\mathcal{OO}$): Objectives of this class are always tried to be minimized. Thus, if $\alpha^{(i)} \cdot \left[\frac{m^{(i)}(v_1)}{\mathcal{T}^{(m^{(i)})}} \right] < \alpha^{(i)} \cdot \left[\frac{m^{(i)}(v_2)}{\mathcal{T}^{(m^{(i)})}} \right]$ holds for two peers v_1 and v_2, v_1 will be considered the better choice regarding Objective $\mathcal{O}^{(i)}$. This approach works for CMA since Objectives in $\mathcal{OO}$ only have to be minimized (e. g. in case of data dissemination delay).
- **Constrained Objectives** ($\mathcal{CO}$): Objectives of this class have a dedicated upper bound which defines their tolerable operation space. This upper bound is expressed through the normalization value $\mathcal{T}^{(m^{(i)})}$ for an Objective $\mathcal{O}^{(i)} \in \mathcal{CO}$. In case $m^{(i)}$ exceeds the upper bound $\mathcal{T}^{(m^{(i)})}$ the peer's state is considered intolerable. Then, CMA tries to react accordingly, e. g. by changing the peer's position in the tree. The upper bounds $\mathcal{T}^{(m^{(i)})}$ are

combined in the set $\mathcal{T}$. In contrast to Objectives in $\mathcal{OO}$, Objectives in $\mathcal{CO}$ are not tried to be minimized as long as they do not exceed their upper bound, i. e. as long as $m^{(i)} < \mathcal{T}^{(m^{(i)})}$ the heuristic will not try to optimize the peer's position in the tree considering metric $m^{(i)}$.

The classification of the Objectives is defined in the set

$$\mathcal{CL} = \{\mathcal{CO}, \mathcal{OO}, \mathcal{T}\}.$$

The definition of Objectives as well as their assignment to classes in Peer Rating is part of CMA protocol configuration.

For all Objectives $\mathcal{O}^{(j)} \in \mathcal{CO}$ an upper bound value $\mathcal{T}^{(m^{(j)})}$ has to be defined in order to properly decide if a bound is exceeded. For all Objectives $\mathcal{O}^{(k)}$ in $\mathcal{OO}$ but not in $\mathcal{CO}$ $\mathcal{T}^{(m^{(k)})}$ is determined per epoch by evaluating the worst value learned in Peer Probing. Since it can be a complex task to define a proper upper bound value, e. g. because the network properties are not sufficiently known, this approach releases from providing a dedicated upper bound value, especially if Objectives are not constrained. Using the worst value learned serves as a basic indicator about a peer's current state in the tree, compared to a subset of other peers.

Heuristic Transformation

Metric measurements are often prone to variations during epochs because network paths' or peers' properties change over time. To consider these changes a weighted sum heuristic evaluated at epoch t for a peer v_{cand} is denoted as $\Psi_t(v_{cand})$ in CMA. In order to consider the different Objective classes introduced above the weighted sum heuristic $\Psi_t(v_{cand})$ has to be transformed into a new heuristic $\widehat{\Psi}_t(v_{cand})$ by using a dedicated transformation function once per epoch. $\widehat{\Psi}_t(v_{cand})$ preserves the requirement that $\sum_{i=1}^{n} \widehat{\alpha}^{(i)} = 1$ in all cases. The *Heuristic Transformation Function* $\mathcal{H}$ at epoch t is[2]

$$\mathcal{H}(\Psi_t, \mathcal{CL}) = \mathcal{H}(\alpha_t^{(1)} \cdot \left[\frac{m_t^{(1)}}{\mathcal{T}^{(m_t^{(1)})}}\right] + \alpha_t^{(2)} \cdot \left[\frac{m_t^{(2)}}{\mathcal{T}^{(m_t^{(2)})}}\right] + \cdots + \alpha_t^{(n)} \cdot \left[\frac{m_t^{(n)}}{\mathcal{T}^{(m_t^{(n)})}}\right], \mathcal{CL})$$

$$= \widehat{\alpha}_t^{(1)} \cdot \left[\frac{m_t^{(1)}}{\mathcal{T}^{(m_t^{(1)})}}\right] + \widehat{\alpha}_t^{(2)} \cdot \left[\frac{m_t^{(2)}}{\mathcal{T}^{(m_t^{(2)})}}\right] + \cdots + \widehat{\alpha}_t^{(n)} \cdot \left[\frac{m_t^{(n)}}{\mathcal{T}^{(m_t^{(n)})}}\right]$$

$$= \widehat{\mathcal{O}}_t^{(1)} + \widehat{\mathcal{O}}_t^{(2)} + \cdots + \widehat{\mathcal{O}}_t^{(n)}$$

$$= \widehat{\Psi}_t.$$

---

[2]For increased readability the argument (v_{cand}) in the formula is omitted but assumed implicitly.

$\mathcal{H}$ considers a peer's state regarding of the Objectives $\mathcal{O}^{(i)}$ together with their class memberships defined in $\mathcal{CL}$. Then, it adapts the weight factors $\alpha_t^{(i)}$ in order to reflect the peer's state at epoch t. The adapted weight factors are denoted as $\widehat{\alpha}_t^{(i)}$ and the resulting new Objectives are denoted as $\widehat{\mathcal{O}}_t^{(i)}$.

Algorithm 3: CMA's Heuristic Transformation Function $\mathcal{H}$

---

1   $ConstraintsExceeded = \{\}$;
2   Classification of Objectives $\mathcal{CL} = \{\mathcal{CO}, \mathcal{OO}, \mathcal{T}\}$;
3   Set of Objectives $\mathcal{X}$;
4   **for** $\{\mathcal{O}^{(i)} \in \mathcal{X}\}$ **do**
     /*Check all objectives*/
5   **if** $\{\mathcal{O}^{(i)} \in \mathcal{CO} \wedge (\mathcal{O}^{(i)}$ *exceeds Constraint* $\mathcal{T}^{(m^{(i)})} \in \mathcal{T})\}$ **then**
       /*Remember Objectives that exceed their
         constraints*/
6        $ConstraintsExceeded \leftarrow \mathcal{O}^{(i)}$
7   **if** $\{ConstraintsExceeded == \{\}\}$ **then**
     /*No constraints exceeded*/
8   **for** $\{\mathcal{O}^{(i)} \in (\mathcal{CO}/\mathcal{OO})\}$ **do**
9   reallocate $\alpha^{(i)}$ to all $\mathcal{O} \in \mathcal{OO}$, preserving relative importance;
10      $\alpha^{(i)} = 0$;
11   **else**
     /*There are exceeded constraints.   Try to repair.*/
12   **for** $\{\mathcal{O}^{(i)} \notin ConstraintsExceeded\}$ **do**
13   reallocate $\alpha^{(i)}$ to all $\mathcal{O} \in ConstraintsExceeded$, preserving relative importance;
14      $\alpha^{(i)} = 0$;

Algorithm 3 sketches the flow of CMA's Transformation Function $\mathcal{H}$. It takes the Objective classification $\mathcal{CL}$ and the heuristic $\Psi_t(v_{cand})$, evaluates which constraints are exceeded at epoch t (lines 4–6), and adapts the weight factors $\alpha_t^{(i)}$, accordingly: If no constraints are exceeded the specific Objectives in $\mathcal{CO}$ are abandoned, reallocating their weight factors to the Objectives in $\mathcal{OO}$ (lines 7–10). In contrast, if there are constraints exceeded the Objectives in $\mathcal{OO}$ are abandoned and their weight factors are reallocated to all Objectives which constraints are exceeded. In case more than one constraint is exceeded the specific Objective's relative importance is preserved (lines 11–14). Finally, the algorithm returns a weighted sum $\widehat{\Psi}_t$ used to evaluate the status of a peer at epoch t.

Mapping CMA Design Goals to Objectives

In Section 5.4 the constraints for a solution have been described with respect to the introduced graph model and in Section 5.5.1 the design goals of CMA have been formulated. In order to follow the Capacity Matching approach these goals and constraints are mappable to four Objectives in CMA's Peer Rating:

1. **Local internal processing capacity constraints of a peer:** A peer may not forward more data than its local value $cap^{(io)}$ allows. Let $\kappa_t(v)$ be the internal processing load at peer v at epoch t, measured by Peer Probing. Then, for epoch t it is

$$m_t^{(1)}(v) = \kappa_t(v)$$

$$T^{(m_e^{(1)})}(v) = cap^{(io)}(v).$$

2. **Egress capacity constraints of a channel:** A peer may not forward more data than its used channel allows. Let $\sum_{e \in out(c)} \beta_t(e)$ be the consumed outgoing capacity in channel c at peer v at epoch t. Then, it is

$$m_t^{(2)}(v) = \sum_{e \in out(c)} \beta(e)$$

$$T^{(m_t^{(2)})}(v) = cap^{(egress)}(c).$$

3. **Egress capacity of a SAM domain:** A peer may not forward more data than its used SAM domains allow. Let $\sum_{c \in channels(s)} \sum_{e \in in(c)} \beta_t(e)$ be the measured consumed egress capacity in SAM domain s at peer v at epoch t. Then, it is

$$m_t^{(3)}(v) = \sum_{c \in channels(s)} \sum_{e \in in(c)} \beta_t(e)$$

$$T^{(m_t^{(3)})}(v) = cap^{(egress)}(s).$$

4. **Video stream dissemination delay:** Since a near-live video stream is targeted the dissemination delay any peer experiences hast to be bounded. Given that an upper bound UB_Δ value has been defined, $\Delta_t(v)$ being the root-to-peer network delay for peer v at epoch t. Then it is

$$m_t^{(4)}(v) = \Delta_t(v)$$

$$T^{(m_t^{(4)})}(v) = UB_\Delta.$$

In the scenario where a video stream is disseminated to all peers, modeling the ingress capacity constraints of SAM domains and channels is correct but less important than the remaining constraints for the following reason. A constant bandwidth video stream is disseminated and observed in the scenario and each peer receives the stream exactly once. Hence, each peer has exactly one parent peer in the tree (except the root peer, which has none). Therefore, constraints considering ingress channel and SAM capacities are trivial in the scenario and left out for the sake of simplicity in the following. The resulting weighted sum heuristic $\Psi_t(v)$ for a peer v in CMA is[3]:

$$
\begin{aligned}
\Psi_t = {} & \alpha_t^{(1)} \cdot \left[\frac{m_t^{(1)}}{\mathcal{T}^{(m_t^{(1)})}} \right] + \alpha_t^{(2)} \cdot \left[\frac{m_t^{(2)}}{\mathcal{T}^{(m_t^{(2)})}} \right] + \alpha_t^{(3)} \cdot \left[\frac{m_t^{(3)}}{\mathcal{T}^{(m_t^{(3)})}} \right] + \alpha_t^{(4)} \cdot \left[\frac{m_t^{(4)}}{\mathcal{T}^{(m_t^{(4)})}} \right] \\
= {} & \alpha_t^{(1)} \cdot \left[\frac{\kappa_t}{cap^{(io)}} \right] + \alpha_t^{(2)} \cdot \left[\frac{\sum_{e \in out(c)} \beta(e)}{cap^{(egress)}(c)} \right] \\
& + \alpha_t^{(3)} \cdot \left[\frac{\sum_{c \in channels(s)} \sum_{e \in in(c)} \beta(e)}{cap^{(egress)}(s)} \right] + \alpha_t^{(4)} \cdot \left[\frac{\Delta}{UB_\Delta} \right] \\
\hat{=} {} & O_t^{(1)} + O_t^{(2)} + O_t^{(3)} + O_t^{(4)}.
\end{aligned}
$$

The objective classification of the four involved Objectives is defined to be

$$
\mathcal{CL} = \{\mathcal{CO} = \{O^{(1)}, O^{(2)}, O^{(3)}, O^{(4)}\}, \mathcal{OO} = \{O^{(3)}, O^{(4)}\}, \mathcal{T}\}.
$$

This classification considers that local processing capability bounds are constraint but do not have to be minimized ($O^{(1)}$). This classification is chosen since processing load is not focused to be balanced in any way, rather the existing potential of the peers should be used. The same applies to outgoing capacity consumptions in case of channels ($O^{(2)}$). In contrast, SAM capacity consumption and video stream dissemination delay are constrained and also are tried to be minimized ($O^{(3)}, O^{(4)}$). This ensures that the capacity bounds of the SAMs and the targeted upper delay bounds are not exceeded. Concurrently, both metrics are tried to be balanced. The classifications of $O^{(3)}$ and $O^{(4)}$ will be modified during the evaluations to show the effects of parameterization. It will be denoted in the specific parts. If not stated differently, the relative importance values $a_t^{(i)}$ are all set to $\frac{1}{|\mathcal{CO} \cup \mathcal{OO}|} = 0.25$.

---

[3]For increased readability the argument (v) is omitted but implicitly assumed.

Peer Rating selects those peers from $\mathcal{R}$ which fulfill the constraints and combines them in a new set $\hat{\mathcal{R}}$. The new set is passed to the Maintenance & Refinement part.

5.5.2.4 Maintenance & Refinement

The *Maintenance & Refinement* part in CMA targets three major goals:

- First, it picks the best appropriate peer as new parent out of the candidate set $\hat{\mathcal{R}}$ provided by Peer Rating.
- Second, it repairs the tree in case of lost connection to the parent peer. This is accomplished by remembering the non-optimal alternatives provided in Peer Rating as fallback parent peers. In case connection to the direct parent peer is detected to be lost, these alternate peers will be probed (descending in quality) in order to repair tree connectivity. This approach is proactive (similar to the approach proposed in [236]) but the required information can be collected in Peer Rating "on the fly" without inducing additional overhead.
- Third, it tries to limit tree fluctuations due to parent switches in the tree, since these fluctuations also induce packet loss or inconsistencies, at worst.

How these aspects are implemented in CMA is briefly described in the following.

Choosing a Parent (CP)

For determining a potential new parent peer in CMA a simple mechanism is used that chooses the best (i. e. the first) candidate out of the provided ordered list of potential parent peers. This candidate is kept but the actual tree change decision is postponed until all mechanisms in Maintenance & Refinement have finished.

Determining Fallback Candidates (FB)

For enhanced robustness also the remaining potential parent peers are stored as fallback parents in case of error. All peers in the ordered list but the peer chosen in CP are stored. If the current parent peer fails these fallback candidates are probed in descending order of their quality (with respect to the weighted sum heuristic) to determine an alternate parent peer.

Considering Position in the Tree (RF)

Single trees are naturally fragile, since a failing peer or a tree change may lead to all peers residing below this peer in the tree will experience packet loss. Clearly, the higher a peer resides in the tree the more other peers will be influenced by this peer's change decisions indirectly. To mitigate this effect a mechanism is used in the CMA protocol that considers the current position of

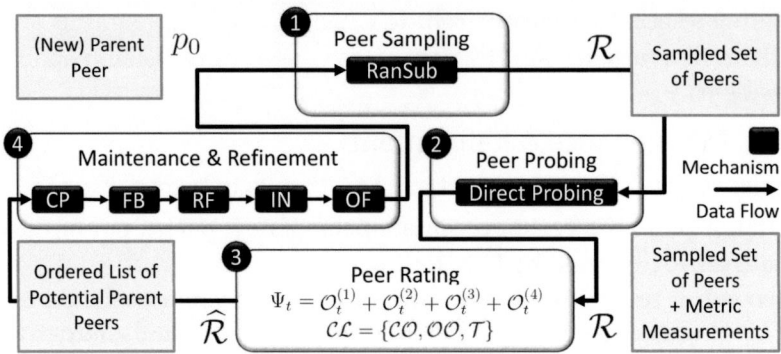

Figure 5.7 CMA Protocol Parts and Data Flow Overview

a peer in the tree and uses this information in the tree refinement process. The RanSub mechanism in Peer Sampling inherently provides knowledge about the estimated number of peers below a given peer in the tree via up-tree aggregation. Also, the estimated total number of participants is collected in the root peer and distributed via down-tree signaling. These two values can directly be used to estimate the overall fraction n_{sub} of sub-tree children. Then, a new weighted sum heuristic value for comparing the current peer v with the probed peers is determined and used. It is computed through

$$\widehat{\Psi}_{new}(v) = (\widehat{\Psi}_t(v))^{log_e(n_{sub})}.$$

Since $\widehat{\Psi}_t(v) \in [0,1]$, the new value is in the same bounds, decreasing with higher exponent. Because the new value indicates the heuristic bound that has to be underrun by a potential new parent peer the protocol will as a result only change parents if the benefit resulting from that change is comparably high. $log_e(n_{sub})$ is called *Responsibility Factor (RF)* here.

Mute Fluctuations (IN)

In case the network environment is very dynamic (due to mobility or churn) or part of the involved metrics in the Objectives is prone to fluctuations it is necessary to mute the arising tree changes to some extent in order to preserve tree stability. The idea is preventing peers from change decisions in case the same peers decided to change their position often in a short period of time before. Hence, a mechanism is used here that introduces a backoff to the estimated weighted sum heuristic value, degrading its value depending on the number of tree changes attempted before. This mechanism is called *Inertia (IN)*. The Inertia value is initially set to zero. In case the peer changed parents for the first time in an epoch the value is increased by a small amount

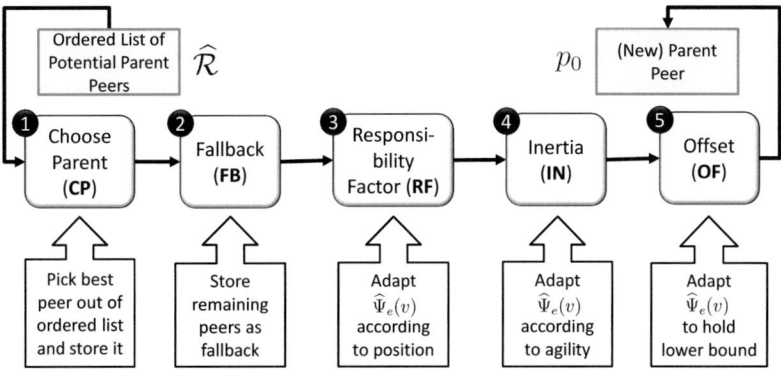

Figure 5.8 Maintenance & Refinement Mechanisms in CMA

(0.1). In every epoch the peer decides to remain stable the value is degraded again. Otherwise, if the peer decides to change position, the value will be exponentially increased for every epoch in which it changes in row (i being the number of change epochs in a row):

$$Inertia_{new} = Inertia_{old} * (2^i).$$

Finally, the value is subtracted from the current weighted sum heuristic value in order to accordingly raise the hurdle for a tree change:

$$\widehat{\Psi}_{new}(v) = \widehat{\Psi}_{old}(v) - Inertia_{new}.$$

The Inertia value decreases the local weighted sum heuristic and hence makes it harder to find remote parent peers with a lower value which will be considered a better parent choice.

Define Lower Bound for Operation (OF)

As a last mechanism to reduce fluctuations CMA uses a small comparison value called *Offset (OF)*. It defines a lower bound that indicates how big the difference between the two heuristic values $\widehat{\Psi}(v_0)$ and $\widehat{\Psi}(v_i \in \widehat{\mathcal{R}})$ (local peer state versus potential parent value) has to be, at least. The Offset helps to avoid alternating tree changes in which a peer changes parents frequently due to only small benefits in the heuristic. These frequent changes may occur especially if the values measured through Peer Probing tend to be prone to high fluctuation (like e. g. network latency measurements).

The mechanisms are used inside CMA as a chain of mechanisms once per epoch. Figure 5.8 gives an overview of the overall Maintenance & Refinement part in CMA and recalls the single functional sub-parts that are accomplished, also executed as a chain. Finally, Figure 5.7 again shows the whole CMA protocol flow in more detail together with its configuration to be used in the following protocol evaluations, also indicating the flow of information.

5.6 Protocol Evaluation

In this section the CMA protocol is evaluated and analyzed with respect to the described scenario (cf. Section 5.1) in a simulated environment. The goal is to observe the protocol's ability to cope with its induced higher traffic load while maintaining important performance measures of the target service. Section 5.6.1 describes this network scenario. Then, the used simulation environment is depicted in Section 5.6.2. Important performance measures used for evaluation are presented in Section 5.6.3, before in Section 5.6.4 the parameterization of the simulation is given. Afterwards, the behavior of CMA as well as the impact on the network and the service quality are evaluated in-depth with respect to different aspects.

5.6.1 Network Scenario

For evaluating the usage of the tree-based ALM protocol CMA for the video streaming case a network scenario is chosen in which all peers are able to access the Internet through cellular access networks (like 3G/4G) exclusively, since the problem of access network traffic congestion is mainly found in such access networks in dense urban environments. The case of multi-access communication possibilities (WiFi and cellular communication at the same time) is observed in Chapter 6.

Cellular Access in Dense Urban Environments

Figure 5.9(a) exemplarily shows the locations of cellular access towers in the core city of Karlsruhe, Germany, for the service provider Vodafone [223] in November 2010. While these real placements are bound to population density, building development, and permissions, an idealized but simple and general cellular environment can be modeled as a grid of cells. In this grid every cell reflects a spatial coverage area, each with exactly one access tower. Figure 5.9(b) exemplarily shows such a grid. The introduced term SAM directly applies to cellular access networks, therefore it is used to describe the involved 3G/4G cells. Participants interested in receiving the live video stream can be embedded in the grid by attaching each to exactly one SAM, reflecting cellular access tower assignment in a real communication scenario. Figure 5.9(b) also shows eight exemplary participants, one being source peer, and an exemplary ALM dissemination tree connecting them. Since in the scenario peers communicate via cellular access exclusively there is only one channel involved per peer and each peer is connected to exactly one cell (SAM). Furthermore, physical effects like e. g. cellbreathing in UMTS networks are not

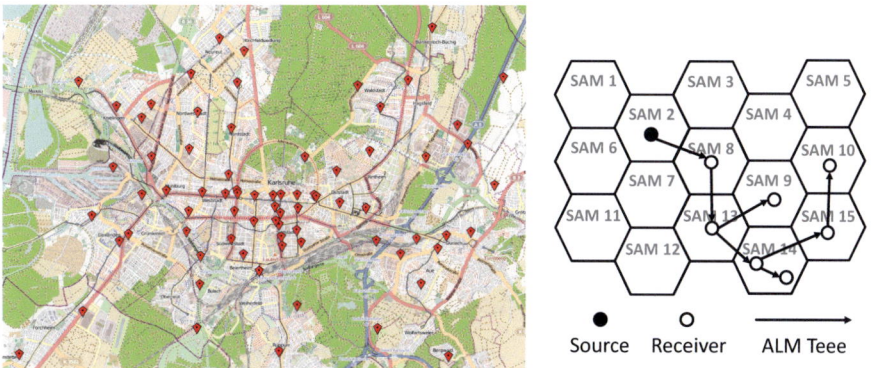

(a) Cellular Towers in Karlsruhe (Vodafone) (according to [163]) (b) SAM Grid with Example ALM Tree

Figure 5.9 Urban 3G Scenario, modeled through a Grid of SAMs

considered, where high numbers of participating users can lead to shrinking UMTS cells and sporadic areas without service provision. Rather, every participant is assumed to have access to at least one cellular access tower at all times.

Modeling Underlay Network Delays

Evaluating a cellular network scenario raises questions like e. g. which exact technology built-out is used, how the underlay is connected, which delays arise, and similar aspects. Acquiring exact data as base for simulations is hard in this context, since the backbone structure of cellular access providers is complex and hidden and providers normally don't provide information concerning the interior workings of their networks. Data dissemination delay is one of the metrics to be observed, so the modeling of these delays has high importance. Hence, in this chapter certain assumptions are made and three different underlay network delay models are observed in the evaluations, shown in Figure 5.10. The different models are used to get an idea of the influence of the underlay delay properties on the service and the Capacity Matching approach.

Each transmission comes with a one-way delay consisting of three delay components $(\delta_1, \delta_2, \delta_3)$. δ_1 describes the transmission delay that arises from the sender's cellular access network (δ_3 analogously describes the receiver's access network delay). δ_2, in contrast, models the backbone transmission delay. The sum of δ_1, δ_2, and δ_3 builds the graph model's $\delta(v_1, v_2)$ property for an edge connecting the peers v_1 and v_2, as introduced in Section 5.4.

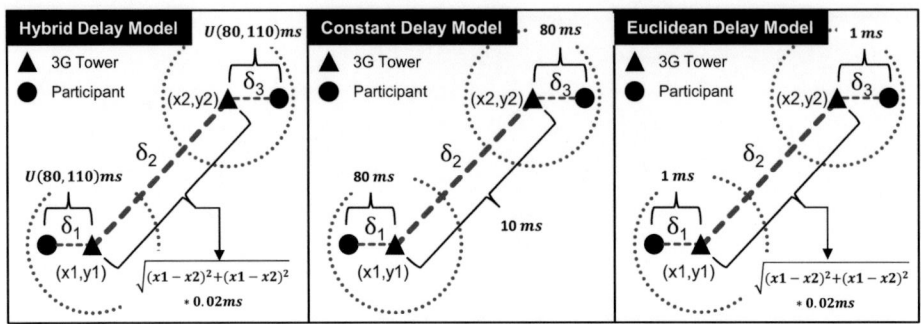

Figure 5.10 Different Underlay Delay Models used in CMA Evaluation

Three configurations are used, being a *hybrid*, a *constant*, and an *euclidean* model. The hybrid approach targets to model a 3G underlay network based on the evaluations in literature: Jurvansuu et al. [122] showed that in 3G-based data transmission, the largest delay source originates from the radio access network, while the Internet-related part roughly estimates as being constant. Cano-Garcia et al. [33] propose a 3G delay model based on testbed measurements. They find that packet losses in the wireless access are not frequent and that delays are in general not prone to high variance, the mean packet delays residing between 90 ms and 110 ms, the median packet delays between 70 ms and 85 ms. The difference between mean and median results from infrequent spikes in data delays. Prokkola et al. [175] provide similar results in their work focusing on the performance gain between WCDMA and HSDPA. Furthermore, own evaluations [17] in the context of a study thesis support the findings in literature. The evaluations have been accomplished in metropolitan 3G networks (in the city of Karlsruhe), measuring end-to-end performance properties in 3G access networks. Following these insights and assuming a HSDPA-enabled underlay network an uniformly distributed access network delay between 80 ms and 110 ms for δ_1 and δ_3 is used in the hybrid model. The backbone delay δ_2 in the hybrid model expresses the euclidean distance between both involved access towers in the field. Each meter of distance in the simulation field induces 0.02 ms of data dissemination delay, resulting in a network delay of 2 ms per 100 m. The goal is to model network delays resulting especially from the involved intermediate systems rather than global Internet packet delays. As the scenario observed is limited to model a city-like environment (cf. Sec. 5.6.4) the assumption leads to comparably high but limited network delays where the access networks induce the highest fraction of overall delays.

The constant underlay delay model assumes constant values for all components, being 80 ms for δ_1 and δ_3 and 10 ms for δ_2. It is used to compare the influence of the hybrid model against an underlay model were the distance of peers has no impact but the difference between access network delays and backbone delays is still considered. Finally, the euclidean model nearly neglects access network delays by setting δ_1 and δ_3 to 1 ms and using the same euclidean distance for δ_2 as in the hybrid approach.

5.6.2 Simulation Environment

For evaluating the CMA protocol in the scenario the *MiXiM* simulator (MiXed SiMulator) [127] is used. MiXiM is an extension to the discrete event simulation framework *OMNeT++* [221]. Although OMNeT++ is designed for network simulations it has no built-in support for wireless or cellular communications. Various extensions have been developed in order to simulate different aspects of wireless and mobile communications with OMNeT++. MiXiM combines some of them in one single simulation framework, including the *Mobility Framework* [158], the *Channel Simulator* [39], the *MAC Simulator* [149], and the *Positif Framework* [149]. As MiXiM—at the time of writing this thesis—does not provide specific communication functionality needed here, like e. g. backbone routing, capacity constraints in cellular networks, or automatic binding of peers to cellular access towers, it is enhanced in order to fit the scenario as described in the following.

MiXiM Enhancements & Modifications

By default MiXiM is a pure wireless point-to-point communication simulator, thus currently there is no infrastructure support, like e. g. interconnected cellular towers. In the scenario a SAM is formed by a cell tower and the peers assigned to it. A simple backbone routing network has been implemented for the evaluations that can be used to transmit messages between cellular towers. On deployment peers are automatically attached to their next tower in range which routes their traffic to the backbone. Towers are implemented as non-mobile network nodes with one (or more) appropriate wireless network interface(s). Furthermore, the towers form a mesh of non-wireless channels, interconnecting all towers and building the backbone network.

Each tower broadcasts *Beacons* to all mobile peers in range. A peer receiving a Beacon from a tower registers at this tower in order to receive the data traffic. If a peer sends data the traffic of this peer is sent to the tower the peer registered at. The tower itself has to resolve the destination network address of an incoming packet to the information on which tower the destination peer is registered. The routing mechanism is kept simple but allows for configurable network delays. For each network address the current tower can query the assigned peer object in the simulation. With this information the sending tower can furthermore request the destination tower where the destination peer is currently registered at. Then, the sending tower can directly pass the data to the destination tower over the non-wireless channel connecting the towers. The destination tower finally passes the data to the destination peer in range. Every tower keeps track of incoming and outgoing traffic to model direction-dependent ingress and egress SAM capacities in the simulation.

In order to model cellular access networks simultaneous transmissions on the same frequency band have been integrated. Cellular connections are abstracted in an own MAC layer implementation as interference-free channels, respecting the SAM capacities. Network delays can be configured for backbone transmissions and access networks separately. This helps getting insights in how the underlay delay properties influence the resulting dissemination tree. Further details of the MiXiM modifications are provided in Appendix B.

5.6.3 Performance Measures

Two performance measures are of specific interest:

- The service to be provided is near-live video streaming, hence an upper bound of dissemination delay should not be exceeded, i. e., the time between sending the video stream from the source peer and reception by all receivers should be bounded.
- The dedicated Capacity Matching design goal of CMA has to be connected to traffic load consideration regarding the involved access networks. Therefore, a measure for the arising data traffic load has to be employed.

Both metrics are introduced in the following sections.

Dissemination Delay

The video stream to be disseminated via CMA's ALM tree experiences a certain delay between being sent by the source peer and being received by a receiver peer. This delay arises from the multiple transmission delays between the peers on the overlay path (hop count). These delays sum up and finally comprise the overall data dissemination delay. The dissemination delay depends on a peer's position in the overlay tree and the underlying network properties.

Two delay metrics are of interest in the context of the evaluation, being the *mean dissemination delay* and the *maximum dissemination delay*. The mean dissemination delay expresses an average source-to-peer-delay for all peers in the tree. It serves as a measure what average video dissemination delay to expect with a specific CMA configuration. The maximum dissemination delay, in contrast, expresses the worst source-to-peer-delay experienced by any peer in the tree. It is important as an upper bound measure to express what delay a user has to expect at worst for a specific CMA tree configuration.

SAM Load Disparity

Besides data dissemination delays, the traffic load disparity in the involved SAMs is of particular interest, since the main focus of the scenario lies on balancing the induced egress traffic load in the access network and on congestion avoidance (Capacity Matching). SAMs may have different communication capacities that express their technical properties. Furthermore, assigning specific capacities to SAMs can also be used to model concurrent background traffic inside this SAM inherently. Considering these heterogeneous capacities, an efficient dissemination solution should at best balance the data traffic so that each SAM experiences similar traffic load, considering its overall capacity. Hence, the load should be proportional to its capacities. Likewise, the resulting dissemination tree should not increase the video dissemination delays too heavily for the peers.

The ratio of current egress video streams and the capacity limit $cap^{(egress)}$ of a SAM domain s is used as an estimator for current egress traffic load $Load(s)$:

$$Load(s) := \frac{\sum\limits_{c \in channels(s)} \sum\limits_{e \in out(c)} \beta(e)}{cap^{(egress)}(s)}, \forall s \in \mathcal{S}, c \in \mathcal{C}, e \in \mathcal{E}.$$

To reduce simulation complexity a linear capacity model is used: The video stream to be disseminated is assumed to consume a unit bandwidth of 1 per overlay connection. This assumption suffices to evaluate the inherent CMA protocol behavior without simulating complex communication at lower layers.

Based on the Load values of all SAMs in a scenario two tools are used for evaluation: *Lorenz Curves* to visualize disparities, on the one hand, and *GINI Coefficients* to calculate a scalar representation of Lorenz Curves, on the other hand. Both tools are briefly described in the following.

Lorenz Curves: SAM traffic load disparity can be visualized through *Lorenz Curves*[148]. In the context of economics a Lorenz Curve is often used as a graphical representation of the Cumulative Distribution Function (CDF) of an empirical probability distribution of wealth. Since there are similarities between SAM load disparity and wealth distributions with respect to the optimal case of even distribution, Lorenz Curves are employed for visualization

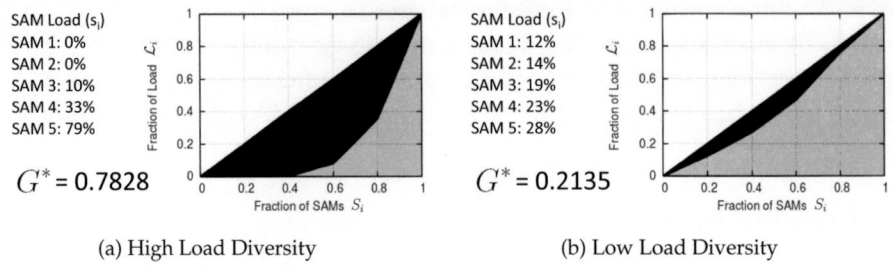

(a) High Load Diversity   (b) Low Load Diversity

Figure 5.11 Lorenz Curves and GINI Coefficients for different Load Diversities

in this work. For each network environment and a CMA dissemination tree in a given scenario there is a Lorenz Curve representation

$$\Xi(\mathcal{L}_i, S_i),$$

being computable as follows: For n SAMs $(s_1, ..., s_n)$ with corresponding load values $Load(s_i), i = (1, ..., n)$, being indexed in non-decreasing order $(Load_j(s_i) < Load_{j+1}(s_k))$, the Lorenz Curve $\Xi(\mathcal{L}_i, S_i)$ is the continuous piecewise linear function connecting the points $(\mathcal{L}_i, S_i)$, and

$$S_i = \frac{i}{n}$$

$$T_i = \sum_{j=1}^{i} Load(s_j)$$

$$\mathcal{L}_i = \frac{T_i}{T_n}$$

with $(\mathcal{L}_0 = 0, S_0 = 0)$.

The Normalized GINI Coefficient G^*: The (normalized) GINI coefficient G^*, in contrast, calculates a scalar value from a Lorenz Curve. Graphically, a GINI coefficient for a given Lorenz Curve expresses the relation between the area between the curve and the angle bisector ("Line of Equality") and the area representing the highest theoretical disparity. Fig. 5.11 gives two examples for Lorenz Curves and GINI Coefficients. Here, example load values are drawn and the corresponding G^* values are calculated. For a sorted set of n SAM traffic load grade values $\{Load_1, ..., Load_n\}$, $G^* \in [0, 1]$ is calculated through

$$G^* = \left(\frac{2 \sum\limits_{i=1}^{n} iLoad(s_i)}{n \sum\limits_{i=1}^{n} Load(s_i)} - \frac{n+1}{n} \right) \cdot \frac{n}{n-1}.$$

In Figure 5.11(a) five SAMs with comparably high diversity are shown. Following the definition of G^*, this results in a GINI Coefficient of approximately 0.8. Figure 5.11(b), in contrast, shows a state in which each SAM experiences more equal traffic load, resulting in a lower G^* value of approximately 0.2.

Lower Bound Estimation: In order to decide on the quality of a CMA multicast tree resulting SAM load disparities have to be compared to a theoretical optimum that could be achieved in a given scenario. Thus, for each network topology and dissemination tree, an optimal (i.e. minimal) GINI Coefficient G^* has to be determined.

The problem of finding such G^* is related to the (NP hard) class of bin-packing problems [44] where objects of given size have to be packed in "bins" of constrained sizes, with, in the classical sense, minimum number of bins used. In the case of SAMs the problem can be formulated as finding a distribution of objects (video streams) on a number of bins with constrained sizes (SAMs, constrained by the number of peers per SAM in the given topology). Each SAM is connected to a current cost, expressed by how adding a peer to the SAM will influence its egress traffic load $Load$. The goal is finding a distribution with minimum G^* (instead of minimum number of SAMs in the common bin-packing problem). To achieve this, a greedy approximation algorithm is used that iteratively chooses the SAM which offers the smallest resulting cost from adding a peer to it (given that peers are left to add in the topology). The solution is optimal in a sense that SAMs are filled up with global knowledge so that the resulting traffic load diversity is minimal with respect to peer distribution and SAM capacities.

Algorithm 4 briefly shows how the minimal G^* is determined: For every peer in the scenario all SAMs are traversed to determine which have egress capacities left (lines 4–8). Also, it is checked whether the contained peers in the SAM have channel capacities left. If both requirements are fulfilled the SAM is treated as a potential candidate. From these candidate SAMs the one with lowest resulting egress traffic load is elected (lines 9–10). From the resulting ALM dissemination tree the theoretical GINI Coefficient G^* is calculated for comparison (lines 11–12). The result from this algorithm for each simulation

---

Algorithm 4: Calculating the minimal GINI Coefficient G^*

---

1   $\mathcal{S}$; /*All SAM domains in the scenario*/
2   $\mathcal{V}$ = /*All peers in the scenario*/
3   $\hat{\mathcal{S}}$ = {} /*Candidate SAM domains*/
4   **for** {$v_1 \in \mathcal{V}$} **do**
     | /*Iterate through the number of peers*/
5 | **for** {$s \in \mathcal{S}$} **do**
     | | /*Iterate through all SAMS for each peer*/
6 | | **if** {s has egress capacity $cap^{(egress)}(s)$ left} **then**
7 | | | **if** {any peer $v_2 \in s$ has channel capacity $cap^{(egress)}(c)$ left} **then**
     | | | | /*Take as candidate*/
8 | | | | $\hat{\mathcal{S}} \leftarrow s$;

9 | Find SAM s_{min} with minimal cost in $\hat{\mathcal{S}}$;
10 | $cap^{(egress)}(s_{min})$++; /*Increment used egress capacity for s_{min}*/
     /*All egress stream edges have been applied to SAMS*/
11   Sort egress traffic load $cap^{(egress)}(s)$ $\forall s \in \mathcal{S}$;
12   Calculate GINI Coefficient G^*;

---

is used in the evaluations as a theoretical load disparity optimum that could be reached at best. It can be used to compare the resulting CMA tree against the theoretical optimum regarding load balancing in the access networks.

5.6.4   Simulation Parameters & Methodology

For evaluating the CMA protocol the parameters given in Table 5.2 are used (as long as not stated differently in the respective sections). A simulated square field with an edge length of 4000 m is used. For network latencies between peers the hybrid approach described in Section 5.6.1 is chosen: Peers experience a specific network delay for exchanging data with the cellular tower they are currently attached to. Additionally, the network delays between these cellular towers (backbone delay) are modeled according to their euclidean distance in the field.

100 SAMs are simulated, placed as a uniform grid across the field. Each SAM has a random linear egress capacity of 10 to 30 video streams, being uniformly distributed. The capacities of the involved channels are randomly set between 2 and 6, also uniformly distributed. As epoch a period of 10 s is defined. An overall time of 1800 s is simulated in which the peers are added randomly in a time frame being half as long as the number of peers (in seconds). Each configuration is simulated with 30 different runs providing mean values of

Simulation Environment Parameter	Value
Playground Size	$[4000 \text{ m} \, x \, 4000 \text{ m}]$
Number of Peers n	$\{50, 100, 200, 300, ...,1000\}$
Channel Capacities $cap^{(egress)}$	$\mathcal{U}(2,6)$ streams
Number of SAMs	100
SAM Egress Capacities $cap^{(egress)}$	$\mathcal{U}(10,30)$ streams
SAM Size	$(250^2 \cdot \pi) \text{ m}$
SAM Delays δ_1, δ_3	$\mathcal{U}(80,100) \text{ ms}$
Backbone Delay δ_2	$\left[\left(\sqrt{(x_1 - x_2)^2 + (y_1 - y_2)^2} \right) \cdot 0.02 \right] \text{ ms}$
Simulation Time	1800 s
Peer Adding Period	$\frac{n}{2} \text{ s}$
Runs per Config	30
CMA Protocol Parameter	Value
Epoch Length	10 s
RanSub Set Size $|\mathcal{R}|$	$log_e(n)$
Offset (OF)	0.05
$\mathcal{O}_t^{(1)}$	Peer Processing Capacity $cap^{(io)}$
$\mathcal{O}_t^{(2)}$	Local Channel Capacity $cap^{(egress)}(c)$
$\mathcal{O}_t^{(3)}$	SAM Egress Capacity $cap^{(egress)}(s)$
$\mathcal{O}_t^{(4)}$	Video Dissemination Delay Δ
Upper Delay Bound UB_Δ	$\{1000, 1500, 2000, 2500, 3000\} \text{ ms}$

Table 5.2 CMA Evaluation Parameters

these runs' results. Additionally, in each run the 95 %-confidence intervals are shown.

The evaluations in this chapter cover different aspects: First, the influence of relative priority of CMA Objectives (delay optimization versus Capacity Matching) is examined, analyzing how the CMA protocol generally behaves in the scenario regarding the observed performance metrics. Then, dedicated upper dissemination delay bounds are defined in order to evaluate their influence on traffic load balancing. Finally, the impact of the underlay delay model is discussed.

5.6.5 Analyzing Relative Objective Importance

This section covers the first evaluation, being the analysis of the general behavior of the CMA protocol in the scenario. It evaluates the properties of the ALM dissemination tree with respect to the measures of interest described in Section 5.6.3. Here, the two Objectives in class $\mathcal{OO}$, being $\mathcal{O}_t^{(3)}$ and $\mathcal{O}_t^{(4)}$ (according to Section 5.5.2.3) are put in different relative importance to each

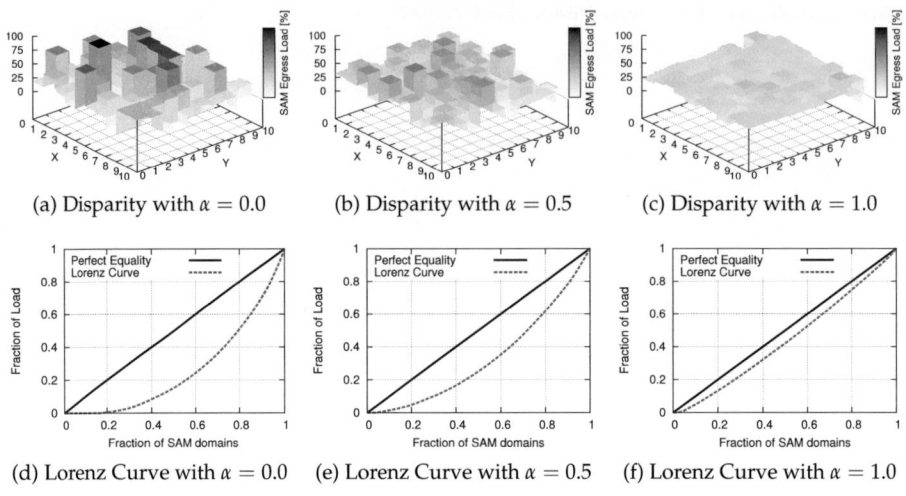

(a) Disparity with $\alpha = 0.0$ (b) Disparity with $\alpha = 0.5$ (c) Disparity with $\alpha = 1.0$

(d) Lorenz Curve with $\alpha = 0.0$ (e) Lorenz Curve with $\alpha = 0.5$ (f) Lorenz Curve with $\alpha = 1.0$

Figure 5.12   Exemplary Influence of trading off Objectives on SAM Load Disparity in CMA

other. They cover the measures of maximum dissemination delay and SAM egress traffic load disparity, respectively. Therefore, the result of trading off these objectives gradually in the scenario is analyzed.

For simplification, in the following the parameter α is used to express the relation between $\mathcal{O}_t^{(3)}$ and $\mathcal{O}_t^{(4)}$ as follows: $\alpha = 0.0$ means there is no traffic load consideration at all while building the multicast tree. $\alpha = 1.0$, in contrast, means traffic load is fully considered, while maximum dissemination delay is of no importance. $\alpha = 0.5$ means both objectives experience the same importance.

5.6.5.1   Basic Influence of Heuristical Traffic Load Consideration

First, to give an impression how trading off $\mathcal{O}_t^{(3)}$ and $\mathcal{O}_t^{(4)}$ affects the resulting access network egress traffic load, three different parameterizations are shown in Figure 5.12. Figures 5.12(a) to 5.12(c) visualize how the egress traffic load values develop for all 100 SAM domains after the ALM tree has been established in a typical scenario. The SAMs are arranged as a two-dimensional field, while for each SAM the corresponding traffic load is indicated as a bar above it. The figures each show a different value for α (ranging from no egress traffic load consideration in Figure 5.12(a) to no dissemination delay consideration in Figure 5.12(c)) with 500 peers in the tree. Clearly to see, a higher consideration of SAM traffic load leads to more even egress traffic load distribution among the involved SAMs. Figures 5.12(d) to 5.12(f) additionally

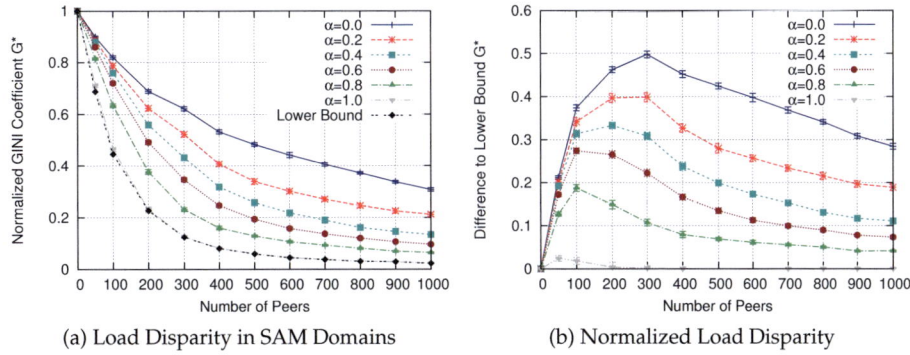

(a) Load Disparity in SAM Domains   (b) Normalized Load Disparity

Figure 5.13   SAM Traffic Load Disparity with different relative Objective Priorities

show the Lorenz Curves for the three scenarios. Here, the absolute optimum (in case of total traffic load equality) as well as the actual Lorenz Curves for each parameterization are shown.

The Lorenz Curves indicate the grade of disparity in SAM egress traffic load graphically. They show that CMA is able to highly balance the load by following the heuristic if the network provides a possibility to learn about the current load situation. In the following this balancing is analyzed in more detail.

5.6.5.2   Load Disparity in the SAM Domains

Following the Capacity Matching idea the disparity of egress traffic load induced by the CMA dissemination tree in the involved SAMs is of particular interest. Evaluations with different numbers of peers have been accomplished where the relative parameter α has been set to different values to see how the resulting ALM dissemination tree influences egress traffic load disparity in the SAMs. Additionally, for each setting the lower bound estimation as described in Section 5.6.3 is provided, indicating the grade of optimality for the multicast tree. The curve with $\alpha = 0.0$ is a case in which the protocol only considers the dissemination delay in the tree and does not care about load balancing. This configuration comes close to typical existing network-agnostic ALM approaches targeting delay optimization. The curve denoted as $\alpha = 1.0$ shows the opposite, being maximum load balancing priority. The "Lower Bound" curve shows the best theoretical load balancing case that could be achieved in the specific scenario, as introduced in Section 5.6.3.

Figure 5.13(a) shows how egress load disparity among all SAMs develops, depending on the number of participating peers and the parameterization via

α. The number of peers and its correlation to the resulting egress load disparity situation in all SAM domains, expressed with help of the GINI Coefficient
G^*, is shown. The lower G^* is the better the egress traffic load is balanced
throughout the involved SAM domains. Each point in the plot stands for the
mean of all 30 runs per CMA protocol configuration and different α values
are analyzed.

What stands out is the fact that obviously increasing the number of peers
leads to a lower G^* in general. This results from involved SAM domains
getting "filled up" with peers. With all SAMs experiencing higher load the
egress load disparity among the SAMs induced by the multicast tree naturally decreases, since all SAMs experience comparably high traffic load. The
small difference between the $\alpha = 1.0$ curve and the lower bound (especially
with little peer numbers) results from the behavior that peers already serving
their full set of potential children do not accept any more children (or change
them in favor of more optimal children) in CMA. Thus, a local optimum is
found rather than a global optimum. Nevertheless, the CMA protocol instance reaches close-to-optimal multicast trees regarding egress load balancing in this configuration in nearly all cases. Between the two extreme cases
of total or no load consideration gradual increases in Objective consideration
reside. Clearly to see, CMA's parameterization directly results in corresponding egress load balancing results, gradually.

The effect of decreasing G^* by filling up SAM domains is rather natural than
due to explicit CMA protocol configuration. To eliminate this effect in the
evaluations normalized values are presented in Figure 5.13(b). Here, the G^*
values of the "Lower Bound" curve are subtracted from the remaining values
in order to eliminate the natural decrease that all curves experience. As a
result it can be observed that in any case increasing the number of peers first
leads to a higher disparity while showing increasingly better load balancing
after some kind of saddle point. The higher the priority for load balancing is
chosen the better the load balancing gets, compared to the lower bound (being
the x-axis in this case). Also, the saddle point is reached earlier the higher the
priority for load balancing is (approximately 300 peers with $\alpha = 0.0$ and 50
peers with $\alpha = 1.0$).

The consideration of SAM egress traffic load in the involved SAM domains
comes with a trade-off against other important metrics, like the dissemination delay in the case observed here. These implications are discussed in the
following.

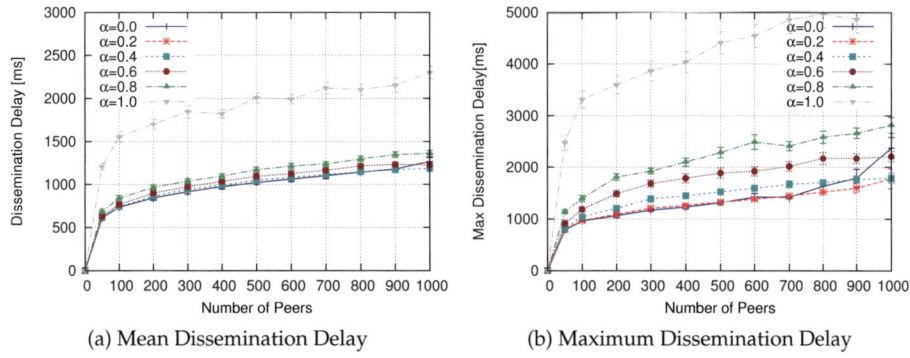

(a) Mean Dissemination Delay   (b) Maximum Dissemination Delay

Figure 5.14 Dissemination Delays with different relative Objectives

5.6.5.3 Data Dissemination Delay

Figure 5.14(a) shows the mean dissemination delay, averaged over all peers in the tree. Figure 5.14(b), in contrast, shows the maximum dissemination delay, i.e. the worst delay experienced by any peer in the tree. In both figures the number of peers and its correlation to the arising delays is shown.

With more peers becoming part of the ALM tree the delays increase because the tree gets deeper. In case of $\alpha = 0.0$, for instance, the mean as well as the maximum dissemination delay approximately doubles between 50 and 700 peers. However, the figures also show that carefully considering traffic load balancing in the weighted sum heuristic only implies small increase in delays both for the mean and the maximum case. As soon as the importance of load balancing is set high the resulting dissemination delays increase significantly. This can be observed in the figures for the cases with $\alpha > 0.8$, for instance. The explanation is the fact that peers in the tree increasingly choose parent peers that have a high source-to-peer delay Δ but a good SAM traffic load situation. As a result the ALM tree starts to degenerate, creating very deep paths in the tree. But, as careful load balancing consideration (i.e. low α values) shows only low delay penalty in the scenario, at least employing the CMA protocol with low α parameterizations is promising regarding the trade-off between load balancing and data dissemination delay penalty. With growing numbers of peers it can also be seen in the figure that (especially with $\alpha = 0.0$) the delays start to grow stronger, for instance with > 800 peers. The evaluations have shown that in these cases the SAMs are partially full (cf. Section 5.6.5.4) so that its harder for the RanSub mechanisms to find appropriate new parents since the heuristic does not consider load balancing unless SAMs are filled up. As a result, at least one peer does not find a position with lower delays in the tree (in Figure 5.14(b) always the worst case peer is shown).

5.6.5.4   Peak Traffic Load

The GINI Coefficient G^* and its development gives an idea about how well egress traffic load among involved SAM domains can be balanced. Anyway, it is hard to judge on the physical grade of egress traffic load in the SAMs since G^* implies only a comparison of the access network domains' state. Of high interest is especially the worst traffic load situation experienced by any SAM domain. This value is referred to as *Peak Traffic Load* here, reflecting the highest value $Load(s)$ as introduced in Section 5.6.3 among all SAM domains $s \in S$ in the scenario. The Peak Traffic Load is important since it gives an impression how high egress traffic really gets at worst in the scenario. It also influences other communication services being used at the same time in the involved SAMs because congestions also affect these. Even despite good load balancing SAMs may experience congestions if no forwarding capacities are left among the access networks.

Figure 5.15(a) shows the Peak Traffic Load for different heuristic parameterizations and changing number of peers. The Peak Traffic Load increases with growing numbers of peers for all parameterizations. However, the number of peers that leads to a specific Peak Traffic Load differs.

A can be observed, ignoring the traffic load situation in SAM domains leads to high egress load in any of the SAM domains comparably fast (case $\alpha = 0.0$). Here, at least one SAM domain experiences above 80 % of traffic load already with approximately 250 peers. Increasing traffic load consideration in heuristic parameterization, in contrast, keeps the Peak Traffic Load considerably lower. The effects can already be observed with low α, and the increase of the Peak Traffic Load is gradually lower in correlation to α. This observation shows that traffic load consideration not only leads to a good egress load balancing among the involved SAM domains (as has been observed in Section 5.6.5.2) but also maintains a lower Peak Traffic Load at the same time. This is especially important with respect to other users in the SAM domains that are not part of the CMA video dissemination service as they would be impaired by congested access network domains.

5.6.5.5   Performance versus Cost Estimation

The evaluations in the predecessing sections showed that trading off egress traffic load in the SAM domains against the resulting video dissemination delay is promising, given that the load consideration is parameterized accordingly. In this section a closer look is taken on the question how the trade-off really behaves. Figure 5.15(b) gives an complete overview on the relation between egress load balancing (the GINI Coefficient G^*) and mean and maximum dissemination delays for different numbers of peers, respectively. It

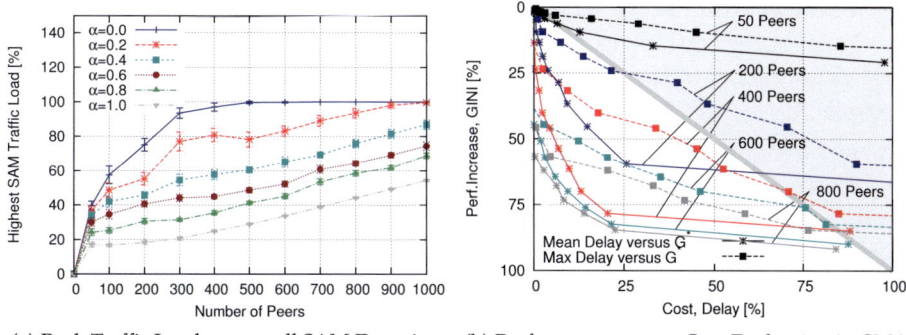

(a) Peak Traffic Load among all SAM Domains   (b) Performance versus Cost Evaluation in CMA

Figure 5.15 Peak Traffic Load and Performance versus Cost Estimation

is evaluated in form of a performance versus cost comparison [137] which helps giving a hint on what to expect in which CMA parametrization. Here, the gain in egress load balancing is treated as the performance, while the loss in dissemination delay (mean and maximum) is defined to be the cost. All three metrics are shown as percentage values, also provided in Table 5.3 for the respective numbers of peers. The 10 points in each line indicate the full set

Peers \ α	0.1	0.2	0.3	0.4	0.5	0.6	0.7	0.8	0.9	1.0
Traffic Load Disparity (Performance Gain) [%]										
50	0.5	1.2	1.7	2.1	3.0	4.3	6.2	9.5	14.7	20.8
200	4.7	9.5	13.4	18.8	24.1	28.6	36.7	45.4	59.2	66.6
400	13.6	23.5	31.7	40.1	45.9	53.7	61.5	70.1	78.4	84.9
600	20.0	31.9	44.6	50.8	57.1	64.5	70.0	76.1	82.5	90.0
800	19.1	34.0	45.6	56.7	62.0	67.8	73.3	78.4	84.6	91.7
Mean Data Dissemination Delay (Performance Loss) [%]										
50	-0.2	0.1	0.2	0.5	1.6	2.9	6.4	12.7	33.1	97.7
200	0.5	0.7	1.4	2.4	3.8	6.7	9.1	14.7	25.7	102.4
400	0.0	0.4	1.4	2.3	4.3	6.7	9.7	13.0	20.4	88.1
600	-0.9	-0.4	0.0	1.9	3.0	5.8	9.3	14.2	21.4	87.6
800	-1.9	-1.3	-0.8	0.2	2.7	6.2	8.1	13.9	22.5	84.1
Maximum Data Dissemination Delay (Performance Loss) [%]										
50	0.5	1.1	1.8	3.0	5.8	15.9	29.0	45.0	85.4	215.6
200	0.9	2.4	7.3	13.6	21.4	39.8	48.0	70.4	89.9	238.9
400	-0.4	2.4	9.2	17.8	33.8	45.2	52.5	70.9	85.0	228.4
600	-7.2	-2.8	2.6	12.2	20.3	35.2	46.1	75.6	81.3	220.1
800	-9.9	-7.0	0.5	4.5	20.4	33.2	41.8	58.6	76.4	205.1

Table 5.3 Performance versus Cost Evaluation in CMA

of parameterizations $\alpha = \{0.1, 0.2, ..., 1.0\}$. The shaded part of the figure indicates parameterizations in which the cost outweighs the performance, while the white part stands for parameterizations in which the performance gain prevails.

The key insights of the covered static heuristic scenario could be summarized as follows: Given the assumptions taken regarding the hybrid underlay delay model, the two metrics delay and SAM egress traffic load balancing can directly be traded off through the α parameter with gains in SAM egress traffic load balancing exceeding resulting delay cost especially in lower α regions. The values are also visualized in Figure 5.15(b) for different numbers of peers ($\{50, 200, 400, 600, 800\}$), indicating that especially in lower α regions (shown in the left part of the figure) the best trade-off between performance and cost in the scenario can be achieved in general. Here, gains in traffic load balancing clearly exceed resulting delay cost. Furthermore, the number of peers in the CMA tree highly influences the grade of performance gain: Since less peers limit the parent choices, trading off load balancing against dissemination delay is less promising in such scenarios. With more peers in the tree the protocol is able to reach far better results. This effect has already been indicated in the load disparity figures and can also be observed in Figure 5.15(b) where the curves approach the point of optimality (100% performance, 0% cost) with higher numbers of peers.

One major drawback of the protocol parameterization so far is the need for a manual choice of α in advance. It has been used to evaluate the influence of trading off both metrics. In a realistic scenario it is hard to anticipate how a protocol will behave regarding a dedicated parameter, since many factors have influence: The choice—in order to be good—requires knowledge about expected participant numbers and the expected delay situation (which depends on the underlay and the network state). A more practical approach is defining upper bounds being tolerable for the video streaming application by configuring the weighted sum heuristic with Constrained Objectives, as described in Section 5.5.2.3. In the next sections, this case is analyzed by defining upper delay bounds UB_Δ in the scenario.

5.6.6   Defining Upper Delay Bounds

The predecessing sections gave an impression of how the two important metrics of egress traffic load and dissemination delay relate with defined relative importance. Since in real environments it is more common to have dedicated bounds which the CMA protocol has to consider, this section focuses on the definition of such bounds. Here, different maximum dissemination delay bounds UB_Δ are defined that should not be exceeded in order to provide a near-live video streaming service of good quality. In the following

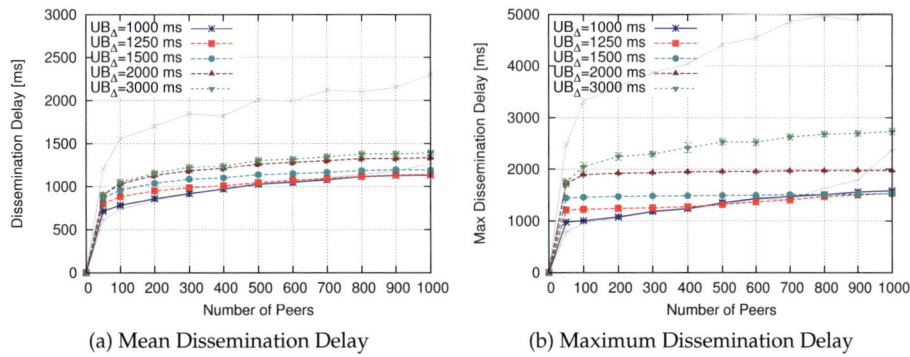

(a) Mean Dissemination Delay   (b) Maximum Dissemination Delay

Figure 5.16 Dissemination Delays with defined Upper Bound Objectives

CMA's ability to hold given delay bounds in its dissemination tree is evaluated. Then, the bounds' influence on egress traffic load balancing is investigated.

Dedicated Upper Delay Bounds

Once defined, the CMA protocol has to hold the upper dissemination delay bound UB_Δ with high priority. Naturally, it depends on the underlay delay properties, the dissemination tree structure, and the number of peers whether this goal is accomplishable, and how much optimization space is left for other considerations besides the delay.

Figure 5.16 shows an evaluation with different upper delay bounds UB_Δ defined. Mean and maximum dissemination delays are shown in Figure 5.16(a) and Figure 5.16(b), respectively. Five different upper delay bounds are defined, being $UB_\Delta = \{1000, 1250, 1500, 2000, 3000\}$ ms. The bounds are chosen with respect to how the CMA protocol performs in the given scenario in order to cover cases in which the protocol holds the delay bound easily, while in other cases it's not reachable at all. This helps evaluating how the egress load balancing, being the second optimization goal, is influenced by the network delay situation in the current ALM tree. Additionally, the minimum and maximum ($\alpha = \{0.0, 1.0\}$) curves from the static parameterization are provided as grey lines to ease comparison.

Regarding mean dissemination delays (Figure 5.16(a)) it can be observed that the bounds can be held in nearly every case. An exception is in case of $UB_\Delta = 1000$ ms with too many peers taking part in the dissemination tree (approximately > 500). This is due to the fact that the ALM tree depth does not allow for shorter mean dissemination paths, being not solvable by ALM tree rearrangements.

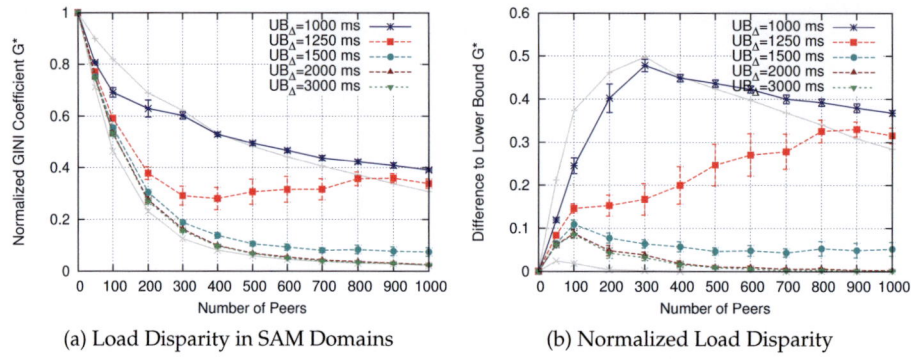

(a) Load Disparity in SAM Domains   (b) Normalized Load Disparity

Figure 5.17 SAM Traffic Load Disparity with Upper Bound Objectives

A more interesting behavior can be observed in case of the maximum dissemination delays (Figure 5.16(b)): For $UB_\Delta = 3000$ ms the bound is not reached
in any of the peer number configurations. In contrast, the hard bound of
1000 ms is reached very early and is naturally not underrun at any time with
growing peer numbers beyond approximately 100. The upper delay bounds
that have been defined to reside between these two cases are held nearly in
every configuration. Only in case of 1250 ms with high peer number (> 500),
the bound is exceeded.

The observations show that the CMA protocol is able to hold the given upper
delay bounds UB_Δ in case the network situation and the number of participating peers allow for it. By using Constrained Objectives (dissemination delay)
and Optimization Objectives (load balancing) a tree can be built and refined
that considers the defined bounds while also balancing the load among the
SAM domains. If the delay bounds are chosen to be too restrictive the protocol aims for delay optimizations as far as possible. If they are chosen very
relaxed the protocol shows low delay consideration, accordingly. The definition of the upper delay bound UB_Δ has influence on the grade of egress traffic
load consideration. This is observed in the following.

Egress Load Balancing with Delay Bounds

Figure 5.17(a) and Figure 5.17(b) show the GINI Coefficients G^* with the defined upper delay bounds UB_Δ as described above. Again, the overall egress
load balancing is shown as well as the normalized values (i. e. the comparison to the theoretical GINI minimum). Also like above the load balancing
results from the static configuration in Section 5.6.5—shown as gray lines—
are provided for comparison.

It can be observed that the easier the CMA protocol is able to accomplish the given delay bound UB_Δ the more consideration falls to egress load balancing. In cases with the bound being above 1500 ms, the load balancing is close to optimal, compared to static importance configuration. In contrast, if the delay bound is chosen to be low, the protocol reacts with exclusive delay optimization very early. This can be seen in case of 1000 ms, where the worst possible GINI Coefficient G^* is reached with 300 peers and above. In case of 1250 ms the load balancing first is comparable to cases with even higher bounds but then switches to average values and with growing peer numbers increasingly turning to a bad load balancing situation. This reflects the growing difficulties in holding the delay bound with increasing numbers of peers.

5.6.7 The Influence of the Underlay Delay Model

In the previous evaluations the hybrid underlay delay model introduced in Section 5.6.1 to model per-hop overlay delay has been assumed. Of course, it is arguable what influence the underlay assumptions have on the observed protocol metrics, therefore further studies in that direction have been conducted. For comparison, the impact of the two other underlay delay models—the constant delay model and the euclidean model—are also analyzed. While the hybrid approach behaves as described, the constant model always assumes a one-way delay of 170 ms and the euclidean model nearly neglects access network delays (set to 1 ms) and only considers euclidean backbone delays. The whole set of experiments with static configurations of α as well

Delay Model	α	GINI [%]	Mean Data Delay [%]	Maximum Data Delay [%]
Hybrid	0.2	-29.76	0.27	0.91
Constant	0.2	-30.76	-0.16	-7.76
Euclid	0.2	-28.78	0.70	4.30
Hybrid	0.4	-46.52	2.64	16.15
Constant	0.4	-46.24	1.62	11.83
Euclid	0.4	-46.48	2.66	16.61
Hybrid	0.6	-59.91	6.81	43.75
Constant	0.6	-64.11	5.35	31.48
Euclid	0.6	-59.59	6.53	41.44
Hybrid	0.8	-73.38	14.50	74.50
Constant	0.8	-73.69	11.44	56.77
Euclid	0.8	-74.22	13.78	66.72
Hybrid	1.0	-87.76	96.40	236.14
Constant	1.0	-87.58	96.03	228.23
Euclid	1.0	-87.83	103.52	279.90

Table 5.4 Underlay Delay Model Comparison Study, 500 Peers

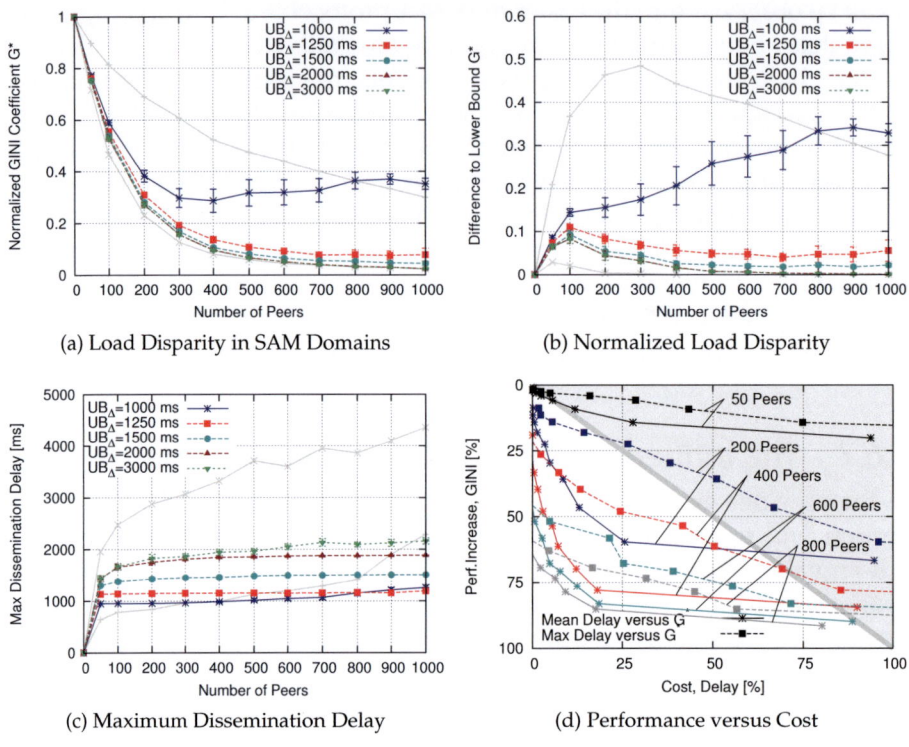

(a) Load Disparity in SAM Domains

(b) Normalized Load Disparity

(c) Maximum Dissemination Delay

(d) Performance versus Cost

Figure 5.18 Upper Delay Bound Behavior with Constant Underlay Delay Model as well as Performance versus Cost Estimation

as with upper bound definitions has been conducted with all three underlay models. Table 5.4 shows a comparison of the performance versus cost behavior for all three model for the case of 500 peers. The results show that in all cases a comparably low α value leads to the most promising tree configurations. In case of the constant delay model the SAM egress load balancing shows best results which is due to no penalty in choosing a parent peer located in a SAM far away, thus making it possible to freely choose the parent in the tree to increase load balancing. The euclidean delay model happens to be the one with slightly less benefit compared to the other two models. Here, the backbone distance has the highest influence on the results. Therefore, choosing SAMs far away in the network increases the drawbacks more obvious.

The underlay comparison shows that the CMA protocol performs the better the less delay increase results from choosing a parent of higher distance in the field. In environments with a high penalty in choosing alternative SAM

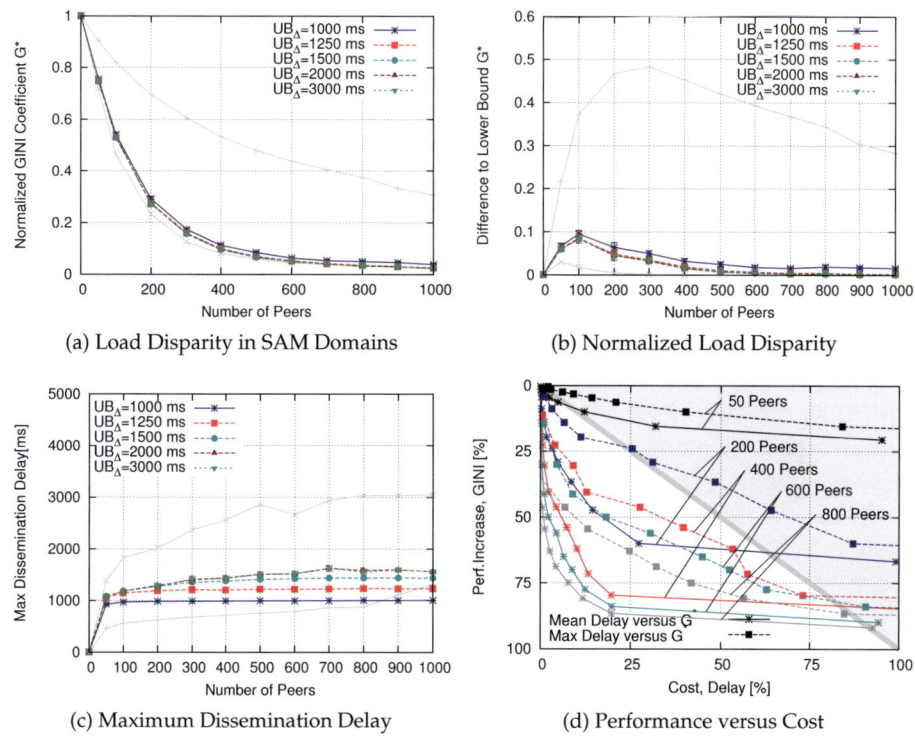

Figure 5.19 Upper Delay Bound Behavior with Euclidean Underlay Delay Model as well as Performance versus Cost Estimation

domains for tree parent search there might still be high potential in doing so if the overall delays are still low.

Figure 5.18 shows the results from evaluations with the constant delay model and defined upper bounds UB_Δ as well as the performance versus cost estimation in case of static α parameterization. Since delays are lower compared to the hybrid underlay model CMA puts higher priority to load balancing. With growing number of peers it gets harder to hold the bound $UB_\Delta = 1000$ ms. Hence, the protocol switches to delay priorization. The remaining upper bound values allow for focusing on load balancing. This behavior can be observed even more clearly in case of the euclidean underlay model, shown in Figure 5.19. Here, even the upper bound $UB_\Delta = 1000$ ms can be accomplished easily since the underlay delays are lower.

The experiments show that in cellular networks as we find them today (being similar to the hybrid delay model) there is high potential of improving SAM egress traffic load balancing without incurring too much additional delay in the dissemination tree. For networks with lower delays, like e. g. the upcoming mobile access network generations, the delays will allow for even better load balancing consideration since the delay penalties will easier stay below given delay constraints.

5.7   Conclusion

In this chapter a case for P2P to implement a near-live video streaming service has been analyzed. A tree-based ALM protocol called CMA has been described that aims at considering traffic load in the involved access networks in order to avoid possible traffic congestions. Inherently, using P2P in the video streaming scenario does not offer much potential to balance incoming traffic load in access networks, since in single-tree environments each peer has to receive the stream exactly once. This fact leads to at least one incoming stream per peer. Furthermore, using P2P even increases traffic load, because peers have to forward the stream, inducing additional outgoing traffic load in the access networks. Therefore, the main question is whether the additional traffic load can be controlled in order to gain the flexibility of P2P-based stream forwarding in video dissemination without incurring too much additional traffic load.

Regarding this question the evaluations in this chapter have shown the following:

- Given that tree-based ALM protocols have access to underlay-related capacity information, this can actively be considered in the tree building and maintenance process.
- Tree-based ALM protocols offer the flexibility to adapt the dissemination structure to defined goals at the cost of inducing additional traffic load in form of egress streams in access networks.
- This additional load can be balanced to high extent if the capacity situation in the networks allows it. This load balancing comes with increased dissemination delays. The increase is comparable low if the protocol is configured accordingly.

In the next chapter, the protocols described in Chapter 4 (NICE) and this chapter (CMA) will be further enhanced to consider communication possibilities via different access technologies. These considerations allow to enhance the efficiency in communication, especially with respect to the traffic load problem explained in this chapter.

6. Multi-Access Discovery and Integration

Today's modern laptops integrate wired and wireless communication devices. Likewise, smartphones come with built-in devices for more than one wireless technology in many cases, e. g. IEEE 802.11 (WiFi) derivates, 3G/4G, and Bluetooth. The active consideration of these multiple communication possibilities can be utilized in ALM protocols in order to gain several benefits: WiFi domains can be used as a broadcast medium in many cases, saving communication overhead, on the one hand. Regarding the load balancing issues discussed in Chapter 5, multiplexing traffic load to different network domains could also be a key driver for alleviating access networks from high traffic load, on the other hand.

In this chapter a rendezvous mechanism is presented for looking up alternative WiFi peer reachabilities in tree-based P2P protocols. Furthermore, this mechanism is exemplarily integrated in the ALM protocols introduced in the predecessing chapters of this thesis. The chapter is structured as follows: In Section 6.1 the rendezvous mechanism is motivated, described, and analyzed. Subsequently, the two ALM approaches NICE and CMA are enhanced by the integrated use of the mechanism. In case of NICE (cf. Chapter 4) the consideration of WiFi domains—both in infrastructure and ad-hoc mode—as well as their integration in the hierarchical clustering is described in Section 6.2. For the tree-based Capacity Matching (cf. Chapter 5) public WiFi domains in dense urban areas are discovered and integrated in the video stream dissemination. This can help to multiplex traffic load among the different access technologies to avoid overload situations.

6.1   Wireless Multi-Access Proximity Probing

In this section an approach denoted *Wireless Multi-Access Proximity Probing (WIMP)* is presented. WIMP targets to support the integration of WiFi networks into tree-based P2P overlay networks through a dedicated overlay refinement mechanism. In order to allow for local wireless connections between peers using a WiFi network such networks and connection opportunities must first be detected in a distributed manner. Following the IEEE 820.11 WiFi Standard document [70], an infrastructure-WiFi BSS is defined as a set of stations (peers) controlled by a single coordination function, the latter implemented as a single access point (AP). All peers in the same BSS are associated with the same AP. The goal of the WIMP mechanism is to provide every peer in the overlay with knowledge about the number of peers in proximity, potentially reachable through WiFi communication. WIMP intends to ease the decision which WiFi network to join for communication.

In the following a problem description is derived from today's deployment situation regarding wireless networks in dense urban areas. Subsequently, related work in the field of WiFi integration in P2P communication is described, before the WIMP mechanism is introduced.

6.1.1   Wireless Networks in Dense Urban Environments

The growing ubiquity of wireless technologies is characteristic for today's big cities (especially in developed countries). The large number of people equipped with modern end-systems naturally increases the user density in these areas. Additionally, the coverage of infrastructure-based wireless networks is constantly growing. This applies to cellular networks (commonly reaching almost 100% coverage) as well as to license-free technologies, like e. g. WiFi. In the latter case, networks are not only deployed by operators but also by private users for home usage.

Recent studies by Valadon et al. [219, 220] and Jones et al. [120] showed that in big cities around the world the per-km^2 count of detectable WiFi networks already reached $\approx$ 1900 in Manhattan in 2006, $\approx$ 3000 in Tokyo in 2007, and $\approx$ 4000 in Paris in 2007. These numbers are increasing considerably every year: According to JiWire [119], the total number of public infrastructure-WiFi locations has more than doubled between 2009 and 2011. Furthermore, a trend can be observed where free WiFi hot spots make out a remarkable fraction of WiFi networks, although the situation highly differs between countries. In the U.S., free WiFi networks outnumbered paid offers for the first time in the end of 2010 and constituted approximately 75% of WiFi networks by the end of 2011. In other countries (especially in Europe), in contrast, free offers made out approximately 25% by that time [119]. Finally, some cities even aim for a 100% coverage with WiFi [46, 119]. Part of them—like e. g. Singapore—offer city-wide free and unrestricted WiFi already [200], while also European cities are planning strong buildouts in that direction for 2012 [23, 147].

As already outlined in Chapter 5 the growing peer density leads to higher risk of network congestion in shared media networks. Given that peers can potentially use local WiFi networks as alternatives to communicate with other peers, higher density increases the chance of direct WiFi connectivity. To exploit these opportunities, e. g. for data traffic offloading, the main question to be answered is: how can peers learn about others in proximity to peer with each other wirelessly using a common WiFi network? While WIMP provides an answer to this question, it does not determine how a P2P protocol uses information about other peers in proximity. It rather defines how the actual detection of proximity is accomplished.

In the following related work in the field of WiFi integration in P2P overlay networks is described. Afterwards, WIMP is described in detail.

6.1.2 Related Work

In order to exploit local area communication possibilities and preserve the 3G access networks Choi et al. [38], Lee et al. [134, 135], and Handa [96] pointed out the efficiency of low-cost WiFi networks in this context, especially in metropolitan areas. Collins et al. [45] motivated WiFi networks as promising and easily deployable communication domains in large controlled environments by example of an entertainment park.

Multihoming support with WiFi consideration is well studied in related work. However, early considerations were limited to single host observations [237]. *Wiffler* [10] is a system to support fast switching between 3G and WiFi on a local peer to reduce 3G usage. Tsao and Sivakumar [218] proposed a strategy called *Super-aggregation* in order to achieve better multihoming performance on local hosts compared to the plain sum of bandwidths when using 3G and WiFi at the same time.

As a step towards distributed wireless communication consideration, *CUBS* [214] targeted bandwidth sharing between neighbors, motivated by increasing bandwidth demands in P2P applications. PatchPeer [61] aims at increasing the cellular link capacity by exchanging parts of a video between peers being interconnected via ad-hoc P2P connections. Similarly, Stiemerling and Kiesel [207, 208] proposed a cooperative P2P system for near-live video streaming for the application case of fast-moving trains: Peers receive different chunks of data via 3G and exchange their parts in an ad-hoc WiFi-based P2P manner. Hanano et al. [95] proposed a hybrid 3G/ad-hoc WiFi system for video ads dissemination. Nahrstedt et al. presented *iShare* [224], a system for the collaborative usage of cellular and ad-hoc WiFi communication. iShare also aims at 3G relief, but enhances the general approach by the integration of an incentive scheme. Further approaches for the integration of WiFi communication in distributed networks have been proposed in the context of opportunistic networks [94, 152], not relying on any predeployed infrastructure components at all. However, opportunistic communication is generally incapable of providing low dissemination delays, for instance, since peer density and mobility are not dependably predictable.

Most of these approaches take the straightforward approach of detecting other peers in wireless proximity by establishing a WiFi ad-hoc network and constantly scan the environment for other peers using this network. As soon as any peer in the same ad-hoc WiFi network is detected the peers can start using the network to communicate directly. While this approach is simple, it has two major drawbacks: First, permanently sending beacons and scanning the environment results in significant overhead with—in most cases—low chance of success. Since energy consumption in WiFi ad-hoc mode is significantly higher than in infrastructure mode [69], this approach can be considered infeasible for many applications executed on mobile devices. Second, most smartphones shipped today do not offer the possibility to connect via ad-hoc[1].

In contrast to ad-hoc connectivity the high availability of infrastructure-based wireless networks in metropolitan areas could be used as an alternative to ad-hoc communication. Infrastructure-based WiFi—as found e. g. in public places—does not share the drawbacks stated above. Yoon et al. presented *MOVi* [239], a system that aims at video streaming services in infrastructure-WiFi networks by exploiting the downlink and P2P capacities of peers in order to increase efficiency. However, MOVi targets VoD services and depends on a centralized management component to be always available in the network.

Furthermore, exploiting infrastructure-based WiFi networks imposes other problems, like e. g. the decision which concrete WiFi network to join and use: In big cities, most places are commonly covered by dozens of infrastructure-based WiFi networks concurrently. Arbitrarily joining networks for searching other peers is not promising in such environments. Hence, a mechanism is

---

[1]Some devices allow to act as an access point. This also comes with comparably high additional energy overhead.

necessary to coordinate the process of joining and testing among the peers. WIMP offers such a mechanism and is described in the following.

6.1.3   The WIMP Approach

Instead of detecting neighbors in local proximity WIMP merely aims at providing hints on possible WiFi connectivity between peers. WIMP is designed to provide information for the refinement of P2P systems that construct tree-based overlay networks. Hence, it assumes a tree-based overlay network to be established in advance.

In WIMP every peer in the overlay periodically scans the WiFi networks currently in range. Subsequently, it sends *visibility information* about these networks to its parent in the tree. For each WiFi network an ID Θ is used (e. g. the MAC address of the WiFi access point). In this process all IDs are aggregated until they reach the root peer. Finally, the root peer redistributes the (relevant) visibility information down the tree. After one full period—which is called *epoch* here in accordance with the terminology used in predecessing chapters—every peer in the overlay has received the visibility information about relevant WiFi networks detected by peers in the overlay. This process is repeated periodically in each epoch.

On reception of a list of visibility information containing multiple WiFi IDs $\overline{\Theta} = \{\Theta_1, ..., \Theta_n\}$ a peer can check whether one or more of its locally visible WiFi IDs are contained in the list. Multiple containedness of a WiFi ID Θ_i indicates potential wireless proximity between peers in this specific WiFi network.

The number of peers concurrently detecting the same WiFi network is denoted as *cardinality* ρ. To save overhead in WIMP multiple identical WiFi ID entries Θ_i in the list are cut down to one entry with a corresponding *cardinality* ρ_i value attached. Furthermore, the root peer in the tree eliminates WiFi ID entries with a cardinality value $\rho = 1$ from the list. Those IDs are no longer relevant in WIMP since they are detected by only one peer in the overlay and therefore hold no potential to be used as a P2P connection medium. This optimization is called *adjustment* in the following.

Figure 6.1(a) provides an example for this WiFi visibility distribution where 8 peers are arranged in a small tree and 5 WiFi networks are deployed in the environment. The peers detect their locally visible WiFi networks and aggregate the specific IDs Θ_i up the tree. Doing so, the root peer learns the whole set of IDs $\overline{\Theta} = \{\Theta_1, \Theta_2, \Theta_3, \Theta_3, \Theta_4, \Theta_5\}$. The set in the example indicates that WiFi network Θ_3 is locally visible for two peers in the tree, although the identities of these peers are not known. Since the goal is to indicate shared WiFi visibilities only those networks which are visible by at least two peers concur-

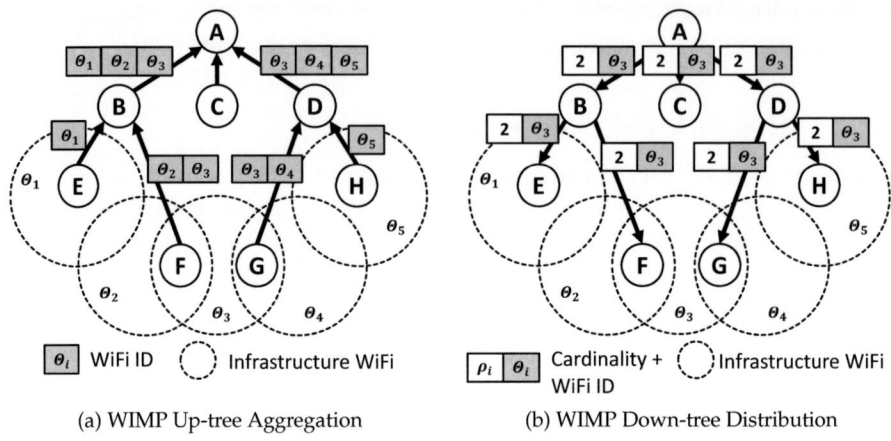

(a) WIMP Up-tree Aggregation   (b) WIMP Down-tree Distribution

Figure 6.1 Up- and Downtree WiFi Visibility Distribution in WIMP

rently affect peer decisions: Hence, as a result of adjustment, the root in the example only distributes the ID Θ_3, together with the cardinality value $\rho_3 = 2$ (cf. Figure 6.1(b)). Based on this information peers F and G could consider to join the WiFi network Θ_3 in order to directly communicate in the shared WiFi network.

Besides the function of indicating common WiFi visibilities the cardinality ρ can also be used as a rating mechanism: In case a peer learns through WIMP that it has shared visibilities in more than one WiFi network it can choose the network with higher cardinality in order to find more overlay peers. In case cardinalities are equal it is up to the concrete decision algorithm of the protocol how to behave, as this is not part of WIMP. Every peer learns the set of WiFis which presumably are in range of at least one other peer in the overlay. The protocol using WIMP can decide which WiFi to join and try to reach other peers inside the specific network. Should no answer be received the peer can leave the network and try a different one in the next epoch.

6.1.4   WIMP Overhead Analysis

In this section the overhead created by WIMP is quantified both from a global point of view as well as per individual overlay peer. Here, overhead is defined as the number of WiFi IDs to be distributed in the tree periodically (i. e. per epoch). The actual amount of data can be derived easily, depending on how IDs are encoded in the system. Furthermore, inclusion of all detected WiFi networks is assumed in distribution, i. e. no detected networks are left out due to access restrictions or similar limitations.

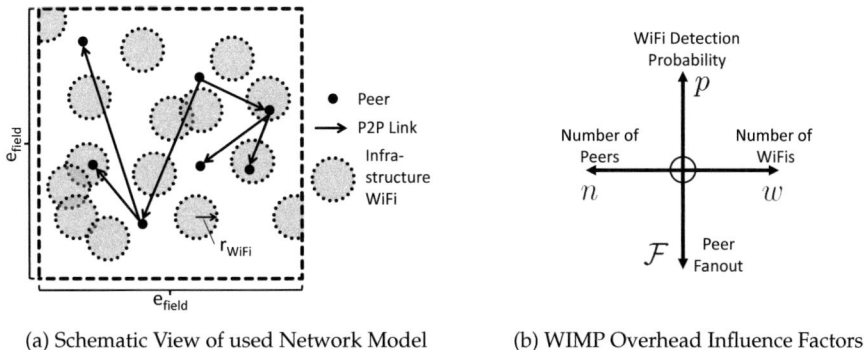

(a) Schematic View of used Network Model   (b) WIMP Overhead Influence Factors

Figure 6.2 Used Network Model and Overhead Influence Factors

As overhead per epoch is discussed, its total amount per time naturally depends on the length of the epoch. The concrete choice for the epoch highly depends on the specific application case. In the following, the network model being used for overhead estimation is described.

6.1.4.1 Network Model

A square field with edge length e_{field} is used. In this field a number of peers is deployed uniformly at random. Furthermore, w WiFi networks are deployed to the field, also placed uniformly at random and each network providing a coverage radius of r_{WiFi}. The WiFi networks may overlap. Effects arising from near-border placement are neglected. Among the peers an overlay tree is established with each non-leaf-peer having the same number of children. Since WIMP is working on prebuilt trees it is out of scope how these trees are established. A tree with randomly selected children for each node is used. In realistic scenarios the placement of peers and WiFis in the field may not follow complete randomness but rather follow specific probabilistic (social) distributions. These aspects are not considered. For analytical evaluations the tree is assumed to be full (i. e. the tree is balanced and each non-leaf peer has its full set of children). For a given out-degree of a peer its local uptree overhead only depends on the number of peers in its subtree. The downtree overhead, in contrast, does not depend on the tree structure.

Figure 6.2(a) shows a schematic view of the used network model. In this example 7 peers have been deployed to the field together with 15 WiFi networks. Among the peers a tree structure with an out-degree of 2 has been established, i. e. with every non-leaf peer having two children.

Besides the epoch four factors have influence on WIMP overhead (cf. Figure 6.2(b)): (1) The number of participating peers n, (2) the number of WiFi networks w in the system, (3) the probability of a peer to detect a WiFi network p, and (4) the number of children per peer in the tree $\mathcal{F}$ (fanout). The overall number of peers, together with the fanout, determine the tree height, the number of overall P2P links, and also the number of detected WiFi networks (because more peers increase detection probability). The number of detected WiFi networks influences the overall amount of information to be distributed. This also applies to the probability of WiFi detection. The peer fanout determines a peer's local overhead.

All four overhead dimensions will be considered in the following in order to answer the question how they influence the overall generated additional communication overhead as well as the per-peer overhead in WIMP. First, the mathematical basis for overhead estimation is described.

6.1.4.2   Stochastic Overhead Analysis

In the following the network model described in Section 6.1.4.1 builds a basis for this analysis. Given a tree with depth d and an out-degree (fanout) $\mathcal{F}$ per peer. Then, there are

$$n = \sum_{x=0}^{d-1} \mathcal{F}^x \tag{6.1}$$

peers in the tree. Each peer falls into a specific WiFi network (and therefore is able to detect it) with a probability p of

$$
\begin{aligned}
p(\text{WiFi Detection}) &= \frac{\text{WiFi coverage area size}}{\text{Global field size}} \\
&= \frac{(r_{\text{WiFi}})^2 \cdot \Pi}{(e_{\text{field}})^2}.
\end{aligned}
\tag{6.2}
$$

Since all WiFi networks and peers are placed completely independent and may overlap the probability p applies to each WiFi network in the field. The probability for a given WiFi network to be detected by exactly x peers can be modeled as a Bernoulli Process $\mathcal{B}$ with parameters (n, p, x), n being the number of peers and p being the probability of detection given in (6.2):

$$
\begin{aligned}
\mathcal{P}(\text{Exactly } x \text{ detections}) &= \mathcal{B}(n; p; x) \\
&= \binom{n}{x} \cdot p^x \cdot (1-p)^{n-x}.
\end{aligned}
\tag{6.3}
$$

Average Overhead

In each layer $i = \{1, ..., d-1\}$ of the tree a peer propagates the set of WiFi network IDs detected by all peers in its subtree (including itself) towards the tree's root, adjusted by aggregation. The maximum number of peers in a subtree of layer i is $n_{sub}^i = \sum_{x=0}^{d-i} \mathcal{F}^x$ and the number of detected WiFi networks in this subtree (with duplicates) is $w_{sub}^i = n_{sub}^i \cdot p \cdot w$. Since every peer removes duplicates in this set each peer in layer i of the tree finally sends

$$\Theta_{noduplicates}^i = \left[1 - \mathcal{B}(n_{sub}^i; p; 0)\right] \cdot w$$
$$= \left[1 - (1-p)^{n_{sub}^i}\right] \cdot w \qquad (6.4)$$

WiFi IDs to its parent in the tree. Then, the overall number of WiFi IDs being sent in the process of up-tree aggregation is

$$\Theta_{UpTree}^{Prob} = \sum_{x=1}^{d-1} \left[\mathcal{F}^{d-x} \cdot \Theta_{noduplicates}^x\right]. \qquad (6.5)$$

The final adjusted set that has to be distributed to all peers in the tree holds $\Theta_{adjusted}^{\mathcal{D}}$ elements, being the adjusted set of WiFi IDs collected by the root peer. Since the root peer eliminates all WiFi IDs that have been detected by only one peer in the tree (in the process of adjustment) the final set evaluates to

$$\Theta_{adjusted}^d = W_{noduplicates}^d - \mathcal{B}(n_{sub}^d; p; 1) \cdot w$$
$$= \left[1 - \left[(1-p)^{n_{sub}^d} - n \cdot p \cdot (1-p)^{n_{sub}^d - 1}\right]\right] \cdot w. \qquad (6.6)$$

Then, the overall communication overhead in down-tree direction evaluates to

$$\Theta_{DownTree}^{Prob} = \sum_{x=0}^{d-1} \left(\mathcal{F}^{d-x} \cdot \Theta_{adjusted}^d\right). \qquad (6.7)$$

The average global overhead in the tree per epoch is (6.5) + (6.7), being

$$\Theta_{UpTree}^{Prob} + \Theta_{DownTree}^{Prob}.$$

Each individual peer in the tree distributes the WiFi IDs up-tree and down-tree once per epoch. The leaf peers as well as the root peer do not have to accomplish one of these two steps, respectively. Thus, the overhead for a leaf

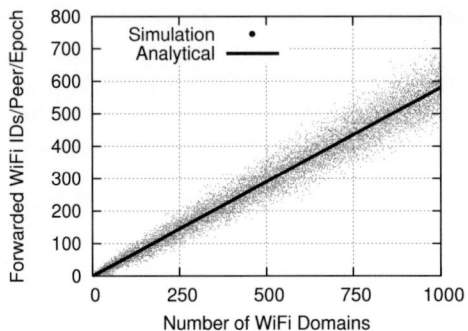

Figure 6.3 Comparison between analytical Average and Simulation: Per-Peer Overhead in the Root Peer of the Tree

peer is $1 - \mathcal{B}(1, p, 0)$ and the overhead for the root is $(\Theta^d_{\text{adjusted}} \cdot \mathcal{F})$. For peers in layer $i \in \{2, ..., d-1\}$ the probabilistic overhead estimates to $\Theta^i_{\text{noduplicates}} + (\Theta^{\mathcal{D}}_{\text{adjusted}} \cdot \mathcal{F})$.

Worst Case Overhead

The highest possible overhead to be generated in WIMP occurs for the case when each leaf peer in the tree detects all WiFi networks in the system. Then, the whole set of IDs has to be distributed up and down through the entire tree. This (unlikely) case serves as an upper bound estimate here. The worst case global overhead per epoch is given by

$$\Theta^{Worst}_{DownTree} + \Theta^{Worst}_{UpTree} = 2 \cdot \left[\sum_{x=1}^{d-1} \left(\mathcal{F}^{d-x} \cdot w \right) \right]. \tag{6.8}$$

Similarly, the worst case local peer overhead is given by

$$(\mathcal{F} + 1) \cdot w. \tag{6.9}$$

It represents a peer that has to send all WiFi IDs up once and additionally has to distribute them to its children.

6.1.4.3   Simulative Validation

The proposed overhead calculations compute probabilistic values. To validate the findings simulations have been accomplished in addition based on the network model described in Section 6.1.4.1. For this purpose a JAVA-based simulation has been created that implements the network model, randomly deploys peers and WiFi domains to the field, and finally builds an

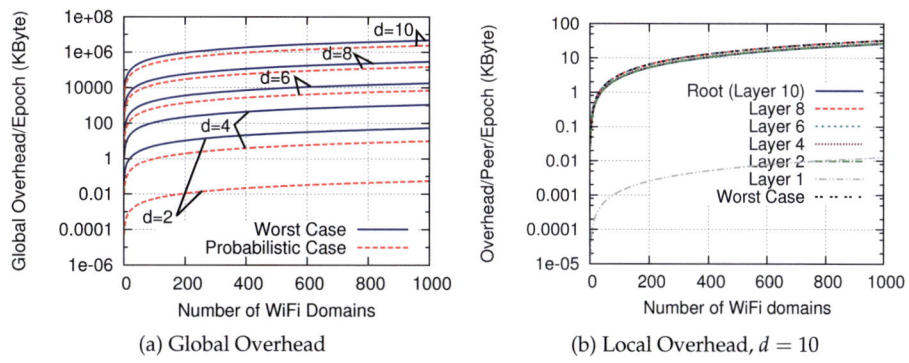

(a) Global Overhead   (b) Local Overhead, $d = 10$

Figure 6.4 Influence of the Number of WiFi Domains on WIMP Overhead

overlay tree. Figure 6.3 shows a comparison between simulation results and values calculated analytically. As an example, it shows the average number of locally forwarded WiFi IDs per epoch for the root peer in a tree with 341 peers and fanout $\mathcal{F} = 4$ (resulting in tree height $d = 5$). A field of length $e_{\text{field}} = 4000\,\text{m}$ and WiFi domains with radius $r_{\text{WiFi}} = 100\,\text{m}$ have been used. The results are based on the analytical calculation and 20 simulation runs. As can be observed from the figure the analytical approach fits the simulative cases very well. Similar comparisons (not presented here due to space limitations) have been accomplished with all relevant overhead dimensions, showing that the analytical approach models empirical overhead behavior. In the following the analytical model is used to analyze WIMP-generated overhead from several perspectives.

6.1.4.4 Resulting WIMP Overhead

For overhead considerations WiFi IDs are assumed to be represented through 48 bit (access point) MAC addresses. Furthermore, cardinalities ρ are encoded by a 4 bit field for each ID Θ, allowing to differentiate cardinalities of up to 15 peers. A cardinality of this dimension is assumed to be high enough in order to efficiently differentiate the peering potential of WiFi domains. For the field an edge length of $e_{\text{field}} = 4000\,\text{m}$ is assumed. If not stated differently a WiFi domain has a coverage radius of $r_{\text{WiFi}} = 100\,\text{m}$. Finally, the tree is always assumed to be full and the fanout $\mathcal{F}$ for each peer is assumed to be 4^2.

Impact of the number of WiFi Domains

Figure 6.4(a) shows the global amount of data that has to be transferred in one epoch, depending on the number of WiFi domains in the field. The worst

---

[2]This value has been chosen as a calculation base. The general influence of the peer fanout $\mathcal{F}$ is discussed later in this section.

cases and probabilistic cases are shown for different tree height values d. A logarithmic scale for the y-axis has been chosen to improve readability. Depending on the number of WiFi domains in the field the global overhead increases linearly in all cases. However, the global overhead generated by WIMP quickly grows with increasing tree height because the number of peers grows exponentially (a tree height of $d = 10$ results in $\approx 350\,000$ peers under the given assumptions). How the probabilistic case relates to the worst case is discussed later in this section. Figure 6.4(b) shows the local overhead per peer, differentiated by the peers' positions in the tree. A tree of height of $d = 10$ is shown as representative for a scenario with a high number of participating peers. Obviously, leaf peers experience very low overhead due to the fact that they only have to forward IDs connected to their locally visible WiFi networks once. The root peer has to sent the adjusted set of IDs $\Theta^d_{adjusted}$ to all of its children. Peers inside the tree have higher overhead since they always have to sent the adjusted sets received from below (up-tree) as well as the final set from the root peer (down-tree). Depending on the number of WiFi networks w, the overhead per peer can easily reach several kilobytes per epoch, growing linearly. Furthermore, all layers except the leaf layer generate a similar amount of overhead, as visible in the figure. Overall, the number of WiFi networks w directly influences how many WiFi IDs Θ have to be distributed in the tree since more WiFi domains result in a higher fraction being detected by peers. Hence, the global overhead as well as the local overhead per peer increase linearly in WIMP.

Influence of the Number of Peers

Figure 6.5(a) shows the global overhead with different numbers of peers in the tree. Additionally, three different numbers of WiFi domains deployed to the field are shown in the figure. The figure makes clear that growing numbers of peers also lead to a linear growth in global overhead. This is due to the fact that more peers need to forward the WiFi IDs over more P2P links. Furthermore, a higher number of peers also increases the probability of detecting a specific WiFi domain, resulting in more IDs being distributed in the tree.

Figure 6.5(b) shows how the local peer overhead correlates to a growing number of peers. The number of WiFi domains is fixed at $w = 1000$. With growing number of peers the local overhead quickly reaches worst case regions in higher layers of the tree. The reason is that the worst case applies if all WiFi network IDs Θ have to be distributed and the probability to detect all WiFi domains increases with the number of peers. Furthermore, the higher a peer resides in the tree (except the root) the more overhead it will experience.

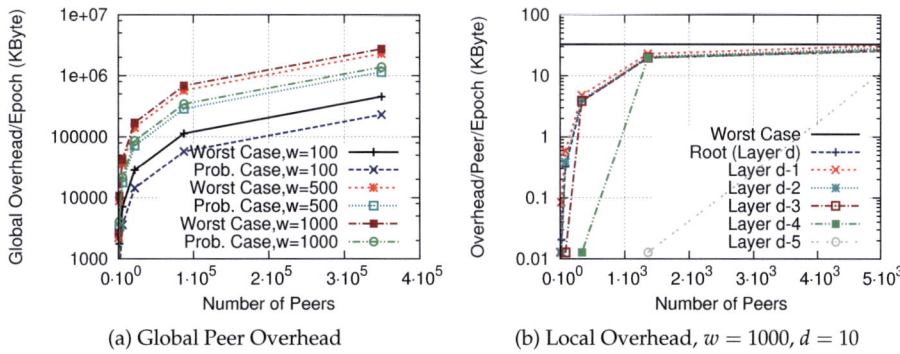

(a) Global Peer Overhead   (b) Local Overhead, $w = 1000$, $d = 10$

Figure 6.5 Influence of the Number of Peers on WIMP Overhead

Overall, with a fixed number of WiFi domains but growing number of peers
the global overhead grows linearly, while the per-peer overhead additionally
converges quickly against the worst case (i. e. the case when distributing all
WiFi domain IDs).

Impact of the WiFi Detection Probability

The third factor that influences WIMP overhead is the probability p of a peer
to detect a WiFi domain in the field. Figure 6.6(a) shows the local overhead
for peers residing in the different layers of the tree. The number of WiFis is
set to $w = 1000$, while the tree height is $d = 10$. The figure shows that the
local overhead in each layer (except the root layer) converges to a fixed worst
case value. This worst case value is lower for the root peer compared to the
remaining layers. The convergence speed is determined by the height of the

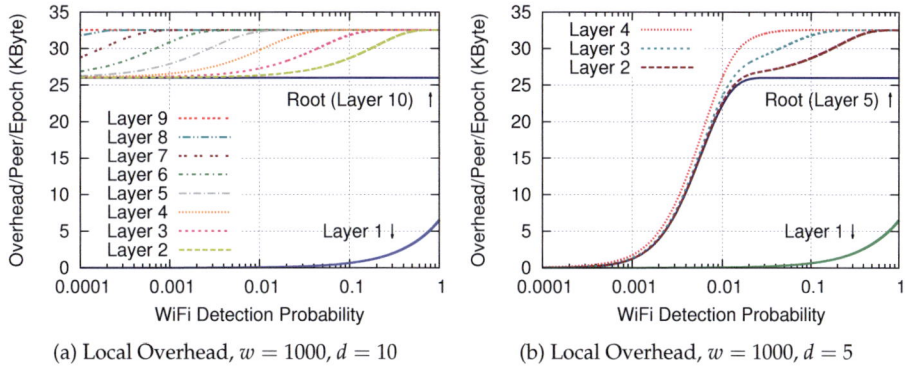

(a) Local Overhead, $w = 1000$, $d = 10$ (b) Local Overhead, $w = 1000$, $d = 5$

Figure 6.6 WiFi Detection Probability Influence on local WIMP Overhead

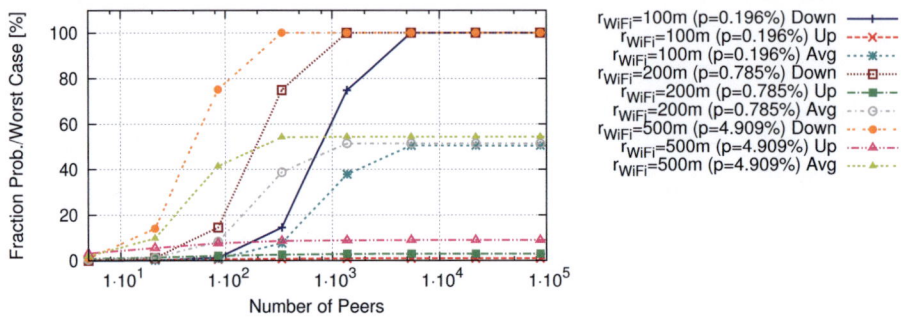

Figure 6.7 Relation between Probabilistic and Worst Case Global Overhead

specific layer, with layer 1 naturally growing slowest. Figure 6.6(b) shows the same behavior for a tree with height $d = 5$. The convergence behavior is the same for the shown layers as in Figure 6.6(a) with higher WiFi detection probability (e. g. $p > 0.01$), while it differs with lower probability. The reason is that in the tree with more peers (i. e. the case shown in Figure 6.6(a)), the probability that the root peer has to send down a higher fraction of WiFi IDs is higher than in the (lower) tree with less peers. This leads to a higher influence for down-tree distribution with lower WiFi detection probability. Hence, the number of peers has influence on early convergence, while it does not affect the per-layer overhead when the WiFi detection passes a certain threshold. Furthermore, the number of WiFi domains only affects the worst case to which the overhead converges. In the following the relation between the probabilistic overhead and the worst case overhead is further examined.

Relation between Probabilistic and Worst Case Overhead

Figure 6.7 shows the fraction of probabilistic global overhead in WIMP, compared to the worst case. Three different WiFi radiuses r_{WiFi} are considered, resulting in three different WiFi detection probabilities. Additionally, the resulting detection probabilities p are provided.

The figure shows the relations for the up-tree direction, the down-tree direction, and the average (up and down) case, separately. For $r = 100\,\text{m}$ the fraction in up-tree direction is below 1 %, while the down-tree overhead converges to the worst case with growing number of peers. Hence, the overall overhead (being the average of both) converges to a value near 50 %. The higher the probability of detection gets (cf. $r = 500\,\text{m}$, for instance), the faster the overhead in down-tree direction converges to the worst case and

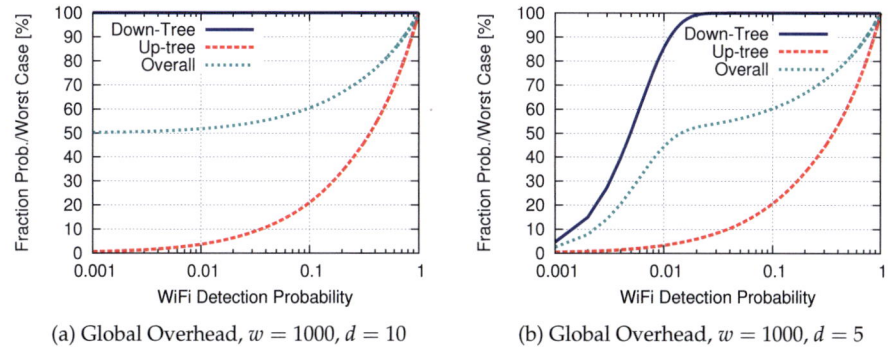

(a) Global Overhead, $w = 1000, d = 10$ (b) Global Overhead, $w = 1000, d = 5$

Figure 6.8 Convergence of Global Probabilistic Overhead to Worst Case

the higher the fraction of up-tree direction and worst case gets. As a result, the overall probabilistic overhead converges against the overall worst case.

This behavior results from the fact that with more peers joining the overlay tree and WiFi domains with higher radiuses r_{WiFi} the fraction of detected WiFi domains (and therefore both down-tree and up-tree overhead) increases. The worst case overhead in down-tree direction is reached if all WiFi domains have been detected during up-tree aggregation. The up-tree overhead is comparably low compared to the worst case but naturally grows with increasing detection probability p. Obviously, the relation between probabilistic and worst case overhead does not depend on the number of WiFi domains w (as both grow in same dimensions), while with growing number of peers n the relation converges to a fixed value. Figure 6.8 shows how this converged relation between probabilistic and worst case behavior develops with growing detection probability. Here, the down-tree overhead relation converges against worst case very fast in case of $d = 10$, while it grows slower in the lower probability regions in the tree of height $d = 5$. In both cases the up-tree overhead relation grows slowly since the number of WiFi networks being detected lower in the tree has less influence and is independent of the overall tree size when considering local overhead. The overall fraction (being the average of down-tree and up-tree fraction) hence converges to the worst case, being mainly influenced by the down-tree development.

Comparison of Overhead Increase

As described above, WIMP global overhead shows linear behavior with both growing peer numbers and WiFi domain numbers. The question remains which one of these two factors has higher impact on overhead growth. The number of WiFi domains affects the overall worst case since the number of

WiFi detections grows with it, although the probability to detect a specific single WiFi domain stays constant. The number of peers, in contrast, influences two aspects: On the one hand, the WiFi detection probability p grows because more peers detect more WiFi domains. On the other hand, the tree grows, resulting in more P2P links and a higher overhead to distribute the WiFi IDs throughout the whole tree. Hence, it is claimed that the number of peers has higher influence on global WIMP overhead growth than the number of WiFi domains in the field.

Proof: Let $y := \Theta^{Worst}_{DownTree} + \Theta^{Worst}_{UpTree}$, with number of peers x, number of WiFi domains w, tree height d, and peer fanout $\mathcal{F}$. Then, the global overhead as given in (6.8) is:

$$
\begin{aligned}
y &= 2 \cdot \left[\sum_{i=1}^{d-1} \mathcal{F}^{d-i} \cdot w \right] \\
&= 2 \cdot w \cdot \left[\sum_{i=1}^{\log_{\mathcal{F}}(1-(1-\mathcal{F})x)-1} \mathcal{F}^{\log_{\mathcal{F}}(1-(1-\mathcal{F})x)-i} \right] \\
&= 2 \cdot w \cdot \left[\sum_{i=1}^{\log_{\mathcal{F}}(1-(1-\mathcal{F})x)-1} (1-(1-\mathcal{F})x) \cdot \mathcal{F}^{-i} \right] \\
&= 2 \cdot w \cdot (1-(1-\mathcal{F})x) \cdot \left[\sum_{i=0}^{\log_{\mathcal{F}}(1-(1-\mathcal{F})x)-2} (\tfrac{1}{\mathcal{F}})^{i+1} \right] \qquad (6.10) \\
&= \frac{2w}{\mathcal{F}} \cdot (1-(1-\mathcal{F})x) \cdot \left[\frac{1-(\tfrac{1}{\mathcal{F}})^{\log_{\mathcal{F}}(1-(1-\mathcal{F})x)-1}}{(1-\tfrac{1}{\mathcal{F}})} \right] \\
&= \frac{2w(\mathcal{F}x - x + 1)}{\mathcal{F}-1} \cdot \left[1 - \frac{\mathcal{F}}{(\mathcal{F}-1)x+1} \right] \\
&= 2w(x-1) \\
&= 2wx - 2w \\
&\Rightarrow \frac{\partial y}{\partial w} = 2x - 2; \quad \frac{\partial y}{\partial x} = 2w \quad \square
\end{aligned}
$$

The estimation shows that the global overhead in WIMP grows similarly in both dimensions with number of peers x having slightly higher impact than the number of WiFis w.

Impact of Fanout

The described overhead considerations all assumed each peer to have exactly 4 children ($\mathcal{F} = 4$), although obviously the fanout has considerable influence on WIMP overhead. While in (6.10) it has been shown that global overhead is independent of $\mathcal{F}$ the peer fanout is the factor with highest influence for per-peer-generated overhead (cf. (6.9)). Since $\mathcal{F}$ scales the local overhead linearly resulting per-peer overhead depends on a peer's number of children in the overlay tree structure. This fact should be considered in the following "real world" overhead estimation.

WIMP Overhead in Real World Environments

Up to now, the linear behavior of WIMP overhead has been pointed out. To get an idea how much overhead is potentially generated by WIMP in real metropolitan areas the 3 example cities New York (Manhattan), Tokyo, and Paris are considered in the following, based on the data given by Valadon et al. [219, 220] and Jones et al. [120]. Since these cities show a considerably high WiFi density an arbitrary city with lower density is also analyzed to give an impression for less dense scenarios. It should be mentioned that the data has been collected between 2006 and 2007. Hence, the evaluation does not try to reflect today's situation but gives a general impression for cities of different WiFi density.

A field of $1\,\text{km}^2$ from the city's core is considered in each case. Figure 6.9 exemplarily provides a visual impression of today's WiFi density in two big U.S. cities. Each red or green dot indicates a single WiFi Hotspot.

Table 6.1 shows the overhead generated by WIMP for three different tree heights ($d = \{4, 5, 6\}$), resulting in different numbers of peers ($n = \{85, 341, 1365\}$). For each city the worst case global overhead (WCG), worst case

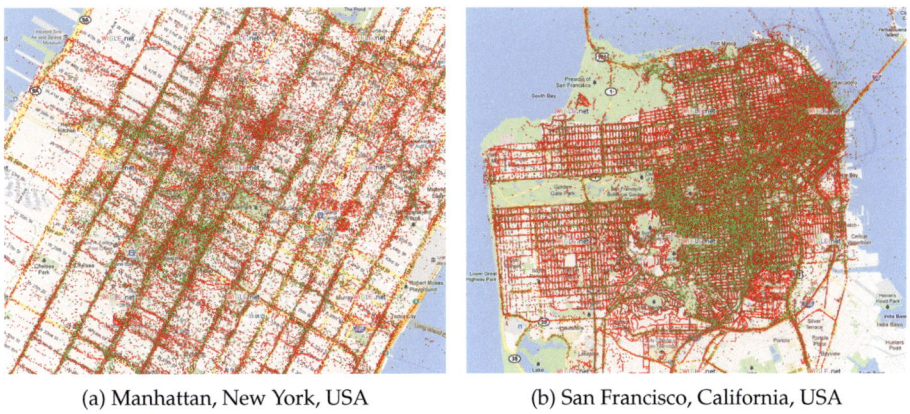

(a) Manhattan, New York, USA   (b) San Francisco, California, USA

Figure 6.9 Exemplary WiFi Hotspot Density in two U.S. Cities, taken from Wigle.net [231] on November 22nd, 2011

City	All Detected WiFis				Open WiFis Only			
	WCG	WCL	PG	PL	WCG	WCL	PG	PL
Tree Height $d = 4$ (85 Peers)								
Smaller Model City (500 IDs/km^2)	$5.5\,E^2$	16.25	55	2.4	36.0	1.1	3.0	0.2
Manhattan 2006 (1900 IDs/km^2)	$20.7\,E^2$	61.75	171	9.0	136.5	4.1	11.2	0.6
Tokyo 2007 (3000 IDs/km^2)	$32.8\,E^2$	97.5	270	14.2	216.2	6.4	17.8	0.9
Paris 2007 (4000 IDs/km^2)	$43.7\,E^2$	130.0	360	19.0	288.3	8.6	23.8	1.3
Tree Height $d = 5$ (341 Peers)								
Smaller Model City (500 IDs/km^2)	$22.1\,E^2$	16.25	$8.6\,E^2$	11.3	145.9	1.1	56.5	0.7
Manhattan 2006 (1900 IDs/km^2)	$84.0\,E^2$	61.75	$32.5\,E^2$	43.0	552.5	4.1	214.0	2.8
Tokyo 2007 (3000 IDs/km^2)	$132.6\,E^2$	97.5	$51.4\,E^2$	68.0	875.2	6.4	339.0	4.5
Paris 2007 (4000 IDs/km^2)	$176.8\,E^2$	130.0	$68.5\,E^2$	90.6	1166.9	8.6	452.0	6.0
Tree Height $d = 6$ (1365 Peers)								
Smaller Model City (500 IDs/km^2)	$8.9\,E^3$	16.25	$4.6\,E^3$	16.0	585.2	1.1	301.0	1.1
Manhattan 2006 (1900 IDs/km^2)	$33.7\,E^3$	61.75	$17.3\,E^3$	60.9	2216.5	4.1	1139.9	4.0
Tokyo 2007 (3000 IDs/km^2)	$53.2\,E^3$	97.5	$27.4\,E^3$	96.2	3510.9	6.4	1805.5	6.3
Paris 2007 (4000 IDs/km^2)	$70.9\,E^3$	130.0	$36.5\,E^3$	128.2	4681.2	8.6	2407.4	8.5

Table 6.1 WIMP-generated Overhead in different metropolitan Areas [kbyte/epoch], Peer Fanout $\mathcal{F} = 4$

local overhead (WCL), probabilistic global overhead (PG), and probabilistic local overhead (PL) is provided. Additionally, the case for all WiFi domains in the environment being considered is compared to the case where only free and unrestricted WiFi domains ("Open WiFi") are considered. The fraction of such free WiFi domains is hard to determine and can strongly differ between cities and countries (cf. Section 6.1.1). In accordance to the work of Valadon et al. [220] a statistical fraction of 6.6 % is assumed to be free and unrestricted[3], here. These WiFi domains are additionally assumed as the fraction of net-

---

[3]While the authors found approximately 10 % of WiFis being unrestricted in their studies, part of the domains were connected to a portal webpage. These cases are excluded in this chapter's evaluations.

works that permit direct P2P connections to give an impression how WIMP overhead develops with only those networks being considered.

The PL columns in Table 6.1 have the highest relevance for user acceptance since they show the per-peer probabilistic overhead. As the table shows, with consideration of all detected WiFi domains in the environment the local overhead per peer can grow over 100 kilobytes per epoch in environments with high WiFi domain density. These values of course result from the high WiFi densities considered but also in less dense environments overhead can be expected that easily exceeds the bounds that most users will likely accept for a P2P refinement extension mechanism like WIMP. To mitigate the problem of high communication overhead with plain adjusted ID lists in WIMP the following section presents an ID encoding extension that is able to reduce communication overhead.

6.1.5   Enhancing WIMP Scalability

The generated overhead in WIMP may reach the bounds of acceptance from user side in case of high numbers of users or WiFi domains. To support higher numbers of both this section presents an extension that is able to slow down the linear growth, although not eliminating it completely. The basic idea is to use *Bloom Filters* as sophisticated data structures that considerably exceed the space-efficiency of plain WiFi ID lists (which have been used in the evaluations above). The concept of Bloom Filters is described in the following before their integration in WIMP is explained subsequently.

6.1.5.1   Bloom Filters

Bloom Filters [29] offer a space-efficient randomized data structure to support content queries. A survey covering various application scenarios is given by Broder and Mitzenmacher [30]. A Bloom Filter is a one-dimensional array of bits in which given content values (elements) can be encoded. The length of the array is l. For an element x to be encoded in the Bloom Filter k independent hash functions $\{h_1, ..., h_k\}$ are used, determining which bits $h_i(x)$ in the filter are set to 1. Afterwards, an element can easily be tested on containedness in the Bloom Filter if all corresponding bits are set to 1. This approach may lead to false positives (if different hash results overlap), therefore potential application scenarios have to be tolerant to such cases. However, false negatives are not possible. In the following a Bloom Filter with one bit per field in the array is called *Standard Bloom Filter (SBF)*.

In general, for an input set of size n, the false positive probability σ in a Bloom Filter can be asymptotically approximated by

$$\sigma = \left(1 - e^{-\frac{kn}{l}}\right)^k.$$

The choice for the number of hash functions k directly influences σ since more bits being set in the array per element decrease the probability of overlapping on the one hand, but also decrease the number of possible elements in the Bloom Filter. According to [30], the number of hash functions is optimal if

$$k = \frac{m \cdot \log(2)}{n}.$$

Assuming k has been chosen accordingly, the length l of a Bloom Filter with expected false positive probability σ can be calculated through

$$l = \frac{n \cdot \log(\frac{1}{\sigma})}{\log^2(2)}.$$

The drawback of SBFs is the fact that each element's insertion will only be registered once even if the element has been added more than once to the SBF. Furthermore, deletion of single elements is not possible. To enhance the SBF concept by the possibility to insert an element more than once and delete single elements *Counting Bloom Filters (CBF)* [68] have been proposed (to which the calculations for σ, k, and l also apply). In a CBF each of the l fields in the Bloom Filter does not only hold a single bit but a set of bits to implement a small counter. On insertion the counter is incremented, while on deletion it is decremented. Fan et al. [68] state that 4 bits is a sufficiently high counter value for most application scenarios, resulting in 15 distinguishable insertions per element. The number of bits used per element is called *bucket size b* in the following. If two CBFs have the same length l they can easily be aggregated by adding up the buckets in both filters at the same positions. The bucket sizes do not necessarily have to be the same in both CBFs since cardinalities can simply be added and used to determine a new bucket size.

For supporting changing element sets another class of Bloom Filters, called *Dynamic Bloom Filters (DBF)* [85] has been proposed. DBFs trade off dynamic growth of l against increased false positive probabilities for cases in which l is not known in advance. Since in WIMP element sets are static in downtree distribution and l can be adapted and optimized per epoch (as will be described below) DBFs are not considered here (because they also come with certain drawbacks).

The aggregability of CBFs is the basis for their integration in WIMP. How CBFs are used to decrease WIMP-generated overhead is described in the following.

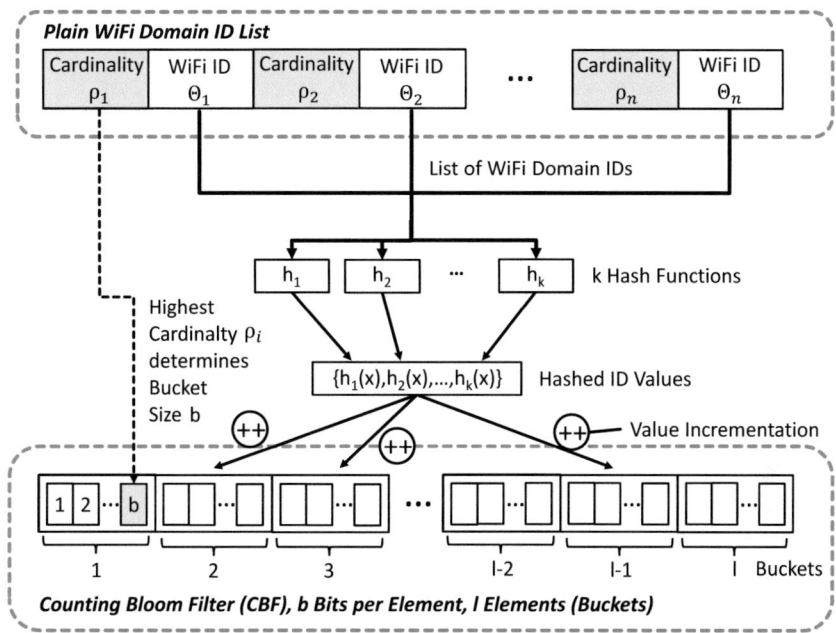

Figure 6.10 From Plain Lists to CBFs for encoding WiFi Visibilities in WIMP

6.1.5.2   Bloom Filter Integration in WIMP

To mitigate the overhead generated by WIMP the integration of Bloom Filters into WIMP is proposed in this section. The idea is to encode the WiFi IDs Θ to be distributed into a CBF, where the highest occurring cardinality ρ determines the bucket size b.

Figure 6.10 gives an overview on how WiFi domain IDs are represented in case of the plain list approach and in case of using a CBF. In the upper part the plain list is shown, where each ID Θ is part of the list and is connected to one cardinality value ρ per ID. With a CBF (shown in the lower part), the IDs are hashed and each hash value points to a specific CBF bucket whose cardinality gets incremented.

Compared to the plain list approach CBFs allow to encode the WiFi IDs in a bit field of bounded length $l \cdot b$, on the one hand. On the other hand, checking for containedness of a WiFi ID is always connected to a risk of false positives. In the CBF-enabled WIMP enhancement either aspect can be considered: If aiming for bounded false positive rates the mechanisms can choose the number of buckets l accordingly, in most cases still being considerably more space efficient than with the plain lists. In contrast, if WIMP overhead per peer should be bounded, l can be fixed. Then, the false positive rate σ will increase nearly linear, being the trade-off to limited communication overhead. The CBF integration in WIMP differentiates between up-tree and down-tree direction as described in the following.

Algorithm 5: WIMP Bloom Filter Extension Algorithm for Root Peers

---

1 $\Theta^d_{adjusted}$; /*Adjusted Set of WiFi IDs to be distributed*/
2 ρ_{max}; /*Highest occurring Cardinality in $\Theta_{adjusted}$*/
3 b /*Bucket Size*/
4 $Width_\Theta$; /*Space required per WiFi Domain ID Θ*/
5 UB_σ; /*Upper Bound for False Positive Rate*/
  /*Determine b:*/
6 $\lceil log_2(\rho_{max}) > 4 ? b = 4 : b = \lceil log_2(\rho_{max});$
  /*Calculate Space Requirement for Plain List:*/
7 $Space_{List} = \left|\Theta^d_{adjusted}\right| \cdot Width_\Theta + b \cdot \left|\Theta^d_{adjusted}\right|;$
  /*Calculate Space Requirement for Bloom Filter with
    UB_σ:*/
8 $Space_{CBF} = \dfrac{\left|\Theta^d_{adjusted}\right| \cdot log(\frac{1}{UB_\sigma})}{x} \cdot b;$
9 **if** $(Space_{CBF} < Space_{List})$ **then**
  | /*Bloom Filter Approach takes less Space*/
  |
10 | $l = \dfrac{\left|\Theta^d_{adjusted}\right| \cdot log(\frac{1}{UB_\sigma})}{x}; k = \dfrac{m \cdot log_{10}(2)}{\left|\Theta^d_{adjusted}\right|};$
11 | Send (CBF, l, k, b) down Tree;
12 **else**
  | /*Plain List Approach takes less Space*/
13 | Send Plain List down Tree;

Down-Tree Direction

On reception of all adjusted WiFi domain ID lists the tree's root peer can decide whether to use a CBF or just send an aggregated plain list down the tree. For this decision it calculates the number of buckets l, the bucket size b, and the number of hash functions k (in case the false positive rate σ should be bounded). If the overhead should be bounded l is given. The used algorithm for the case of bounded false positive rate[4] is shown in Algorithm 5. Based on the highest occurring cardinality ρ in the WiFi ID list the root peer determines the bucket size b as the needed number of bits to encode the cardinality. The resulting value is bounded by 4 here (line 6). Then, the root peer calculates

---
[4]The case for bounded l is omitted here but considered in the evaluations provided later.

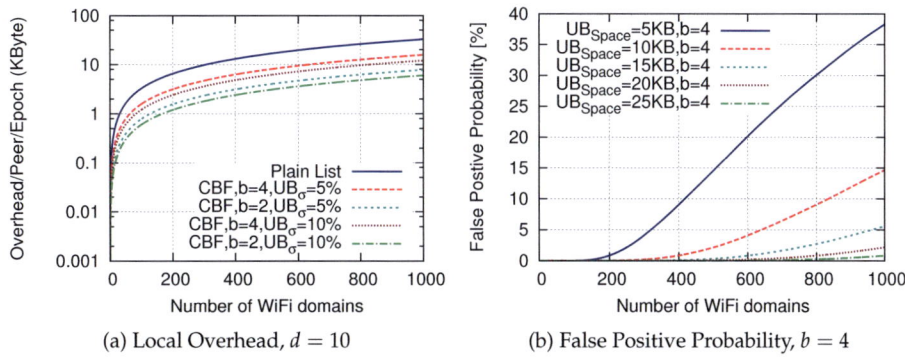

(a) Local Overhead, $d = 10$ (b) False Positive Probability, $b = 4$

Figure 6.11 Overhead and False Positive Probability with CBF-enabled WIMP

the space requirement of the aggregated plain list (line 7) and the resulting CBF (line 8). If the CBF's space requirement is lower it is used and sent down the tree (lines 9–11). Additionally, the root peer has to provide the values l, k, and b, which are required by all down-tree peers in order to eventually use CBFs as well and correctly interpret the received CBFs. If the plain list is more space-efficient it will be sent down instead of a CBF (line 13).

Up-Tree Direction

In up-tree direction every peer can decide autonomously whether a CBF is more space-efficient than sending up an aggregated plain list. In contrast to the root peer decision a peer lower in the tree cannot calculate its own value l. The reason is that in order to ensure all CBFs being sent up the tree can be summed up they have to have the same number of buckets l. Therefore, the root peer sends a unified l down-tree which will be used for decisions taken by any peer below the root. In contrast to l, the bucket size b can be decided autonomously as buckets with different sizes can still be summed up. Algorithm 6 shows the behavior of non-root peers with the CBF extension in WIMP. On reception of either a plain list or a CBF from above the peer simply forwards the data down-tree (line 4). If sending up-tree, a peer calculates an own bucket size value b (line 9) and compares the plain list space requirement against the CBF space requirement (lines 10–11). If the CBF is more space-efficient it is sent up the tree (line 14), while a plain list is sent up, else (line 16).

Algorithm 6: WIMP Bloom Filter Extension Algorithm for Non-Root Peers

---

1 $Width_\Theta$; /*Space required per WiFi ID*/
2 l, k; /*Values learned from Root Peer*/
3 **if** (*Sending Down-Tree*) **then**
4 | Send down what has been received from Parent, either Plain List or CBF;
5 **else**
6 | $\Theta^i_{noduplicates}$; /*Duplicate-free Set of WiFi IDs to be sent up*/
7 | ρ_{max}; /*Highest occurring Cardinality in $W_{noduplicates}$*/
8 | b /*Bucket Size*/
   | /*Determine b:*/
9 | $\lceil log_2(C) > 4 ? b = 4 : b = \lceil log_2(C);$
   | /*Decide what to send up the Tree*/
   | /*Calculate Space Requirement for Plain List:*/
10 | $Space_{List} = \left| \Theta^i_{noduplicates} \right| \cdot Width_\Theta + b \cdot \left| \Theta^i_{noduplicates} \right|;$
   | /*Calculate Space Requirement for Bloom Filter of length l:*/
11 | $Space_{CBF} = l \cdot b;$
12 | **if** ($Space_{CBF} < Space_{List}$) **then**
   | | /*Bloom Filter Approach takes less Space*/
13 | | Send Bloom Filter with Bucket Size b up Tree;
14 | **else**
   | | /*Plain List Approach takes less Space*/
15 | | Send Plain List up Tree;

6.1.5.3   Evaluation

To evaluate CBF integration in WIMP the generated overhead is compared to the plain list approach before also the real world scenario as described in Section 6.1.4.4 is reconsidered.

Analytical Comparison

Figure 6.11(a) shows the local worst case overhead generated by WIMP in a tree with height $d = 10$. In the figure the plain list approach is compared to different CBF cases. Two different false positive rate upper bound values UB_σ are provided (5 % and 10 %), and for both, two different bucket sizes ($b = 2$ and $b = 4$) are shown. As can be seen in the figure, with growing number of WiFi domains the CBF approach's overhead grows linear (just like in the plain list approach) but is always considerably smaller than the generated overhead with plain lists.

City	Plain List PL	CBF, bounded False Positive Probability σ			
		$UB_\sigma = 5\%$	Savings	$UB_\sigma = 10\%$	Savings
Smaller City ($500\,\text{IDs}/\text{km}^2$)	11.3	5.83	47%	4.48	59%
Manhattan 2006 ($1900\,\text{IDs}/\text{km}^2$)	43.0	22.17	47%	17.04	59%
Tokyo 2007 ($3000\,\text{IDs}/\text{km}^2$)	68.0	35.00	47%	26.90	59%
Paris 2007 ($4000\,\text{IDs}/\text{km}^2$)	90.6	46.67	47%	35.87	59%

Table 6.2 WIMP-generated Overhead in different metropolitan Areas [kbyte/epoch] with and without CBF Usage, bounded False Positive Probability

City	Plain List PL	CBF, bounded Overhead			
		$UB_{\text{Space}} = 10\,\text{KB}$	Savings	$UB_{\text{Space}} = 25\,\text{KB}$	Savings
Smaller City ($500\,\text{IDs}/\text{km}^2$)	11.3	$\sigma = 0.01\%$	12%	$\sigma = 3\,\text{E}^{-6}\%$	-112%
Manhattan 2006 ($1900\,\text{IDs}/\text{km}^2$)	43.0	$\sigma = 26\%$	77%	$\sigma = 0.03\%$	42%
Tokyo 2007 ($3000\,\text{IDs}/\text{km}^2$)	68.0	$\sigma = 42\%$	85%	$\sigma = 12\%$	63%
Paris 2007 ($4000\,\text{IDs}/\text{km}^2$)	90.6	$\sigma = 53\%$	89%	$\sigma = 20\%$	72%

Table 6.3 WIMP-generated Overhead in different metropolitan Areas [kbyte/epoch] with and without CBF Usage, bounded Overhead per Peer

As discussed, the CBF approach also allows to define a bounded overhead (UB_{Space}). This bound results in an increasing false positive probability σ. Figure 6.11(b) shows how the false positive probability develops with growing number of WiFi domains for different upper bound overhead values. Here, a bucket size $b = 4$ is assumed. Clearly to see, strictly limiting the overhead comes with considerable false positive probabilities which have to be traded off against the bandwidth savings. If a smaller bucket size b can be used due to lower cardinalities ρ the space requirement for the resulting CBF decreases, allowing for considerably lower false positive probability σ with fixed size. The concrete application scenario always has to be considered when deciding in which mode and with which parameters the CBF extension should be used.

Real World Scenario Comparison

In addition to analytical comparison CBF integration in WIMP is also analyzed in the real world scenario given in Section 6.1.4.4. Table 6.2 compares the local overhead in WIMP with CBF usage against the plain list approach. With bounded false positive probabilities of $UB_\sigma = 5\%$ and $UB_\sigma = 10\%$ overhead saving of $\approx 50\%$ and $\approx 60\%$ could be achieved in all considered city scenarios, respectively.

Table 6.3 evaluates the influence of bounding the WIMP-generated overhead per peer. Two different bounds, $UB_{Space} = 10\,KB$ and $UB_{Space} = 25\,KB$, are used. The static bounds lead to different false positive probabilities σ, depending on the number of WiFi domains in the environment. σ can reach high values in case a high number of WiFi domains is detectable and the bound is chosen to be low, like e. g. in case of "Paris" with a bound of $10\,KB$ in the table. Furthermore, choosing a high bound in scenarios with low density of WiFi domains can lead to overhead loss instead of saving since the CBF will take more space than it would in case of using plain ID lists. In Table 6.3 this case can be observed with the "Smaller City" example and the bound of $25\,KB$. Hence, the false positive probability σ always has to be traded off against the overhead savings when using the CBF extension in WIMP.

6.1.6   Conclusion

Integrating infrastructure-based WiFi networks in P2P-based protocols can help to increase communication efficiency, e. g. with respect to data offloading or broadcast usage. To fully exploit the potential of this approach a rendezvous mechanism is required that assures that peers connect to the same WiFi network if multiple of such are available. To support WiFi integration *Wireless Multi-Access Proximity Probing (WIMP)* as a solution to this rendezvous problem has been proposed.

WIMP can be applied to any P2P application that either maintains a tree-based overlay structure directly or allows embedding of such a structure into its overlay. The tree is used to aggregate and distribute information that helps to decide to which WiFi network a peer should connect to in order to maximize the probability for discovering other peers. To this end, it learns about the number of peers that are in range of the WiFi networks it can discover by scanning. After successful discovery such peers can directly peer in the respective WiFi domain in order to optimize the structure of the P2P overlay. WIMP can either supply accurate information or compress information while tolerating a certain probability of false positives using Counting Bloom Filters.

WIMP has been evaluated analytically in a defined tree scenario in this chapter. The tree has been assumed to be balanced and full (i. e. each non-leaf peer holds a defined number of children). The stochastic evaluations show that WIMP induces linear overhead with respect to the overall number of WiFi domains, the overall number of peers, and the WiFi detection probability. However, the local peer overhead has been evaluated to be about 8.5 kilobytes per protocol epoch even with high numbers of peers and WiFi domains if only open networks are considered in real metropolitan environments (cf. the case of Paris in Table 6.1). Applying Counting Bloom Filters can reduce the overhead by 59 % if a false positive rate of 10 % is tolerated (cf. Table 6.2). While the assumed trees in the evaluations were balanced and full, the findings regarding WIMP can be applied to tree-based P2P protocols in general to some extent: In unbalanced trees, for instance, the overall global overhead is unaffected by the structure of the tree. The local peer overhead, in contrast, highly depends on the tree structure and is affected by the position of a peer in the tree and its fanout, for instance. However, the local peer overhead will always result in an overhead value below the calculated worst case and the probabilistic value presented in the evaluations can be used to get an impression of WIMP's generated overhead.

As further aspects not discussed the use of Bloom Filters for WiFi ID encoding offers additional benefits, e. g. increased privacy due to the fact that WiFi IDs are not visible to anyone but to peers that already know them. Furthermore, Bloom Filter integration could be further optimized for saving even more bandwidth, e. g. by using *Compressed Bloom Filters* [30]. These aspects are subject to future research. While WIMP has been used with focus on WiFi integration in this chapter, the possibilities to enhance it are manifold: Integrating end-system GPS or similar approaches like PlaceEngine [171] may be used as additional proximity indicator (encoded in the IDs), offering potentially to save overhead or increase proximity estimation precision. Also, other wireless technologies could be considered and integrated, e. g. Bluetooth or WiFi Direct.

Finally, although a high fraction of deployed infrastructure-based WiFi domains in real metropolitan areas today is access restricted, there has been a trend towards open and unrestricted WiFi in the U.S., which is in some countries also pushed by several initiatives (e. g. FON [74] or Freifunk [77]). These trends are promising for WIMP to increase the peering opportunities and therefore the benefit of the approach. However, in the end the availability of spontaneous WiFi connectivity is the key driver for an approch like WIMP and highly depends on the environment, as mentioned in Section 6.1.1.

In the next sections of this chapter the ALM protocols described in Chapter 4 and Chapter 5 are enhanced by the integration of WiFi domains with the help of WIMP in order to increase communication efficiency.

6.2   WiFi Integration in Cluster-based Application-Layer Multicast

The cluster-based ALM approach NICE (cf. Chapter 4) intends to provide an Internet-wide group communication service. Peers are clustered considering a given distance metric which is network latency in the common case. It can be assumed that the growing ubiquity of WiFi access leads to NICE also being partly used in wireless networks, either home networks or public free WiFi, for instance. The NICE protocol traffic as well as the data to be disseminated will impact these networks concerning capacity usage and collisions. If NICE would be aware of the employed underlay connectivity it could exploit certain access technology properties, like e. g. the broadcast capabilities of WiFi networks. Furthermore, the access technology of a peer could directly influence its role in the hierarchy, e. g. by preventing wireless peers from becoming Cluster Leaders. This can help to increase the communication efficiency by lowering the traffic load and the risk of collisions in the shared medium.

In this part of the chapter NICE is enhanced by the integration of WIMP. To this end, the use of WIMP is assumed and the original protocol is enhanced by the dedicated consideration of WiFi reachability between peers. Therefore, the question how NICE can use the information provided by WIMP is answered. The goal is to organize WiFi-enabled peers in broadcast domains, lowering communication overhead and excluding them from the NICE hierarchy. The resulting enhanced protocol, referred to as *NICE-WLI* (NICE with Wireless Integration), is described in the following sections and is published in [99, 107, 198].

6.2.1   NICE-WLI Structure and Operation

In contrast to existing works that focus on ALM usage in pure WiFi ad-hoc environments (like e. g. Local Broadcast Clusters [20]) the approach described here aims at the integration of different access networks and communication domains in a single ALM protocol instance. This enhances the ALM protocol's applicability to heterogeneous networks, consisting of wired and wireless access networks. The case focused here is the efficient discovery and integration of WiFi-enabled peers in a NICE scenario where part of the peers are connected to the Internet through a fixed network access, while another part uses WiFi technology for Internet access.

NICE assumes end-to-end connectivity between peers and a network unicast service to built upon. In its basic form it does not consider different access technologies in any way. Thus, when using NICE peers in a WiFi domain, data and control messages will be sent via separate unicast transmissions among participants. For more than one peer residing in the same WiFi do-

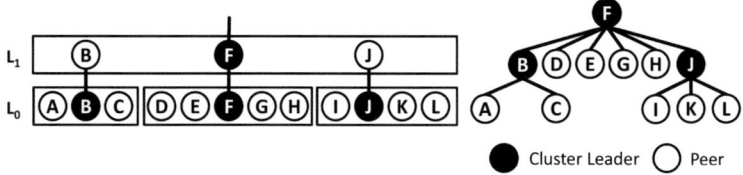

Figure 6.12 Mapping a NICE Overlay Structure to a Tree

main this results in higher medium occupancy, higher risk of collisions, and increased network latencies, at worst. If peers would consider WiFi domains and would use the broadcast[5] property of the medium collisions, traffic load, and dissemination delays could be lowered.

To enhance NICE by the consideration and use of WiFi communication three enhancements have to be included: (1) The protocol has to be aware of its access communication alternatives, (2) it has to be able to detect other peers with the same possibilities in order to take decisions which alternative to choose, and (3) it has to provide means for bridging between wired and wireless domains and employ the medium-specific functionality only where applicable.

For (1) a peer can detect its visible WiFi networks locally if it is equipped with a WiFi device. For (2) WIMP can be used: Figure 6.12 shows an example how a given NICE hierarchy structure is mappable to a tree that can serve as a WIMP control structure. On this structure WIMP can operate and provide all participating peers with knowledge about surrounding peer WiFi visibilities. How (3) is accomplished is the main question to be answered.

NICE-WLI enhances NICE by bridging between wired and wireless domains and using the WiFi broadcast capabilities where available. Peers being connected through WiFi access networks are no longer integrated in the cluster hierarchy but are rather loosely coupled to wired peers. Figure 6.13 shows an example of how NICE-WLI behaves in contrast to the unmodified protocol version: In Figure 6.13(a) a NICE structure is shown where part of the peers are connected through WiFi but are still part of the clustering. This example case would be the result of using wired and WiFi peers in access technology-agnostic NICE. Figure 6.13(b) shows a NICE-WLI structure, resulting from the same given set of peers. Here, all WiFi peers (except one) are excluded from the cluster hierarchy to form a so-called *WLI domain*. WLI domains are WiFi broadcast domains which are represented by a dedicated broadcast peer called *Gateway Peer*. These Gateway Peers are described in the following.

---

[5]Since single WiFi access networks are considered broadcasting results in the same behavior as using MAC layer multicast. Hence, broadcast is the only dissemination technique considered in the remainder of this chapter.

6.2.1.1   Gateway Peers

The bridging between wired and wireless network parts is accomplished by specific Gateway Peers in NICE-WLI. With their help NICE is enhanced by a loose coupling between both technologies. From a wired peer's perspective (being part of the cluster hierarchy) Gateway Peers are transparent representatives of WLI domains. Common NICE hierarchy members do not have any knowledge about the existence of WiFi-enabled peers taking part in NICE-WLI. Gateway Peers receive data messages from the wired overlay part and forward (broadcast) them to the WiFi peers in WLI domains. Thereby, each Gateway Peer represents exactly one such WLI domain. In contrast, if WLI domain peers wish to send data messages to the overlay structure they broadcast it inside the WLI domain they reside in. The respective Gateway Peer of this WLI domain forwards them to the wired overlay part, while the remaining WiFi peers in the WLI domain receive the data through the broadcast.

Although Gateway Peers act as cluster members in the NICE hierarchy structure they have special properties concerning their role: Recalling that Gateway Peers are always connected through WiFi, all data and protocol traffic sent or received by them will automatically traverse the respective wireless network domain. Hence, network traffic should be avoided in order not to impact the WiFi domain more than necessary. Therefore, in NICE-WLI Gateway Peers are not considered in Cluster Leader election in their L_0 cluster since leadership always comes with higher communication overhead. Likewise, Gateway Peers will neither be elected as Cluster Leaders in higher layers of the NICE structure. To ensure this Gateway Peers use enhanced *Cluster Join* and *Heartbeat* messages that contain a flag indicating their role as a Gateway Peer. Details on all enhanced NICE protocol messages can be found in Appendix A.

The cluster leadership avoidance is not always enforceable. If the fraction of WiFi-enabled peers in a NICE-WLI instance is comparably high it may occur that the Gateway Peer's L_0 cluster does not hold any wired peer to be chosen alternatively. Then, the Gateway Peer will automatically become Cluster Leader. The integration of NICE-WLI with both infrastructure-mode WiFi and ad-hoc WiFi is described in the following.

6.2.1.2   Infrastructure-Mode NICE-WLI

The first WiFi mode to be considered in NICE-WLI is infrastructure mode. Here, WiFi peers are attached to one single centralized access point per WiFi domain. In infrastructure-mode NICE-WLI the qualification of a peer to become Gateway Peer is determined by its *Signal-to-Noise-Ratio (SNR)*. This value indicates the quality of a peer's connection to the WiFi access point and is pro-

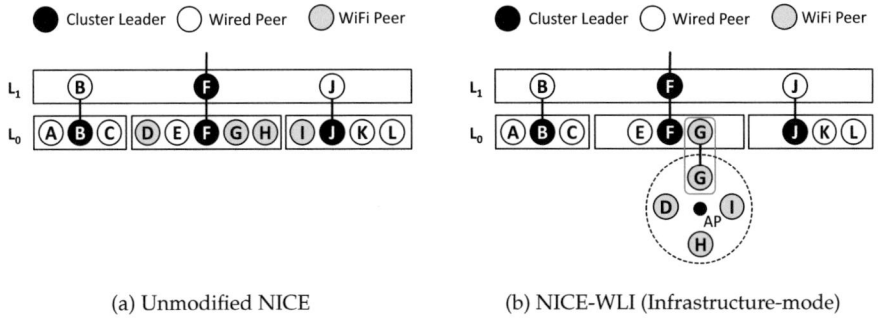

(a) Unmodified NICE   (b) NICE-WLI (Infrastructure-mode)

Figure 6.13 Example NICE and NICE-WLI Scenario with WiFi-enabled Peers

vided through operating system functions. As Gateway Peers have higher responsibility and higher data forwarding load than common (Non-Gateway) WLI peers, the WLI peer with highest SNR should be chosen as Gateway Peer to ensure minimal packet loss and best robustness achievable. In the following the relevant protocol aspects of NICE-WLI (and differences to common NICE) are covered for the infrastructure-mode case.

Joining Peers

WiFi-enabled peers wishing to join NICE-WLI can start by connecting to any WiFi network in range that provides Internet access in order to become part of the overlay. Then, they are integrated into the hierarchy structure and start receiving WIMP information. With it they can potentially refine their connectivity in order to choose the WiFi network in range with the most overlay peers already residing in. On joining a WiFi network a peer first has to check for the existence of a Gateway Peer in this specific WLI domain. This is accomplished by broadcasting a dedicated *WLI Gateway Discovery* message in the WLI domain. This message contains the address and the current SNR of the joining peer.

If a Gateway Peer receives such a message it compares its own SNR to the value contained in the message. If the Gateway's SNR is higher than the joining peer's the Gateway answers with a dedicated *WLI Welcome* message, indicating its role to the joining WiFi peer. On reception of the WLI Welcome message the joining peer is loosely attached to the Gateway, not joining the cluster hierarchy. In case the SNR of the joining peer is higher than the Gateway's the joining peer is considered the better Gateway Peer. The current Gateway in this case sends a *Gateway Transfer* message to the joining peer, containing the address of the Cluster Leader of the L_0 cluster the Gateway currently resides in. Afterwards, the current Gateway leaves the cluster by sending a *Remove* message to the Cluster Leader, accordingly. Finally, the joining peer becomes

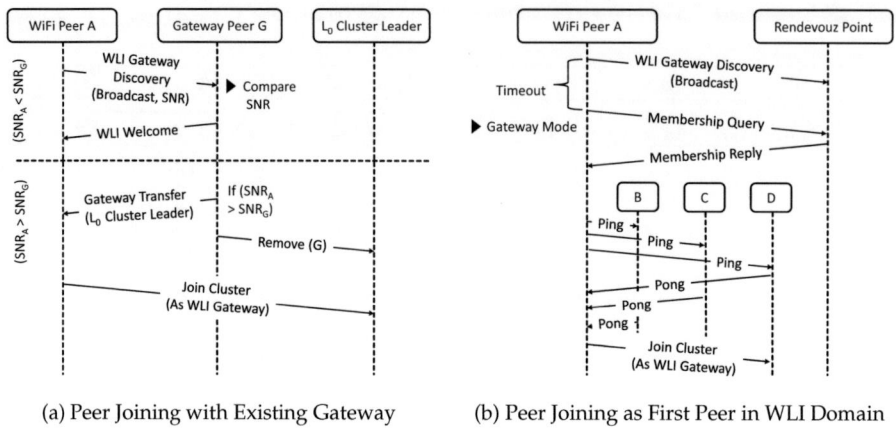

(a) Peer Joining with Existing Gateway   (b) Peer Joining as First Peer in WLI Domain

Figure 6.14 WiFi Peer Joining in NICE-WLI

new Gateway Peer and joins the same L_0 cluster by sending a *Join Cluster* message to the Cluster Leader it has learned from the Gateway Transfer message. The communication in peer joining for both described cases is shown in Figure 6.14(a).

If no Gateway Peer exists in a WLI domain a peer is joining the latter does not receive any WLI Welcome message. After a timeout the peer assumes to be Gateway itself and starts a regular joining process to the cluster hierarchy structure. Therefore, it polls the respective information from the Rendezvous Point and starts stepping down the cluster hierarchy until the nearest L_0 cluster is determined. Finally, it joins this cluster, indicating its role as a Gateway Peer. This behavior is also shown in Figure 6.14(b).

WLI Heartbeat Messages

Similar to NICE, WLI domain peers in NICE-WLI exchange periodic *Heartbeat* messages. Unlike NICE, these messages do not hold information about all peers in the WLI domain. This information is not necessary because data is always broadcasted via the access point. Thus, Heartbeat messages in a WLI domain are only used to indicate a peer's liveliness and to hold a peer's current SNR, used for Gateway election. One further benefit is that this way the size of Heartbeat messages can be reduced, being preferable in wireless domains to reduce risk of collisions and decrease the time of medium occupancy.

Gateway Election

Gateway election is one of the crucial parts in NICE-WLI due to the Gateways' responsibility. Gateway Peers forward data from and to the WLI domains they represent. As described above, SNR values serve as the metric for determining the Gateway role in a WLI domain. All WLI domain peers' Heartbeat messages hold their current SNR values, being collected by the Gateway Peer. The latter periodically compares its own SNR to the other WLI peer's values. If a peer with a higher SNR is detected the Gateway initiates a Gateway Transfer to that peer, similar to the case in the join process described above.

Due to protocol concurrences, inconsistent states concerning Gateway roles are always possible in NICE-WLI. If two Gateways concurrently exist in the same WLI domain (what may happen as a result of packet loss, for instance) this is detected through Heartbeat messages: A Gateway receiving such a message from another Gateway in the same WLI domain detects the inconsistency and compares the contained SNR value with its own SNR. The result of this comparison determines which one stays Gateway Peer. The decision is indicated to the other peer which changes its own role in the WLI domain, accordingly.

During the period between two Heartbeat messages two Gateway Peers may still exist concurrently for a short time. Since both assume responsibility to forward messages to the cluster hierarchy forwarding loops may occur since the other Gateway will again forward the messages to the WLI domain. Loops will persist until the Gateway inconsistency is resolved, potentially resulting in high forwarding stress. To avoid this all data messages being forwarded from a Gateway to a WLI domain are specifically marked. If a Gateway receives such a marked message, it does not forward it back to the cluster hierarchy. Also, the reception of such a marked message indicates the existence of another Gateway Peer. Mechanisms to resolve this can then be triggered directly without having to wait for the next Heartbeat message.

Data Dissemination

In infrastructure-mode NICE-WLI data to be disseminated inside WLI domains is always sent via broadcast. Common non-Gateway peers do not have to forward any data on reception. If a Gateway Peer receives data messages from inside its WLI domain it forwards it to its L_0 cluster following the cluster hierarchy forwarding scheme of NICE. Since broadcasting is accomplished by the access point all peers can be assumed to be in range and hence be reachable. Only the risk of collisions is a possible drawback since no acknowledgment mechanisms are used in medium access in case of broadcasting.

Leaving Peers

In case a non-Gateway WLI domain peer leaves NICE-WLI gracefully (i.e. regularly and on purpose) no dedicated protocol mechanisms have to be triggered. Due to the loose coupling of these peers and the respective Gateway Peer their leaving is inherently recognized by receiving no more Heartbeat messages from that specific peer. If the leaving peer is a WLI domain's Gateway Peer it has to signal its leave to both the cluster hierarchy as well as the WLI domain. From the L_0 cluster in the hierarchy it has to leave by sending a Remove message to the Cluster Leader. Inside the WLI domain it has to determine a new Gateway Peer that will take its role. Doing so, it compares the collected SNR values and chooses the peer with highest SNR to the access point. If no remaining peers are available inside the WLI domain no further actions are taken.

Should a peer leave ungracefully (due to e.g. software crashes or a canceled WiFi connection) no protocol actions are needed in case the peer is a common non-Gateway WLI peer. If a Gateway Peer leaves ungracefully the cluster hierarchy as well as the peers inside the WLI domain have to react. In both parts the leaving of the Gateway Peer is detected due to the missing periodic Heartbeat messages. In the cluster hierarchy the peers inside the L_0 cluster simply delete the missing peer from their neighborship information. The peers inside the WLI domain, in contrast, compare their collected SNR values (they also got from the Heartbeat messages). The peer with highest SNR then autonomously takes the role as Gateway Peer in this WLI domain. In case more than one peer decides to become Gateway (due to inconsistent SNR information) this is detected and resolved as described in the "Gateway Election" section.

6.2.1.3   Ad-hoc NICE-WLI

Besides the described infrastructure-mode NICE-WLI also ad-hoc WiFi communication is considered in WiFi integration. Here, part of the peers is able to access the Internet and communicate via WiFi ad-hoc concurrently, while other peers are only able to communicate via ad-hoc WiFi. The difference to the described infrastructure-based approach lies in the absence of a dedicated access point to which all WLI domain peers are attached. Thus, the central broadcast capabilities of these access points are not available. Furthermore, a single Gateway Peer cannot be elected based on its SNR value to the specific access point, of course. Finally, a routing scheme to be used in the ad-hoc domain has to be employed because ad-hoc networks may potentially cover a multi-hop area that requires routing strategies to disseminate the data. In ad-hoc NICE-WLI a WLI domain is defined as an ad-hoc WiFi network, comprising all peers communicating wirelessly in that domain. This WLI domain

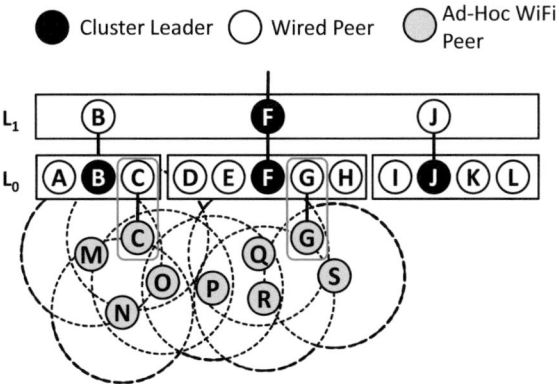

Figure 6.15 Exemplary NICE-WLI Structure with integrated Ad-hoc WiFi Domain

is coupled with the wired hierarchy by the use of existing Internet-capable peers, if existent.

Figure 6.15 shows an exemplary NICE-WLI structure with integrated ad-hoc WiFi domains. Peers C and G are capable of accessing the Internet (and therefore the cluster hierarchy) and take the role as Gateway Peers.

Gateway Election

To accomplish bridging between wired and wireless communication domains part of the participating peers are assumed to be connected through wired connectivity (e.g. LAN in home environments) and have ad-hoc WiFi capabilities as well which can be used at the same time. All such peers that are being attached to a given ad-hoc *SSID* and have Internet connectivity through their wired device automatically take the role of Gateway Peers in NICE-WLI ad-hoc mode. Therefore, in this mode there is no single Gateway determined, rather more than one such Gateway can exist concurrently. In ad-hoc mode a WLI domain spans the whole ad-hoc network, including all WiFi peers with mutual ad-hoc (also multi-hop) reachability.

WLI Heartbeat Messages

In ad-hoc NICE-WLI Heartbeat messages in WLI domains are only emitted by Gateway Peers. Since no SNR-based Gateway election is used, common NICE-WLI peers in the ad-hoc WiFi domains do not have to broadcast their SNR values to the remaining peers. In ad-hoc mode such peers only work as data senders, receivers, and forwarders.

In contrast, Gateway Peers periodically send Heartbeat messages to the ad-hoc WLI domain. These messages are used to publish the Gateway's existence in the domain. Furthermore, these Heartbeat messages hold a special hop count value, indicating how many ad-hoc forwarding steps (hops) have been accomplished before the message reached a specific peer. Every peer in the ad-hoc WLI domain forwarding a Heartbeat messages increments this value and stores the Gateway Peer's address with the lowest hop distance learned.

Joining Peers

A peer joining an ad-hoc WLI domain broadcasts a WLI Gateway Discovery message to its ad-hoc neighbor peers, similar to infrastructure-mode NICE-WLI. This message is forwarded by the neighbor peers until one or more Gateway Peers are reached. The Gateway Peers each answer with a WLI Welcome message, respectively. In contrast to infrastructure-mode NICE-WLI, this message additionally holds a hop count value, just like Heartbeat messages. The hop count values are incremented as the WLI Welcome messages traverse the ad-hoc WLI domain back to the joining peer. They will be used to determine the nearest Gateway in the WLI domain (regarding ad-hoc hops) in data dissemination, assuming symmetric link properties in the wireless medium.

Data Dissemination

Data messages being sent inside ad-hoc NICE-WLI domains are enhanced by a field containing the used Gateway Peer address. In case a Gateway forwarded the data from the cluster hierarchy to the WLI domain it puts its address to the data message. In case a common non-Gateway ad-hoc peer sends data it puts the address of the nearest Gateway Peer (from its own point of view) to the data message. The nearest Gateway Peer can be determined from the learned hop count values acquired through WLI Welcome and Heartbeat messages. Enhancing the data messages with the respective Gateway Peers helps to avoid multiple forwarding through different Gateways: If a Gateway Peer receives a data message being sent from another Gateway Peer (resolved though the Gateway address contained in the message) it does not resend the message back to the cluster hierarchy. Common non-Gateway peers inside the WLI domain only forward data in the ad-hoc domain if the source address matches their nearest Gateway Peer address. In case data messages should reach the WLI domain over multiple different Gateway Peers (due to possible inconsistencies) this reduces forwarding redundancy and overhead.

Since ad-hoc WLI Domains can be spatially distributed (requiring multi-hop data forwarding) further routing mechanisms have to be applied to reach all peers inside the domain. NICE-WLI does not restrict the mechanisms employed for this purpose, in general any ad-hoc routing protocol could be applied for the use in NICE-WLI. The simplest approach to disseminate

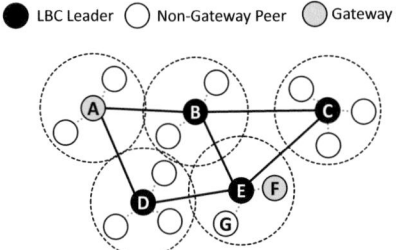

Non-Gateway Peer	Hop Count Gateway A	Hop Count Gateway F	Target Gateway
B	1	2	A
C	2	2	A
D	1	2	A
E	2	1	F
G	3	2	F

(a) Ad-hoc WLI Domain with Local Broadcast Clusters

(b) Nearest Gateway Peers based on Hop Counts

Figure 6.16 Exemplary Ad-hoc Integration and Routing in NICE-WLI

data in the WLI domains is flooding through broadcasting. More sophisticated approaches for multicasting data in ad-hoc environments exist, like e. g.
xScribe [168] or PAST-DM [83]. The ad-hoc routing strategy exemplarily used
here is called *Local Broadcast Clusters (LBCs)*. LBCs have been proposed by
Baumung et al. [21, 22] and aim at efficiently disseminating data in ad-hoc
networks. With LBCs dedicated peers are elected as *LBC Leaders* being interconnected through an overlay mesh but disseminating data to peers in proximity through broadcast. Using this approach considerably reduces medium
occupancy, especially compared to flooding strategies or unicast transmissions.

Figure 6.16(a) shows an example ad-hoc NICE-WLI domain, using the concept of LBCs to disseminate data in an ad-hoc WLI domain. Peers *A* and *F*
are able to reach the cluster hierarchy through wired connections and thus
become Gateway Peers. Peer *A* has been elected as LBC Leader, additionally.
Figure 6.16(b) shows the respective hop count values for a set of the peers in
the example together with the resulting nearest Gateway Peer election.

Data message forwarding in the example ad-hoc WLI domain is shown in Figure 6.17. Here, two cases are covered: First, peer *D* (being LBC Leader) sends
data to its LBC and the other LBC Leaders in order to disseminate it inside
the WLI domain. As soon as the data messages reach the Gateway Peers (*A*
and *F*) the peers check the contained information in order to determine which
of them is intended to forward the messages to the cluster hierarchy part. In
the given case this is peer *A* (being the Gateway with the smallest hop count
value from the sender peer). Gateway Peer *F* receives the data message via
broadcast inside its LBC since it is a common LBC member itself but does not
forward it to the cluster hierarchy.

In the second case the common LBC member peer G is the source of the data message. It sends the message to its LBC Leader which then rebroadcasts the message inside the LBC and also forwards it to the other LBC Leaders. This time, Gateway Peer F takes the task of forwarding the data to the cluster hierarchy since it resides in the same LBC cluster and has the lowest hop count distance from G.

Leaving Peers

Just like infrastructure-mode NICE-WLI non-Gateway peers in ad-hoc WLI domains may leave gracefully or even fail without taking further actions as they do not have any protocol responsibilities. If Gateway Peers in ad-hoc WLI domains leave they have to indicate this to the cluster hierarchy (by properly leaving the L_0 cluster). In the ad-hoc WLI domain no special actions have to be taken since the leaving of peers is detected through missing *Heartbeat* messages. It has to be mentioned that as soon as the last Gateway Peer in an ad-hoc WLI domain leaves communication between the cluster hierarchy and the remaining ad-hoc WiFi peers breaks and both parts are partitioned. This issue can only the resolved by a new Gateway Peer joining the ad-hoc WLI domain, taking the role as bridge peer between both parts.

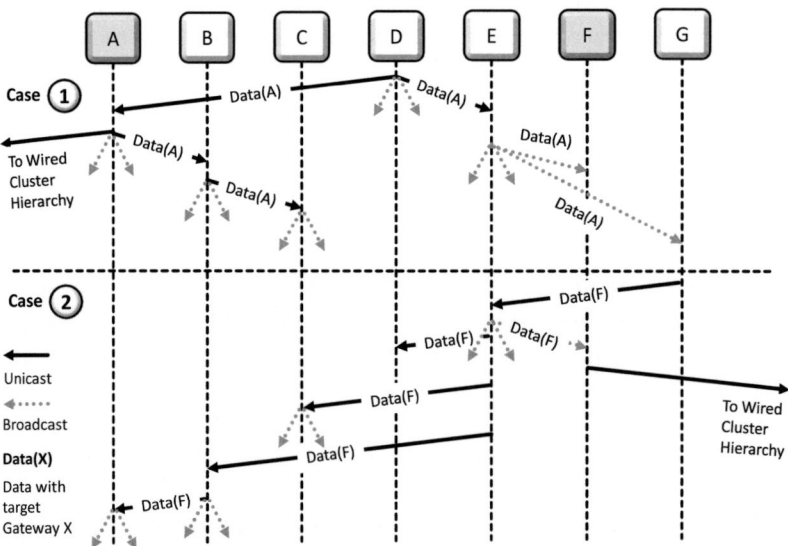

Figure 6.17 Exemplary Data Forwarding in the Ad-hoc NICE-WLI Domain

6.2.1.4   The Influence on the Cluster Hierarchy

In an unmodified NICE version (just like in environments where no WiFi enabled peers participate) the Cluster Leader of the highest cluster peers with a total of

$$\mathcal{O}(k \cdot log(n)) \tag{6.11}$$

neighbors, n being the number of participating peers and k being the cluster parameter ($k \leq$ cluster size $\leq \vartheta k - 1$). This is the worst case assumption concerning protocol overhead as well as data forwarding overhead since the set of peers to exchange messages with is the same in both cases. The height of the hierarchy (i.e. the number of layers) is $k \cdot log(n)$ and the number of application-layer overlay hops a message traverses between any pair of peers in NICE is

$$\mathcal{O}(log(n)). \tag{6.12}$$

Given the asymptotic assumption of a growing fraction of peers being connected via WiFi. Let m be the number of WiFi-enabled participating peers, $0 \leq m \leq n$. If each of these peers is connected via an own WiFi domain no benefit arises since all m peers remain in the cluster hierarchy. Assuming all m WiFi peers reside in the same WiFi domain, then $m - 1$ peers are extracted from the cluster hierarchy by the NICE-WLI approach (one stays in the hierarchy as Gateway Peer). Let w be the number of different WiFi domains the m peers reside in, $0 \leq w \leq m$. Then, the cluster hierarchy height decreases to $k \cdot log(n - (m - w))$, while the number of application-layer overlay hops becomes

$$\mathcal{O}(log(n - (m - w)) + 1) \longrightarrow \mathcal{O}(log(n - (m - w))). \tag{6.13}$$

Accordingly, the worst case protocol overhead decreases to

$$\mathcal{O}(k \cdot log(n - (m - w)) + 1) \longrightarrow \mathcal{O}(k \cdot log(n - (m - w))). \tag{6.14}$$

6.3   WiFi Integration in Dense Urban Tree-based Video Streaming

In Chapter 5 an approach has been described to avoid overloaded 3G access networks by considering the load situation in the access network cells and adapt the dissemination tree, accordingly. It has been shown that the additional traffic load induced by the P2P protocol can be balanced if the network

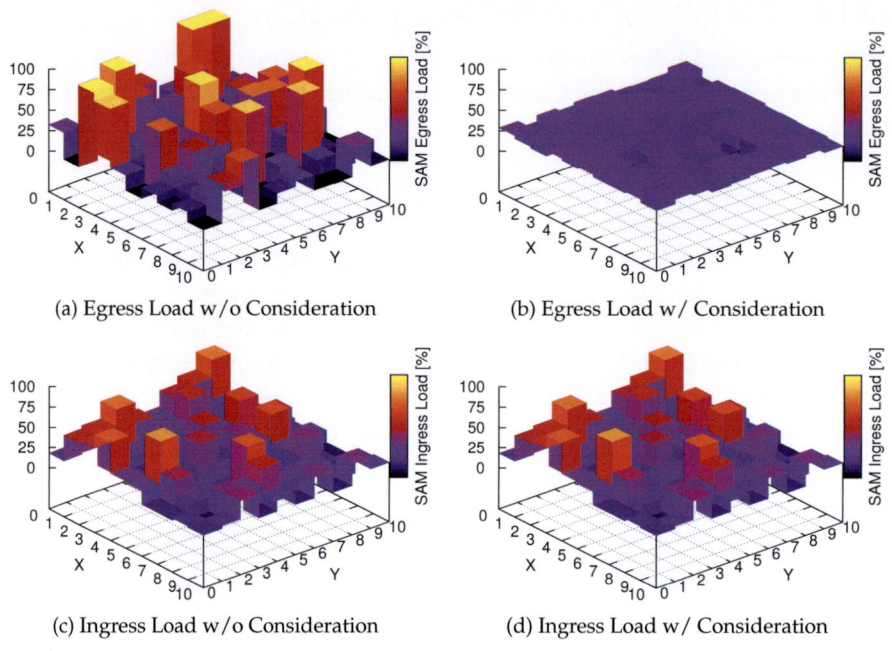

(a) Egress Load w/o Consideration (b) Egress Load w/ Consideration

(c) Ingress Load w/o Consideration (d) Ingress Load w/ Consideration

Figure 6.18 Incoming and outgoing Load Disparities in 3G-only ALM Scenario

capacities allow for it. Unfortunately, incoming data traffic can not be optimized due to the fact that every peer in the tree has exactly one incoming edge. This issue is briefly recalled in Figure 6.18 where Figure 6.18(a) and Figure 6.18(b) compare the egress traffic load in the 3G cells with and without explicit load consideration. Figure 6.18(c) and Figure 6.18(d), in contrast, show the ingress traffic load for both cases, visualizing that no change or optimization can be reached there.

In order to shift traffic load from 3G networks to alternative network domains (in addition to 3G tree adaptation) WIMP can be used to look up peering possibilities in existing public WiFi networks. As has been discussed in the beginning of this chapter, cities and dense metropolitan areas typically offer great potential for such an offloading strategy. The idea is to use the information provided by WIMP to adapt the video stream dissemination tree and distribute part of the video stream in available WiFi networks. How this is accomplished is described in the following.

6.3.1   Offloading Data Traffic from 3G Networks

To reduce traffic load in 3G networks in the single-source near-live video streaming scenario P2P links have to be eliminated from the involved 3G cells. Figure 6.19 shows a schematic view covering two cases: In Figure 6.19(a) the dissemination tree is built via 3G exclusively, although in the lower part of the figure the deployment of two public WiFi domains is shown, indicating the candidate peers for direct WiFi communication. Figure 6.19(b) shows how—with help of these WiFi domains—P2P links can be shifted from 3G to WiFi. Here, one peer per WiFi network remains in the 3G tree as a forwarder, while the others start receiving the video stream from it via WiFi.

Benefit Estimation

To estimate the benefit of WiFi integration in ALM video streaming simulations have been conducted in the MiXiM simulator. In contrast to the CMA-related simulations in Chapter 5 the simulator has been enhanced by infrastructure-based WiFi network domains. This enhancement allows to deploy WiFi network domains to the simulated field. Figure 6.20 shows an example for the observed scenario in this section: The field is partitioned into a set of 3G access network cells where additionally a set of WiFi domains is deployed at random. Then, the participating peers are deployed to the field, establishing the video stream dissemination tree.

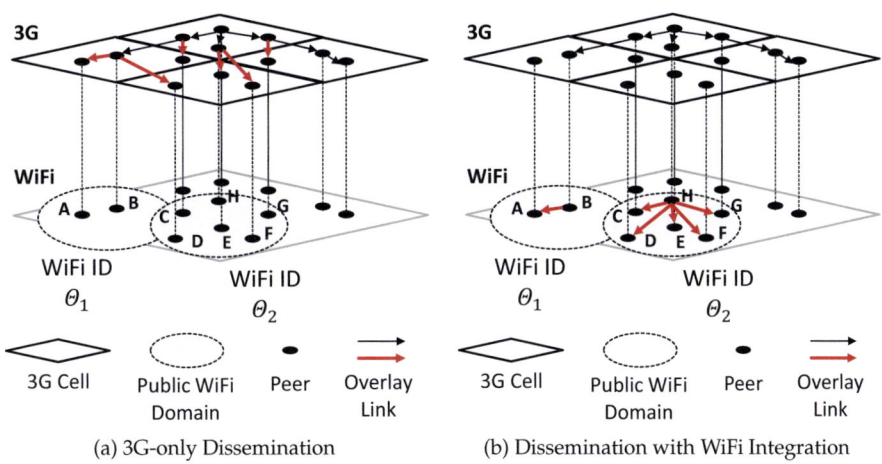

(a) 3G-only Dissemination   (b) Dissemination with WiFi Integration

Figure 6.19   Example Scenario for ALM Video Streaming with WiFi Integration

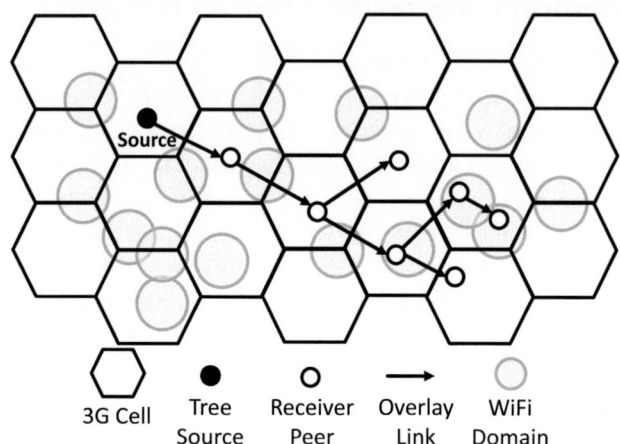

Figure 6.20 Simulation Scenario for WIMP Integration in CMA

Table 6.4 Simulation Parameters

Parameter	Value
Number of Peers n	$\{20,40,...,140\}$
Number of WiFi Domains w	$\{0,20,40,...,100\}$
Number of 3G Cells s	9
Field Size	$[1200\,\text{m} \times 1200\,\text{m}]$
Simulation Time	$1800\,\text{s}$
Node Adding Period	$\frac{n}{2}\,\text{s}$
Seeds per Config	10
3G Cell Range	$250\,\text{m}$
WiFi Domain Range r_{WiFi}	$100\,\text{m}$
3G Cell Capacity $cap^{(egress)},cap^{(ingress)}$	$\mathcal{U}(10,30)$ streams
Peer Capacity $cap^{(egress)}$	$\mathcal{U}(2,6)$ streams

Table 6.4 gives an overview on the used MiXiM parameterization. Different numbers of peers have been observed in scenarios with different numbers of WiFi domains. 10 runs have been evaluated per configuration.

To support decision-making about how and which WiFi domains to use for data traffic offloading WIMP is integrated and used in the CMA video streaming protocol. As has been stated earlier, WIMP is a promising approach especially in environments where a high number of peers is able to detect and integrate a high number of WiFi domains. To estimate the benefit of WIMP integration in the scenario, Figure 6.21 shows two simulation studies considering

WiFi visibilities and WiFi peer reachabilities, respectively. In Figure 6.21(a), 100 peers participate in the tree and different numbers of WiFis are deployed. For each peer the average number of concurrently detectable WiFi networks is shown, together with maximum and minimum values. The number of WiFis reachable by a peer linearly increases proportionally to the number of WiFi domains deployed. This growing set of choices also comes with the burden of choosing the right one. In case of 100 WiFi domains being deployed to the field a peer is in range of approximately 4 WiFi domains at average and above 8 at maximum, assuming uniform placement of WiFi domains in the field, for instance. These values indicate the need for a rendezvous mechanism like WIMP.

Besides WiFi visibilities the expected number of peers able to connect to the same WiFi network is of specific interest as a measure for data offloading potential. Similar to Fig. 6.21(a), Fig. 6.21(b) also shows WiFi reachabilities. In contrast to Fig. 6.21(a), the number of peers is shown here that a peer in a WiFi domain is able to reach directly and wirelessly. For each peer in the field that has already been elected to stay as the 3G forwarder for WiFi peers in range the figure indicates the number of other peers that are reached in the same WiFi domain. The number of WiFi domains has minor influence on these values, hence, a fixed number of 100 WiFi domains is shown. Again, minimum, average, and maximum values are provided.

Finally, the effects of WiFi network integration in the dissemination tree have been studied in simulation. To this end, WIMP has been used to detect WiFi networks with highest peer reachabilities in order to decide to which WiFi network to connect to. Since one peer has to stay in the 3G-based tree as a forwarding peer the peer with the highest network address has been chosen for

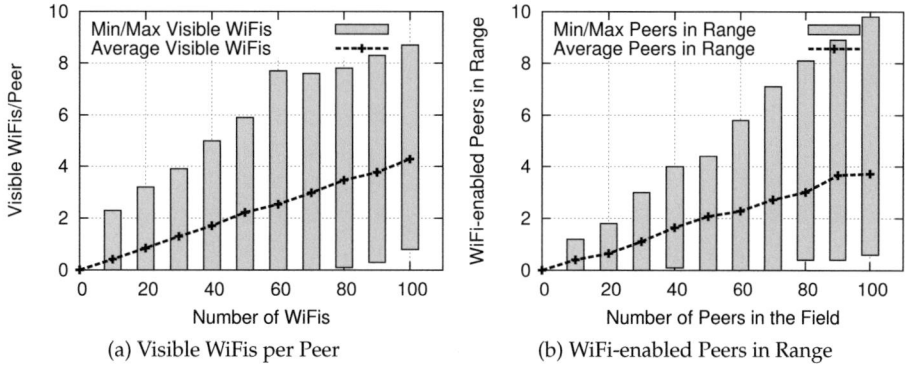

(a) Visible WiFis per Peer (b) WiFi-enabled Peers in Range

Figure 6.21 Effects of Hybrid ALM Dissemination & WiFi Visibilities

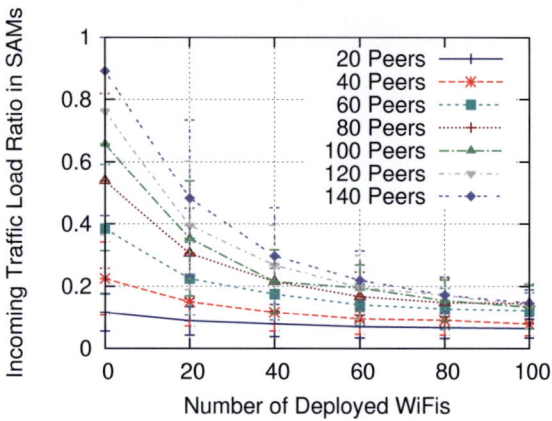

Figure 6.22 3G Traffic Load Alleviation using WiFi

each WiFi domain. After refining the tree with WiFi offloading consideration the average incoming traffic load in the 3G cell has been observed. Fig. 6.22 shows how this incoming traffic load develops in a scenario with different numbers of peers and different numbers of WiFi networks.

As expected, deploying WiFi domains to the field directly results in decreased incoming traffic load in the 3G cells since peers residing in the same WiFi coverage area are able to switch the forwarding technology. The effect of traffic load alleviation is the higher the more peers are involved in the dissemination process, visible especially in case of a comparably small number of WiFi domains. With growing number of such domains the traffic load converges to a comparably low value. Easy to see, increasing the number of peers in the field increases the probability of two peers residing in the same WiFi coverage area. If at least two peers can use the same WiFi domain all but one can leave the 3G overlay dissemination tree, leading to the shown alleviation behavior.

6.4   Conclusion

In this chapter the idea of integrating WiFi networks in ALM protocols has been observed with respect to the two concrete approaches discussed in Chapter 4 and Chapter 5. To this end, a rendezvous mechanism called WIMP for looking up promising WiFi network domains in tree-based P2P overlays has been proposed and studied. It can be used to support P2P overlay peers in the decision which WiFi network in range to connect to in order to peer with other overlay members inside the WiFi domain.

Furthermore, the NICE protocol has been enhanced to support WiFi broadcast communication in order to decrease protocol and data traffic inside WiFi networks. The enhanced protocol is called NICE-WLI and WIMP can be used to support the WiFi peering (i. e., finding other peers in WiFi networks). Additionally, WiFi integration in the P2P-based near-live video streaming protocol CMA, as discussed in Chapter 5, has been exemplarily described. The studies showed the benefit of such a strategy for offloading data from possibly congested 3G access network domains.

The applicability of the proposed mechanisms highly depends on the involved network systems, their configurations, policies, and constraints. This chapter intends to show the benefits of integrating existing infrastructure in the ALM dissemination process for different cases, assuming that e. g. public WiFis allow for direct peering inside one domain or most WiFi networks allow broadcast communication. For using the approaches in real networks one must be aware of the fact that in some router configuration these options may be prohibited. To bypass these limitations, in future work the additional integration of infrastructure-less pure ad-hoc mode can be considered in order to be independent of restrictions. Also, the upcoming *WiFi Direct* [32] Standard is promising to overcome the drawbacks of ad-hoc WiFi and may boost the ideas presented here. Further aspects to be integrated are exploiting potential partial Internet connectivity in public WiFis, like in case a subset of the peers belongs to paying customers. Also, WiFis should not be considered the better choice in all situations since they may also be prone to traffic load congestion. In such situations peers should stick to their existing 3G communication, implementable through enhanced load considerations in the ALM tree building strategy.

7. Summary and Perspectives

Peer-to-Peer (P2P) protocols enable the easy deployment of new communication services in the Internet through overlay technologies. All protocol functionality is accomplished in the end-systems, neither requiring any changes nor dedicated centralized systems in the network. A prominent P2P service class is Internet-wide group communication, implemented via Application-Layer Multicast (ALM) protocols. A large number of Internet applications communicates in groups but a global network support still lacks deployment. ALM protocols can be used to bypass this missing native network support.

Regarding communication efficiency and performance—from a user's point of view as well as from the network's point of view—ALM protocols inherently generate a higher amount of network traffic and provide degraded performance compared to native network solutions. This drawback makes careful and application-case-specific configuration and protocol design essential. Furthermore, mobile access networks already reach their data capacity limits due to heavy usage of content streaming with mobile end-systems. Therefore, it is questionable if ALM protocols worsen the problem or can be used for mitigating the traffic load in mobile access networks.

In this thesis ALM protocols have been presented and analyzed that focus on being used in today's Internet. They consider network heterogeneity and are designed flexibly in order to cope with constant technology changes. While existing ALM protocols mostly assume homogeneous networks and limited applicability to dedicated application scenarios, the protocols developed in this work rather target higher flexibility, configurability, and adaptability to different group communication scenarios.

7.1   Contributions of this Thesis

To get insights into ALM protocol behavior in large and dynamic network environments the cluster-based ALM protocol NICE has been analyzed. While comparable analysis in related work targets the protocol's impact with focus on the network, the evaluations in this thesis have been accomplished with focus on the protocol's peer-perceived performance. Furthermore, related work analyzed medium-sized scenarios with bulky peer fluctuation, while the evaluations provided in this thesis used high numbers of peers and aggressive—but more realistic—peer fluctuation. The evaluations showed that NICE scales well with high numbers of peers. Data dissemination delays in the overlay grow sub-linearly with growing numbers of peers and the per-peer overhead is low. NICE is able to cope even with high peer fluctuations, given the protocol refinement procedures are configured accordingly. Finally, a flexibility extension to NICE has been presented that allows to adapt the cluster size parameter k in order to trade off protocol overhead against data dissemination delays in the overlay structure autonomously at runtime. This extension enables NICE to adapt to changing network conditions, avoiding that predetermined protocol configurations may turn inefficient over runtime.

Furthermore, with CMA a protocol has been designed and presented that targets consideration of access network traffic load in wireless access networks in the context of near-live video streaming. CMA implements a tree-based single-source ALM protocol. It uses a heuristic for tree parent determination based on a weighted sum. As a basis for CMA Capacity Matching has been introduced as a new P2P strategy (in contrast to the common Topology Matching approach). Capacity Matching uses the traffic load state in the involved access networks to refine the dissemination tree while preserving remaining important protocol metrics. The evaluations of CMA showed that the protocol is able to avoid traffic load congestion in cellular access networks, given that remaining capacities are available in alternative cells which can be used for traffic offloading. While offloading data traffic load to alternative cells increases data dissemination delays in the overlay tree, the increase is below 10 % if CMA is configured accordingly and if an underlay network delay model similar to today's 3G networks is assumed.

Although data traffic load can be balanced among access network cells with CMA, the P2P forwarding still induces additional forwarding load to the network. To multiplex data traffic between different access network technologies further mechanisms have to be applied. With WIMP such a mechanism has been developed. It provides reachability information for wireless IEEE 802.11 networks to peers in tree-based ALM overlays. With WIMP peers in the tree can find out about mutual wireless connection possibilities, distributedly. This information can be used to optimize the tree-based data dissemination by consideration of the wireless network domains. WIMP has been applied as an extension to NICE, assigning different roles to peers in order to avoid high protocol maintenance traffic in WiFi networks. Furthermore, the broadcast capabilities of IEEE 802.11 networks have been used to decrease medium occupancy in the wireless networks. WIMP integration in CMA has also been presented. Here, the focus has been put to the integration of dense urban environments' public WiFi networks in the overlay structure. Finding and integrating freely available WiFi networks can help to multiplex data traffic load from cellular access networks in order to avoid congestion.

To provide a basis for the flexible development and deployment of overlay-based services a framework has been presented that has been developed in collaboration with colleagues. The SpoVNet architecture offers an easy-to-use development platform that hides underlay-related network challenges from the overlay developers. Examples for such challenges are user mobility, protocol heterogeneity, middleboxes, and link outages. In the SpoVNet framework's service layer the ALM protocols presented in the thesis can easily be implemented, benefiting from the provided underlay abstraction. Furthermore, it is also possible to develop applications that do not use any higher communication services in SpoVNet or even to use unmodified (legacy) applications with help of the dedicated Legacy Interface.

The protocols presented in this work are a step towards ALM approaches being able to cope with technical developments and changing user demands in today's Internet. Their flexibility, extensibility, and configurability enable the adaptation to different application cases and environments. Also, upcoming access technologies and user demands can be considered more easily, compared to rather static existing ALM proposals. The evaluations of the presented protocols show promising protocol behavior, confirming the claim that P2P protocols can be used to flexibly bring out new communication services and even may support in mitigating current capacity bottlenecks in mobile access networks. Furthermore, by the time of writing this thesis the benefit and potential of ALM protocols is considered by more and more "big players" in the Internet: The Bittorrent protocol is enhanced by a live streaming solution [146], promoted as a promising alternative to common TV. Another example is Adobe, equipping their Flash Player software with RTMFP [194], an integrated protocol to provide peer-assisted networking.

7.2   Perspectives for Future Research

For future research directions the presented protocols and ideas can be enhanced and studied with consideration of several aspects:

While the integration of local wireless networks in ALM-based data dissemination offers great potential, the implications of such an approach should be further studied. In general, user mobility can be considered in future work as an important factor influencing overlay protocol robustness. Furthermore, local wireless domains may themselves be prone to high traffic load already or peer mobility may turn a transient switch to a local wireless technology inefficient. The presented protocols can hence be enhanced by the consideration of an extended switching trade-off. For instance, existing approaches to estimate the mobility of mobile devices [202, 233] can be integrated in order to decide which peer offers the longest residual time in a WiFi domain's range. Such a differentiation can increase the protocols' efficiency by assigning roles as forwarders to more static peers, mitigating overlay fluctuations induced by peer mobility.

In principle, the adaptation of the data to be disseminated offers a further dimension for the ALM protocol strategies. Modern end-systems offer the capacities to adapt the data during the forwarding process, being especially promising with respect to the video streaming context. The stream can be modified accordingly so that it is not sensible to degraded bandwidth but adapts its quality, for instance. Recent studies and proposals, like e. g. *Scalable Video Coding (SVC)* [164], offer potential to adapt the video stream not only to end-system capabilities but also to access network capacities. While these approaches have not been considered in this thesis in favor of constant bandwidth video streams, they fit the idea behind Capacity Matching well and offer further optimization perspectives.

Regarding the used shared medium network models the behavior of the ALM protocols with more realistic assumptions concerning capacities, signal fading, shadowing, and channel assessment has to be evaluated to estimate the effects of local network congestion and find limits of the approach. The impact of low-delay technologies like e. g. LTE, has to be observed because lower delays promise more room for traffic load balancing (since they further limit the negative effect of the inherent metric trade-off). Besides that, the presented concepts can be further enhanced by the integration of wireless technologies that have not been considered in this thesis: Bluetooth, WiMax, Piconets, and WiFi Direct are potential candidates since they will have a higher deployment status in the near future. This integration would considerably increase the number of end-systems that could be used with the protocols.

Regarding WIMP's applicability in real environments the deployment status and development of public wireless access networks in cities around the world should be considered for a more realistic assessment of the approach's benefit and to anticipate if it will experience growing potential in the future. Furthermore, a generic integration of WIMP in diverse ALM approaches (not only tree-based ALM) can be worked out in order to provide general applicability of the mechanisms. Here, new strategies for information aggregation, e. g. based on gossiping or flooding, have to be developed. A generic integration eliminates the limitation to tree-based protocols and opens the approach's potential to a wider group of overlay developers.

For the presented overlay development framework several enhancements for the concepts can be worked out: The SpoVNet architecture is publicly available in form of ariba and is actively maintained and ported to other hardware platforms. Aspects like enhanced security and a bigger set of communication services to be used by applications can be integrated. Also, more communication protocols can be integrated in the Base Communication to increase ariba's usability.

Part III

Appendix

A. NICE Protocol Implementation

The protocol message formats used in the NICE implementation as well as the extensions used in NICE-WLI are listed in the following.

A.1   NICE Protocol Message Formats

The NICE implementation used in this work differentiates 18 protocol message types, defined in the *NICECommand* enumeration:

```
enum NICECommand {

        NICE_QUERY                      // Query Memberships in Clusters
        NICE_QUERY_RESPONSE             // Response to a Query
        NICE_JOIN_CLUSTER               // Join Cluster in specific layer
        NICE_HEARTBEAT                  // Periodic Heartbeat message
        NICE_LEADERHEARTBEAT            // Periodic Leader Heartbeat message
        NICE_LEADERTRANSFER             // Leader Transfer
        NICE_JOINEVAL                   // Distance Evaluation when Joining
        NICE_JOINEVAL_RESPONSE          // Response to JoinEval
        NICE_REMOVE                     // Remove Peer from Cluster
        NICE_PING_PROBE                 // Probe Remote Peer
        NICE_PING_PROBE_RESPONSE        // Response to PingProbe
        NICE_CLUSTER_MERGE_REQUEST      // Request Cluster Merge
        NICE_PEER_TEMPORARY             // Temporary Peer while Joining
        NICE_PEER_TEMPORARY_RELEASE     // Temporary Peering Release
        NICE_POLL_RP                    // Poll Existing RP
        NICE_POLL_RP_RESPONSE           // Response to RP Poll
        NICE_FORCE_MERGE                // Force Merging of Clusters
        NICE_APPDATA                    // Application Data
```

```
};
```

NICEMESSAGE

As a base message class NICE uses a type called *NICEMessage*. It inherits from *BaseOverlayMessage* which is the base class for overlay message formats provided by the OverSim framework. A *TransportAddress* serves as a locator and comprises a network address and an application port:

```
message NICEMessage extends BaseOverlayMessage
{
        fields:
                int command enum(NICECommand);   // Message Type
                TransportAddress srcNode;         // Source Address
                short layer;                      // Cluster Hierarchy Layer
};
```

NICEMEMBERMESSAGE

A *NICEMemberMessage* message is used if a list of addresses of peers has to be disseminated in NICE:

```
message NICEMemberMessage extends NICEMessage {
        fields:
                TransportAddress members[];     // List of Cluster Members
}
```

NICECLUSTERMERGE

A *NICEClusterMerge* message extends a NICEMemberMessage by the address of the new Cluster Leader:

```
message NICEClusterMerge extends NICEMemberMessage {

        fields:
                TransportAddress newClusterLeader; // New Cluster Leader
}
```

NICEHEARTBEAT

A *NICEHeartbeat* message supports intra-cluster refinement and holds all relevant information to decide splitting and merging of a cluster or leadership changes:

```
message NICEHeartbeat extends NICEMemberMessage {

        fields:
                unsigned int seqNo;              // Sequence No. of HB
                unsigned int seqRspNo;           // Responded Seq. No.
                double hb_delay;                 // RTT Estimation
                double distances[];              // Distances to Peers
                unsigned int sublayermembers;    // Peers in Sublayer
}
```

NICELEADERHEARTBEAT

A *NICELeaderHeartbeat* message extends a NICEHeartbeat message by the address of the Supercluster Leader, the members of the supercluster, the current cluster size paremeter k (variable in the proposed adaptation scheme), and the current minimum backoff before changing a Cluster Leader:

```
message NICELeaderHeartbeat extends NICEHeartbeat {

        fields:
                TransportAddress supercluster_leader;    // SC Leader
                TransportAddress supercluster_members[]; // SC Members
                unsigned int k;                    // Clustersize Parameter k
                unsigned int sc_tolerance; // Change Backoff
}
```

NICEAPPDATA

The *NICEAppData* message extends a NICEMessage and is used to disseminate application data throughout the overlay structure:

```
message NICEAppData extends NICEMessage {

        fields:
                const char* data;      // Application Data
                unsigned int k;        // Data Length
}
```

A.2   NICE WLI Protocol Message Formats

In NICE-WLI changed or extended protocol messages are used to extend NICE by WiFi domain integration and consideration.

```
enum NICEWLICommand {

        NICEWLI_JOIN_CLUSTER            // Join Cluster in specific layer
        NICEWLI_HEARTBEAT               // Periodic Heartbeat message
        NICEWLI_GATEWAY_TRANSFER        // Leader Transfer
        NICEWLI_GATEWAY_DISCOVERY       // Discover GW
        NICEWLI_WELCOME                 // WLI Welcome
};
```

NICEWLIMESSAGE

The *NICEWLIMessage* extends a NICEMessage as base class and integrates a flag for Gateway role indication.

```
message NICEWLIMessage extends NICEMessage
{
        fields:
                int command enum(NICEWLICommand);      // Message Type
                boolean isGw;                          // Gateway Role
};
```

NICEWLISNR

The *NICEWLISNR* message extends a NICEWLIMessage and is used to indicate a peer's SNR in a WLI domain. This message is used e. g. for WLI Heartbeats or for Gateway discovery:

```
message NICEWLISNR extends NICEWLIMessage
{
        fields:
                unsigned int snr;       // Own Signal-to-Noise-Ratio
                unsigned int hopcount;  // Hopcount (Ad-hoc)
};
```

NICEWLIGWTRANSFER

The *NICEWLIGWTransfer* message extends a NICEWLIMessage and is used transfer the Gateway role in a WLI domain to a different peer. It holds the address of the Cluster Leader in the lowest layer of the cluster hierarchy to which the new peer has to join subsequently:

```
message NICEWLIGWTransfer extends NICEWLIMessage
{
        fields:
                TransportAddress L0Leader;        // Leader of L0 Cluster
};
```

NICEWLIAppData

The *NICEWLIAppData* message extends a NICEWLIMessage and is used to disseminate application data throughout the WLI domain:

```
message NICEWLIAppData extends NICEWLIMessage {

        fields:
                const char* data;                // Application Data
                unsigned int k;                  // Data Length
                TransportAddress targetGw;       // Target GW
}
```

B. MiXiM Modifications & CMA

MiXiM has been modified and enhanced by a set of mechanisms and concepts to adapt its functionality for this thesis' observations.

B.1   Lower Layer Modeling

The presented evaluations targeted inherent ALM protocol behavior and did not aim at realistic modeling of lower layers of communication. Hence, the MAC layer and the physical layer in MiXiM have been simplified in order to reduce time and memory consumption of the simulations, especially with higher numbers of peers. Collisions, normally occurring in case of simultaneous sending of data in the MAC layer, have been removed in order to accomodate the CDMA scheme's ability of simultaneous medium occupancy. Shadowing and fading issues have been neglected as well. A Unit-Disc-Model is used to determine wireless transmission ranges.

Cellular tower assignment of peers is accomplished by the use of Beacon messages, emitted by the towers. In case of static peers Beacons are sent once. However, mobility is also supported in the modified MiXiM version, although not explicitly considered in this thesis. In case of mobility Beacons are emitted periodically by the towers with a configurable period length.

B.2   Peer Addressing and Multihoming

The unmodified MiXiM version used in this work only supports one network access device per peer. Such a device is called *Network Interface Card (NIC)* in MiXiM. However, multihoming is one of the central aspects considered in this thesis. Therefore, the simulation framework has been extended by the possibility to provide every peer with a configurable number of NICs. This extension raises the problem of peer addressing since each peer is potentially reachable via each NIC it has.

To handle this the concept of *MIP (Multi-NIC IP) addresses* has been introduced in the modified MiXiM version. They replace the common addressing scheme by means of providing multihomed communication. The decision which NIC to choose for outgoing data traffic is based on a routing table implemented in each peer. If no entry exists for a destination or a specific NIC is chosen a configurable default NIC is used. A MIP address consists of a tuple, holding a peer's MiXiM-specific unique object ID and the destination NIC. The object ID serves as a locator, while the NIC address specifies the target network device.

MIP addresses can be used in MiXiM like normal IP addresses. A source peer sending data to a destination peer provides the target MIP address. Then, the cellular tower responsible for the source peer retrieves the destination object ID from the MIP address, requests the responsible cellular tower responsible for the destination peer, and passes the data to this tower. WiFi access domains have been modeled as modified cellular towers. To differ between Internet-enabled WiFi access points and WiFi domains prohibiting Internet access a flag is used to indicate whether the access point should forward data traffic to the simulated underlay backbone.

B.3 CMA Evaluation Results

α Peers	0.0	0.1	0.2	0.3	0.4	0.5	Lower Bound
50	0.898	0.894	0.887	0.882	0.879	0.859	0.687
100	0.819	0.800	0.787	0.775	0.759	0.743	0.446
200	0.688	0.656	0.623	0.596	0.559	0.522	0.227
300	0.621	0.562	0.522	0.475	0.432	0.384	0.124
400	0.531	0.459	0.406	0.363	0.318	0.287	0.080
500	0.482	0.397	0.339	0.286	0.258	0.225	0.056
600	0.442	0.354	0.301	0.245	0.217	0.189	0.045
700	0.405	0.323	0.270	0.216	0.190	0.158	0.037
800	0.372	0.301	0.245	0.202	0.161	0.141	0.030
900	0.337	0.284	0.224	0.179	0.145	0.122	0.028
1000	0.307	0.255	0.211	0.163	0.133	0.114	0.022
	0.6	0.7	0.8	0.9	1.0		
50	0.859	0.842	0.813	0.766	0.711		0.687
100	0.720	0.687	0.633	0.542	0.464		0.446
200	0.491	0.436	0.376	0.279	0.230		0.227
300	0.346	0.289	0.230	0.173	0.125		0.124
400	0.246	0.205	0.159	0.115	0.80		0.080
500	0.193	0.163	0.128	0.094	0.056		0.056
600	0.157	0.133	0.106	0.077	0.045		0.045
700	0.136	0.144	0.092	0.064	0.038		0.037
800	0.120	0.099	0.080	0.057	0.031		0.030
900	0.106	0.087	0.070	0.050	0.028		0.028
1000	0.096	0.080	0.064	0.044	0.022		0.022

Table B.1 GINI Coefficients with α Variations, Hybrid Delay Model

Peers \ α	0.0	0.1	0.2	0.3	0.4	0.5
50	610.515	609.556	611.152	611.460	613.697	620.452
100	733.754	733.393	734.752	736.277	741.783	747.928
200	840.821	844.654	845.762	852.965	860.964	872.894
300	913.058	916.150	917.998	927.722	943.012	953.110
400	968.542	968.892	972.239	981.971	991.039	1010.020
500	1021.422	1021.091	1024.135	1033.564	1048.370	1067.267
600	1061.215	1051.194	1057.260	1061.226	1080.834	1092.896
700	1096.606	1089.660	1088.118	1094.204	1114.440	1130.798
800	1140.870	1119.674	1126.334	1131.426	1143.572	1171.478
900	1215.283	1162.321	1154.184	1156.948	1169.649	1180.129
1000	1332.186	1251.788	1181.453	1169.699	1183.807	1206.855

	0.6	0.7	0.8	0.9	1.0	
50	627.961	649.277	687.934	812.349	1207.068	
100	765.864	786.696	837.242	959.159	1552.480	
200	897.249	917.486	964.346	1056.551	1701.363	
300	972.566	1003.995	1038.759	1126.620	1845.816	
400	1033.606	1062.497	1094.623	1166.176	1821.513	
500	1090.969	1106.162	1169.558	1224.168	2006.046	
600	1123.011	1159.959	1211.904	1288.791	1990.990	
700	1161.490	1206.844	1237.700	1341.656	2118.203	
800	1210.992	1233.419	1298.996	1397.643	2100.413	
900	1230.045	1243.567	1347.677	1453.249	2152.282	
1000	1223.585	1287.445	1363.099	1476.901	2300.116	

Table B.2 Mean Data Dissemination Delays with α variations [ms], Hybrid Delay Model

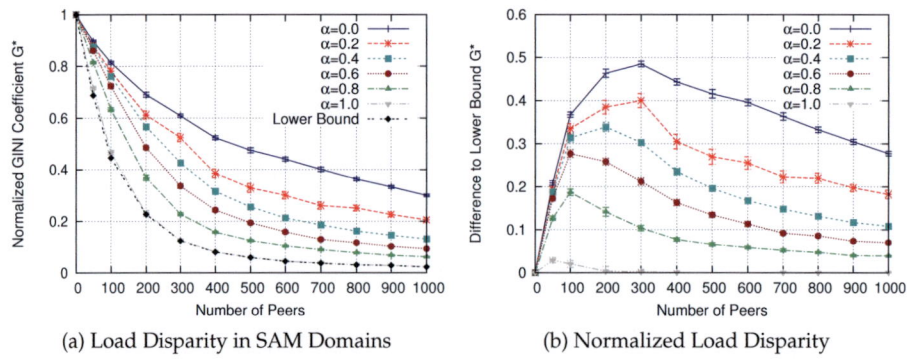

(a) Load Disparity in SAM Domains   (b) Normalized Load Disparity

Figure B.1 Load Disparity in SAM Domains with Constant Delay Model

α / Peers	0.0	0.1	0.2	0.3	0.4	0.5
50	786.111	789.790	794.674	800.491	809.693	831.888
100	958.639	960.319	963.872	978.506	1039.646	1071.917
200	1061.087	1070.597	1086.655	1138.002	1205.113	1288.037
300	1167.295	1179.460	1203.951	1266.668	1386.742	1500.211
400	1228.420	1224.168	1258.189	1341.324	1446.654	1644.042
500	1311.243	1277.701	1323.47	1399.380	1523.013	1792.250
600	1419.208	1316.787	1379.727	1456.484	1592.514	1707.635
700	1417.572	1423.858	1441.359	1501.655	1668.581	1842.664
800	1630.156	1468.441	1515.505	1637.786	1702.635	1962.580
900	1973.483	1686.558	1591.561	1702.240	1761.440	1925.180
1000	2611.540	1981.249	1774.843	1716.555	1786.871	2025.769
	0.6	0.7	0.8	0.9	1.0	
50	911.034	1013.864	1139.858	1457.680	2480.781	
100	1181.581	1262.999	1393.798	1702.953	3311.423	
200	1483.466	1570.804	1807.859	2014.734	3596.106	
300	1679.905	1793.906	1921.136	2226.060	3863.411	
400	1783.875	1872.922	2099.146	2271.964	4033.829	
500	1884.929	1956.954	2288.155	2504.431	4407.612	
600	1918.965	2073.572	2492.304	2573.121	4542.130	
700	2012.864	2224.439	2413.861	2808.958	4854.581	
800	2170.643	2311.721	2585.619	2874.903	4973.798	
900	2167.812	2310.001	2662.003	2999.890	4863.741	
1000	2209.661	2405.338	2818.920	3110.192	5574.703	

Table B.3 Maximum Data Dissemination Delays with α variations [ms], Hybrid Delay Model

UB_Δ / Peers	1000 ms	1250 ms	1500 ms	2000 ms	3000 ms
50	0.806	0.770	0.752	0.748	0.748
100	0.691	0.591	0.555	0.533	0.531
200	0.629	0.377	0.304	0.275	0.269
300	0.602	0.290	0.188	0.162	0.156
400	0.529	0.279	0.138	0.099	0.096
500	0.495	0.306	0.106	0.069	0.068
600	0.467	0.315	0.093	0.054	0.050
700	0.437	0.315	0.080	0.042	0.039
800	0.423	0.356	0.083	0.037	0.033
900	0.408	0.359	0.077	0.031	0.029
1000	0.390	0.338	0.074	0.025	0.024

Table B.4 GINI Coefficients with Upper Delay Bounds, Hybrid Delay Model

Peers \ UB$_\Delta$	1000 ms	1250 ms	1500 ms	2000 ms	3000 ms
50	712.904	797.918	865.260	901.501	900.30
100	781.174	879.842	959.286	1028.670	1049.911
200	856.837	946.818	1036.671	1128.450	1154.069
300	915.821	984.103	1084.308	1181.883	1224.272
400	969.262	1007.401	1100.384	1211.413	1237.870
500	1025.494	1042.894	1136.427	1261.623	1305.844
600	1048.155	1070.283	1148.347	1282.208	1319.328
700	1075.656	1088.233	1162.869	1301.638	1347.317
800	1112.147	1113.840	1184.184	1324.921	1379.865
900	1124.984	1129.958	1193.758	1327.766	1380.293
1000	1129.219	1136.768	1188.656	1334.980	1394.295

Table B.5 Mean Data Dissemination Delays with Upper Delay Bounds [ms], Hybrid Delay Model

Peers \ UB$_\Delta$	1000 ms	1250 ms	1500 ms	2000 ms	3000 ms
50	976.973	1206.225	1440.631	1715.898	1740.795
100	1000.774	1219.389	1455.189	1890.488	2046.060
200	1074.169	1238.298	1469.536	1916.564	2249.220
300	1179.860	1249.010	1478.499	1927.117	2296.120
400	1233.427	1268.679	1482.567	1943.351	2417.633
500	1345.075	1311.665	1489.156	1950.536	2530.327
600	1428.507	1364.159	1493.361	1951.001	2526.345
700	1468.354	1399.953	1505.111	1965.097	2625.159
800	1506.711	1467.316	1508.244	1969.777	2678.980
900	1556.210	1496.443	1514.746	1971.665	2696.336
1000	1581.431	1529.173	1527.666	1967.736	2732.348

Table B.6 Maximum Data Dissemination Delays with Upper Delay Bounds [ms], Hybrid Delay Model

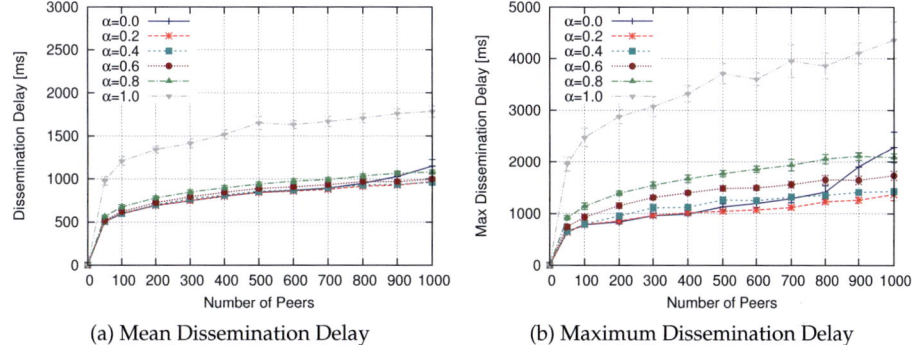

(a) Mean Dissemination Delay   (b) Maximum Dissemination Delay

Figure B.2 Dissemination Delays with Constant Delay Model

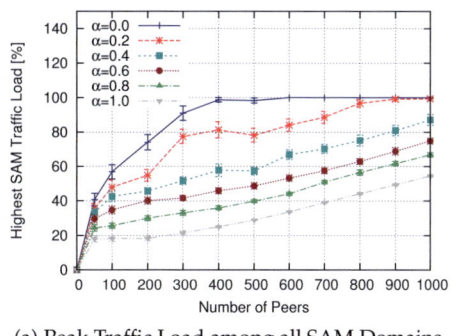

(a) Peak Traffic Load among all SAM Domains

Figure B.3 Peak Traffic Load with Constant Delay Model

α Peers	0.0	0.1	0.2	0.3	0.4	0.5	Lower Bound
50	0.896	0.886	0.880	0.879	0.875	0.869	0.687
100	0.813	0.793	0.781	0.770	0.760	0.746	0.446
200	0.690	0.630	0.611	0.593	0.565	0.535	0.227
300	0.608	0.550	0.524	0.472	0.426	0.377	0.124
400	0.523	0.424	0.385	0.349	0.315	0.272	0.080
500	0.475	0.369	0.329	0.287	0.255	0.218	0.059
600	0.440	0.337	0.300	0.252	0.212	0.184	0.045
700	0.401	0.306	0.260	0.220	0.185	0.157	0.037
800	0.363	0.297	0.250	0.200	0.162	0.135	0.030
900	0.333	0.265	0.226	0.179	0.145	0.119	0.028
1000	0.300	0.234	0.205	0.162	0.131	0.109	0.023
	0.6	0.7	0.8	0.9	1.0		
50	0.859	0.844	0.814	0.769	0.716		0.687
100	0.723	0.688	0.633	0.541	0.466		0.446
200	0.485	0.443	0.368	0.278	0.230		0.227
300	0.336	0.289	0.227	0.169	0.126		0.124
400	0.243	0.202	0.158	0.115	0.081		0.080
500	0.194	0.154	0.125	0.089	0.059		0.059
600	0.158	0.129	0.104	0.074	0.045		0.045
700	0.129	0.111	0.089	0.063	0.038		0.037
800	0.116	0.096	0.078	0.054	0.031		0.030
900	0.102	0.086	0.068	0.049	0.028		0.028
1000	0.092	0.078	0.062	0.043	0.023		0.023

Table B.7 GINI Coefficients with α Variations, Constant Delay Model

Peers \ α	0.0	0.1	0.2	0.3	0.4	0.5
50	503.459	504.870	504.007	503.887	506.447	508.664
100	596.140	596.419	598.083	598.284	599.408	608.221
200	690.093	691.332	690.782	693.229	698.662	713.224
300	745.219	745.888	746.810	752.989	769.113	774.233
400	799.252	799.571	797.703	802.604	810.946	822.488
500	842.018	836.984	840.696	846.947	855.666	879.215
600	865.053	850.956	856.444	861.294	869.611	887.605
700	891.646	874.776	878.032	885.382	896.575	910.872
800	947.115	919.383	912.625	917.304	928.948	940.534
900	1027.514	933.919	926.090	942.330	936.676	946.873
1000	1146.138	951.265	967.655	958.658	959.727	973.090

	0.6	0.7	0.8	0.9	1.0	
50	515.485	531.555	562.974	643.857	975.416	
100	620.118	638.951	674.973	769.051	1209.802	
200	723.389	748.412	779.567	866.423	1343.518	
300	791.418	817.040	846.617	905.626	1416.221	
400	843.380	856.380	896.610	943.705	1518.733	
500	887.031	905.866	938.371	995.848	1650.630	
600	905.879	931.184	971.808	1024.365	1631.329	
700	930.714	970.205	991.304	1085.727	1668.681	
800	967.457	1006.474	1033.107	1113.925	1706.446	
900	967.544	1008.150	1064.947	1137.146	1759.402	
1000	997.706	1025.479	1077.889	1178.391	1784.537	

Table B.8 Mean Data Dissemination Delays with α Variations [ms], Constant Delay Model

α Peers	0.0	0.1	0.2	0.3	0.4	0.5
50	640.295	639.828	638.580	640.978	655.240	671.866
100	782.370	781.056	784.700	782.743	795.923	862.517
200	834.094	848.533	852.727	879.497	953.578	1054.713
300	958.086	934.096	959.742	985.729	1110.973	1169.238
400	989.186	978.096	1012.148	1061.613	1120.964	1230.759
500	1130.310	1009.216	1042.621	1163.804	1263.995	1428.692
600	1194.462	1028.786	1069.725	1166.227	1250.939	1449.960
700	1289.613	1054.916	1116.436	1217.215	1321.865	1474.318
800	1417.619	1188.746	1228.011	1277.719	1354.091	1481.381
900	1903.784	1237.103	1258.233	1325.733	1412.448	1478.169
1000	2286.407	1275.518	1369.100	1373.267	1430.230	1585.908

	0.6	0.7	0.8	0.9	1.0	
50	742.715	823.559	917.408	1119.304	1956.230	
100	927.755	995.685	1141.434	1382.792	2476.935	
200	1151.481	1259.401	1390.850	1633.955	2877.051	
300	1309.691	1417.819	1545.798	1713.277	3070.044	
400	1400.851	1487.590	1672.791	1834.601	3318.460	
500	1486.100	1585.294	1772.008	2006.246	3709.986	
600	1495.355	1658.786	1854.850	2048.190	3600.367	
700	1559.757	1810.532	1934.933	2297.059	3951.081	
800	1653.795	1863.802	2053.848	2218.556	3860.189	
900	1644.964	1881.050	2107.730	2320.651	4105.619	
1000	1731.444	1909.528	2082.626	2531.065	4358.740	

Table B.9 Maximum Data Dissemination Delays with α Variations [ms], Constant Delay Model

UB_Δ Peers	1000 ms	1250 ms	1500 ms	2000 ms	3000 ms
50	0.773	0.761	0.752	0.752	0.752
100	0.590	0.555	0.539	0.529	0.528
200	0.382	0.309	0.280	0.271	0.271
300	0.297	0.192	0.168	0.156	0.156
400	0.287	0.136	0.106	0.096	0.096
500	0.317	0.107	0.081	0.066	0.066
600	0.319	0.092	0.064	0.051	0.051
700	0.326	0.077	0.055	0.040	0.040
800	0.364	0.078	0.053	0.033	0.032
900	0.370	0.075	0.046	0.030	0.030
1000	0.351	0.078	0.045	0.023	0.023

Table B.10 GINI Coefficients with Upper Delay Bounds, Constant Delay Model

UB$_\Delta$ Peers	1000 ms	1250 ms	1500 ms	2000 ms	3000 ms
50	642.634	685.001	709.051	725.051	725.051
100	709.591	764.531	814.147	844.461	847.704
200	763.269	828.567	891.932	913.225	916.644
300	793.094	868.249	923.937	964.665	967.240
400	819.311	891.568	952.484	1001.008	1005.049
500	847.338	917.600	980.794	1024.707	1030.339
600	859.992	928.029	995.049	1056.712	1057.428
700	870.254	935.756	1007.562	1059.990	1069.880
800	903.589	953.534	1029.840	1092.382	1096.440
900	917.918	960.934	1039.114	1099.409	1103.237
1000	929.585	967.112	1051.022	1110.094	1114.929

Table B.11 Mean Data Dissemination Delays with Upper Delay Bounds [ms], Constant Delay Model

UB$_\Delta$ Peers	1000 ms	1250 ms	1500 ms	2000 ms	3000 ms
50	946.497	1129.479	1299.486	1435.788	1435.788
100	950.887	1135.370	1376.503	1657.206	1667.773
200	954.265	1142.431	1426.901	1750.676	1827.357
300	962.165	1147.667	1451.816	1811.843	1864.593
400	980.295	1147.967	1457.839	1845.184	1944.122
500	1015.375	1149.871	1486.189	1856.012	1964.309
600	1043.516	1149.118	1494.684	1869.659	2050.884
700	1066.005	1150.610	1498.257	1877.362	2132.957
800	1150.125	1159.554	1502.972	1878.379	2095.429
900	1210.811	1153.379	1506.608	1882.274	2124.348
1000	1256.649	1187.733	1508.875	1884.725	2161.269

Table B.12 Maximum Data Dissemination Delays with Upper Delay Bounds [ms], Constant Delay Model

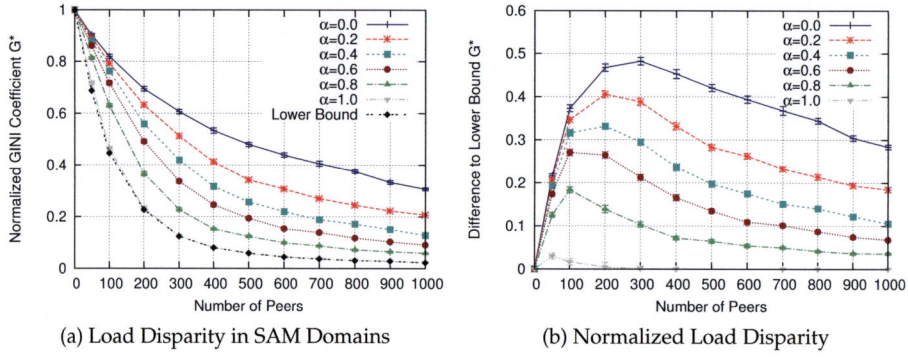

(a) Load Disparity in SAM Domains

(b) Normalized Load Disparity

Figure B.4 Load Disparity in SAM Domains with Euclidean Delay Model

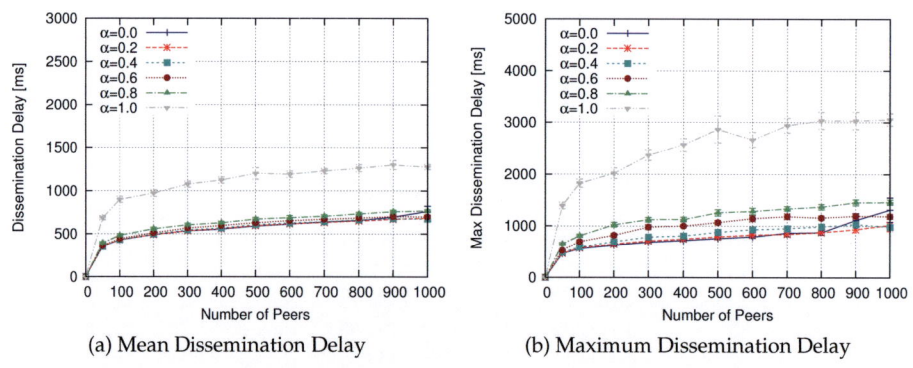

(a) Mean Dissemination Delay

(b) Maximum Dissemination Delay

Figure B.5 Dissemination Delays with Euclidean Delay Model

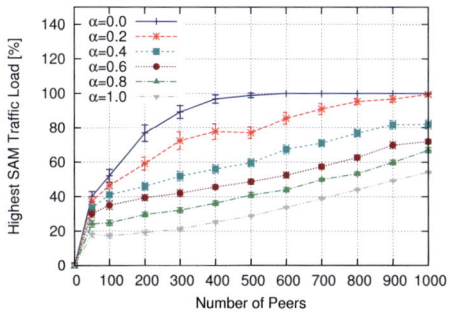

(a) Peak Traffic Load among all SAM Domains

Figure B.6 Peak Traffic Load with Euclidean Delay Model

α Peers	0.0	0.1	0.2	0.3	0.4	0.5	Lower Bound
50	0.903	0.899	0.893	0.889	0.880	0.873	0.687
100	0.819	0.804	0.792	0.778	0.762	0.740	0.446
200	0.694	0.664	0.632	0.596	0.558	0.527	0.227
300	0.606	0.559	0.512	0.466	0.419	0.382	0.124
400	0.533	0.471	0.412	0.370	0.317	0.286	0.080
500	0.479	0.406	0.341	0.295	0.256	0.220	0.058
600	0.438	0.375	0.307	0.258	0.219	0.193	0.044
700	0.405	0.335	0.269	0.224	0.188	0.158	0.037
800	0.375	0.304	0.244	0.201	0.171	0.139	0.030
900	0.332	0.282	0.222	0.179	0.150	0.122	0.028
1000	0.306	0.260	0.207	0.165	0.128	0.110	0.023
	0.6	0.7	0.8	0.9	1.0		
50	0.861	0.845	0.812	0.763	0.717		0.687
100	0.716	0.678	0.629	0.540	0.463		0.446
200	0.491	0.439	0.365	0.278	0.231		0.227
300	0.336	0.286	0.227	0.164	0.125		0.124
400	0.246	0.202	0.152	0.108	0.081		0.080
500	0.194	0.156	0.124	0.086	0.058		0.058
600	0.153	0.132	0.099	0.071	0.044		0.044
700	0.138	0.109	0.087	0.059	0.037		0.037
800	0.117	0.094	0.072	0.050	0.031		0.030
900	0.103	0.084	0.065	0.045	0.028		0.028
1000	0.090	0.076	0.059	0.040	0.023		0.023

Table B.13 GINI Coefficients with α Variations, Euclidean Delay Model

Peers \ α	0.0	0.1	0.2	0.3	0.4	0.5
50	351.704	351.795	353.158	352.380	353.195	355.573
100	427.110	428.947	428.285	427.810	430.339	434.369
200	487.954	489.127	489.134	492.730	496.102	503.507
300	533.544	532.207	533.458	536.920	544.261	553.808
400	555.060	557.334	558.460	560.977	567.542	579.315
500	590.924	590.292	595.072	598.158	606.665	618.193
600	613.728	615.158	615.683	619.493	627.112	640.710
700	637.647	628.072	632.123	635.772	642.150	653.418
800	656.154	651.005	649.659	659.130	664.004	673.041
900	695.407	674.466	669.550	666.257	677.177	682.642
1000	761.664	720.555	682.944	669.867	673.528	686.993
	0.6	0.7	0.8	0.9	1.0	
50	360.304	368.678	394.328	464.465	686.775	
100	441.791	456.685	482.904	556.247	899.196	
200	511.231	529.025	558.195	621.256	971.778	
300	567.034	581.802	604.238	650.650	1076.797	
400	595.695	611.080	628.601	664.171	1123.665	
500	629.515	648.018	672.370	707.708	1202.629	
600	652.984	667.247	689.156	735.408	1193.049	
700	669.043	683.881	705.937	765.363	1229.614	
800	684.055	706.690	732.493	784.937	1264.218	
900	700.019	726.551	758.839	813.359	1301.145	
1000	699.270	723.906	767.328	826.900	1277.931	

Table B.14 Mean Data Dissemination Delays with α Variations [ms], Euclidean Delay Model

α / Peers	0.0	0.1	0.2	0.3	0.4	0.5
50	460.788	470.613	465.816	473.885	488.696	502.680
100	558.060	564.611	571.054	575.863	588.580	626.848
200	622.521	630.270	641.951	662.961	691.646	780.980
300	681.234	688.521	703.557	747.758	783.787	855.868
400	714.070	718.487	742.376	778.426	805.210	911.021
500	753.335	757.745	785.709	817.397	878.444	999.646
600	787.434	793.186	822.680	856.799	930.528	1028.284
700	861.135	810.791	836.980	907.783	950.653	1058.142
800	875.431	856.069	874.391	934.041	989.266	1091.609
900	111.302	982.854	930.025	935.675	1030.178	1124.536
1000	1312.838	1240.182	1018.027	985.584	981.551	1111.407
	0.6	0.7	0.8	0.9	1.0	
50	526.417	556.933	646.993	848.600	1391.994	
100	691.314	762.358	807.542	1023.999	1824.059	
200	816.716	923.945	1022.466	1165.573	2018.846	
300	975.410	1041.253	1120.880	1218.635	2368.232	
400	998.021	1095.045	1125.570	1235.909	2563.250	
500	1065.525	1147.744	1255.981	1372.602	2861.906	
600	1141.485	1200.101	1283.811	1502.921	2661.858	
700	1182.489	1184.970	1334.455	1548.217	2938.251	
800	1158.000	1242.376	1370.539	1616.768	3034.079	
900	1191.429	1334.563	1454.745	1695.239	3031.650	
1000	1184.916	1365.626	1458.868	1747.477	3053.319	

Table B.15 Maximum Data Dissemination Delays with α Variations [ms], Euclidean Delay Model

UB_Δ / Peers	1000 ms	1250 ms	1500 ms	2000 ms	3000 ms
50	0.754	0.748	0.747	0.747	0.747
100	0.541	0.531	0.529	0.529	0.529
200	0.290	0.274	0.271	0.271	0.272
300	0.173	0.159	0.157	0.156	0.157
400	0.112	0.099	0.096	0.095	0.097
500	0.084	0.069	0.068	0.066	0.066
600	0.062	0.051	0.051	0.049	0.049
700	0.053	0.041	0.040	0.040	0.040
800	0.049	0.035	0.034	0.032	0.033
900	0.046	0.030	0.030	0.029	0.029
1000	0.038	0.025	0.024	0.023	0.023

Table B.16 GINI Coefficients with Upper Delay Bounds, Euclidean Delay Model

Peers \ UB$_\Delta$	1000 ms	1250 ms	1500 ms	2000 ms	3000 ms
50	513.699	530.808	534.370	534.370	534.370
100	588.379	613.137	616.885	616.885	616.885
200	637.217	668.886	669.651	669.809	668.826
300	666.736	706.058	713.792	716.054	716.061
400	675.136	716.807	728.636	731.092	731.415
500	701.332	749.761	763.861	765.764	765.764
600	713.305	766.700	779.034	777.701	787.703
700	720.845	772.313	793.751	800.190	800.057
800	734.099	790.060	801.048	812.902	805.890
900	735.989	792.267	808.629	809.851	809.851
1000	736.984	797.075	808.102	810.922	810.367

Table B.17 Mean Data Dissemination Delays with Upper Delay Bounds [ms], Euclidean Delay Model

Peers \ UB$_\Delta$	1000 ms	1250 ms	1500 ms	2000 ms	3000 ms
50	925.220	1052.420	1074.261	1074.261	1074.261
100	965.754	1138.473	1177.682	1177.682	1177.682
200	979.772	1184.953	1270.338	1286.153	1282.424
300	984.848	1204.554	1352.214	1404.701	1420.138
400	989.209	1200.809	1381.962	1443.665	1431.866
500	992.870	1215.975	1413.846	1512.243	1512.243
600	991.433	1215.335	1426.958	1520.593	1527.687
700	997.528	1221.833	1442.038	1626.783	1627.738
800	1002.436	1229.578	1441.874	1586.183	1557.808
900	1001.065	1224.712	1445.050	1599.905	1599.905
1000	1005.466	1227.478	1440.583	1563.463	1563.306

Table B.18 Maximum Data Dissemination Delays with Upper Delay Bounds [ms], Euclidean Delay Model

C. Flexible Tree-based Application-Layer Multicast

In the Chapters 5 and 6 of this thesis a tree-based ALM protocol has been used, respectively. A major benefit of tree-based ALM protocols—compared to e.g. cluster-based approaches like NICE (cf. Chapter 4)—is the ability to directly refine the data dissemination tree with respect to defined optimization goals for each peer in the overlay: Trees allow direct control over a peer's position in the overlay structure, enabling to follow specific constraints for each individual peer more easily.

In order to fit application requirements for the group communication service the tree building and tree refinement strategies between different approaches can vary as much as the application cases may vary. While optimization of a tree regarding one single design goal in a distributed network environment can be accomplished in polynomial time this is no longer the case for more than one goal. The optimization goals can even be contrary to some extent, i.e. optimizing in one direction will degrade the quality of other optimization goals. Optimizing a tree for more than one goal is known to be NP-hard [123, 195, 229]. Therefore, in a distributed environment an overlay building strategy has to be used in the peers that reaches near-optimal results but takes its tree refinement decisions fast and efficient.

In this appendix a family of tree-based protocols, called *MOT-P*, is sketched. It offers high flexibility and extensibility for implementing ALM protocols and it exceeds the existing approaches proposed in literature regarding these aspects. Like CMA (cf. Chapter 5) MOT-P is based on a heuristic refinement strategy. However, it generalizes the approach in order to be highly configurable and extensible and therefore usable to fit various group communication scenarios. CMA can be implemented with the concepts described here. Likewise, the WIMP integration in CMA as presented in Chapter 6 can be implemented with MOT-P.

With AMMO [192] and XPORT [166] two existing generalized tree-based ALM protocols have been proposed in literature following a similar idea like MOT-P. They can be configured and used for various application scenarios, incorporating mechanisms to describe the protocols' optimization criteria. However, both approaches are limited to the specification of tree optimization criteria, while remaining protocol parts (like e. g. overlay refinement and the search for other peers in the overlay) are defined statically. Furthermore, both protocols assume a single communication technology to be used.

MOT-P can be used to implement single-tree ALM protocols. Choosing a single tree over more complex solutions (like e. g. multi-tree or mesh-based protocols) holds benefits and drawbacks: On the one hand, single trees are naturally fragile, a property that has to be compensated through dedicated mechanisms. Fragility may impede a continuous group communication service provision in dynamic environments. On the other hand, single-tree-based protocols are highly flexible in directly adapting the tree to the required multicast service requirements, resulting in high control over the structure. Finally, they are efficient regarding maintenance overhead.

While MOT-P targets single-tree ALM protocols in this appendix, the approach allows for more complex protocol classes (e. g. multi-tree or mesh-first) by design. Its generic structure can be extended for such approaches. These aspects are not discussed here and are hence left for future work. From an architectural point of view MOT-P can be implemented in the service layer of the SpoVNet overlay framework presented in Chapter 3 which allows for easy and fast ALM protocol prototyping and development. MOT-P is published in [109].

C.1   MOT-P

MOT-P (Multi-objective Tree-based Protocols) is a family of distributed ALM-based group communication protocols. It aims at distributedly building and maintaining multicast trees that follow definable optimization goals. The idea behind MOT-P is to provide a generalized approach to the vast set of application cases for single-tree-based multicast. Similar to AMMO [192] and XPORT [166], MOT-P provides a generalization of existing single-tree approaches by offering extensibility and configurability regarding tree optimization goals. It exceeds these approaches by decomposing tree-based ALM

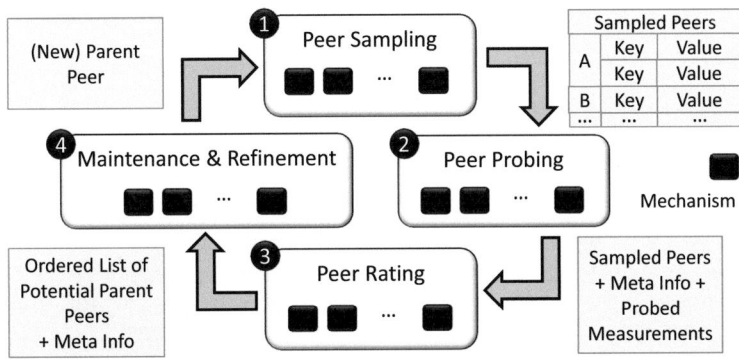

Figure C.1 Functional Building Blocks in MOT-P

protocols into a set of characteristic functional building blocks as described already for the CMA protocol in Chapter 5. MOT-P extends this idea by the aspect that each block can comprise a customizable set of *Mechanisms*, implementing concrete separate functional entities, and improving flexibility.

C.1.1 Functional Building Blocks in MOT-P

The functional blocks in MOT-P directly follow the decomposition of tree-based ALM protocols presented in Chapter 5. While the general task of each block is defined through specified incoming and outgoing parameters (described in more detail in Section C.1.2), the concrete inner workings of each block are left to the protocol designer. This genericness preserves high flexibility and freedom in design of a protocol but also implies a higher grade of initial implementation overhead for protocol designers to implement ALM protocols.

For each functional block the number of Mechanisms is not limited by design. Each block is understood to be a container for a set of Mechanisms, jointly providing the required functionality of the block. The term *Mechanism* expresses an (arbitrarily complex) functional instance that can range from complete protocols to very small functional units, like e. g. a check for a specific local property of a peer. Using a configurable and extensible set of Mechanisms for each functional building block is one of the major differences between MOT-P and existing approaches (including CMA).

Figure C.1 shows an overview of MOT-P covering the functional building blocks comprising exemplary sets of Mechanisms. In the following the incoming and outgoing information per functional building block is described and each part is detailed on, also regarding the protocols presented in predecessing parts of this thesis as examples.

C.1.1.1   Peer Sampling

Peer Sampling in MOT-P is as set of one or more Mechanisms that jointly collect knowledge about other peers in the multicast tree. Given in an ALM implementation n Mechanisms $(\omega_1, \omega_2, ..., \omega_n)$ are used inside this functional building block, providing different sampling sets $(\mathcal{R}_{\omega_1}, \mathcal{R}_{\omega_2}, ..., \mathcal{R}_{\omega_n})$. Then, the overall functional building block provides the joint set $\mathcal{R} = (\mathcal{R}_{\omega_1} \cup \mathcal{R}_{\omega_2} \cup ... \cup \mathcal{R}_{\omega_n})$ to *Peer Probing*. In addition, meta information can be collected, enriching the sampling set $\mathcal{R}$ by further information going beyond plain network addresses, for instance. The meta information is implemented as a generic set of *(key, value)* pairs (cf. Figure C.1) and can be adapted to the application case of the ALM protocol. Taking the protocol presented in Chapter 6 as example, the Peer Sampling functional building block comprises the RanSub sampling mechanism as well as WIMP, both implemented in separate Mechanisms in MOT-P. RanSub provides a sampling set $\mathcal{R}_{\omega_{\text{RanSub}}}$ of peers in the cellular ALM tree. WIMP, in contrast, collects information about directly reachable WiFi peers into a sampling set $\mathcal{R}_{\omega_{\text{WIMP}}}$. All entries in $\mathcal{R}$ are enriched by the communication technology that has been used to reach them as meta information.

C.1.1.2   Peer Probing

In this functional building block the ALM protocol can accomplish measurements to the peers learned in Peer Sampling. It is up to the used Mechanisms if and which peers to measure against and the information or metric to be measured highly depends on the application case. The values gained from measurements are added to the set of sampled peers $\mathcal{R}$. The resulting block of information serves as input to the *Peer Rating* functional building block.

For a protocol integrating different access technologies (like the tree-based protocol in Chapter 6) different Mechanisms in Peer Probing can be used to measure via different technologies: One Mechanism can accomplish direct network measurements via cellular connectivity, while another Mechanism can probe via WiFi, for instance. The benefit is that with differentiation between the technologies also different metrics can be considered for every technology. While e. g. collisions on the wireless medium may be relevant in WiFi domains, this metric does not make sense in cellular technologies with channel assignment. Likewise, measuring network delay inside an infrastructure-based WiFi network may not provide useful insights (but imply additional medium occupancy), while this metric is of high interest in wide-area communication. The decision which probing mechanism to use for each peer is based on the meta information collected and provided via the predecessing functional blocks, comprising the information which peer has been reached via which technology.

C.1.1.3   Peer Rating

In the *Peer Rating* functional building block the information about sampled peers in $\mathcal{R}$ is used to determine if one or more peers provides better properties (regarding the optimization goals) if chosen as new parent peer in the tree. The quality of a tree parent peer is decided based on the optimization goals for the specific ALM application case. These optimization goals are expressed as *Objectives*, like described in Chapter 5. The optimization goals are defined in the Mechanisms used in this functional block. In MOT-P more than one weighted sum heuristic can be used, each defined in an own Mechanism in the Peer Rating functional building block.

C.1.1.4   Maintenance & Refinement

Maintenance & Refinement is the last functional building block in MOT-P's chain. After the collection of sampled peers, measured metrics, and quality evaluations in the predecessing blocks this functional parts comprises functionalities regarding the final decision whether to change the position in the ALM tree or not in the current epoch. Although the Mechanisms in Peer Rating evaluate the optimization goals, they do not decide how to react on the evaluations. In Maintenance & Refinement Mechanisms are located that take this decision. A common approach is to choose the peer with the best heuristic value from $\widehat{\mathcal{R}}$ (holding all potential parent peers after heuristic evaluation) and contact it in the overlay to initiate tree restructuring. A different approach is e. g. choosing a new parent from $\widehat{\mathcal{R}}$ randomly (which is valid since all peers in $\widehat{\mathcal{R}}$ are considered better parents than the current). This can avoid too many peers in the tree choosing the same sampled peer as new parent. Furthermore, Mechanisms enhancing robustness can be located in this functional block. Cycles in the tree can be detected and repaired, for instance. Also, part of the learned potential parent peers can be stored as fallback parent candidates in case of failure or fluctuation, similar to the proactive approach proposed by Yang and Fei [236]. As soon as the Mechanisms in Maintenance & Refinement have been executed MOT-P finishes its epoch. After a definable epoch length timer, it starts over with the Mechanisms in the Peer Sampling functional building block, initiating the next epoch.

C.1.1.5   Functional Building Block Dependencies and Limitations

The flexibility for designing and implementing tree-based ALM protocols with MOT-P enhances its applicability to different application scenarios and its extensibility but also has limitations and drawbacks:

- Information about the target application scenario and the (available) Mechanisms to be used is needed. The Mechanisms for each functional building block have to be chosen. For Peer Rating the configuration has to be accomplished.

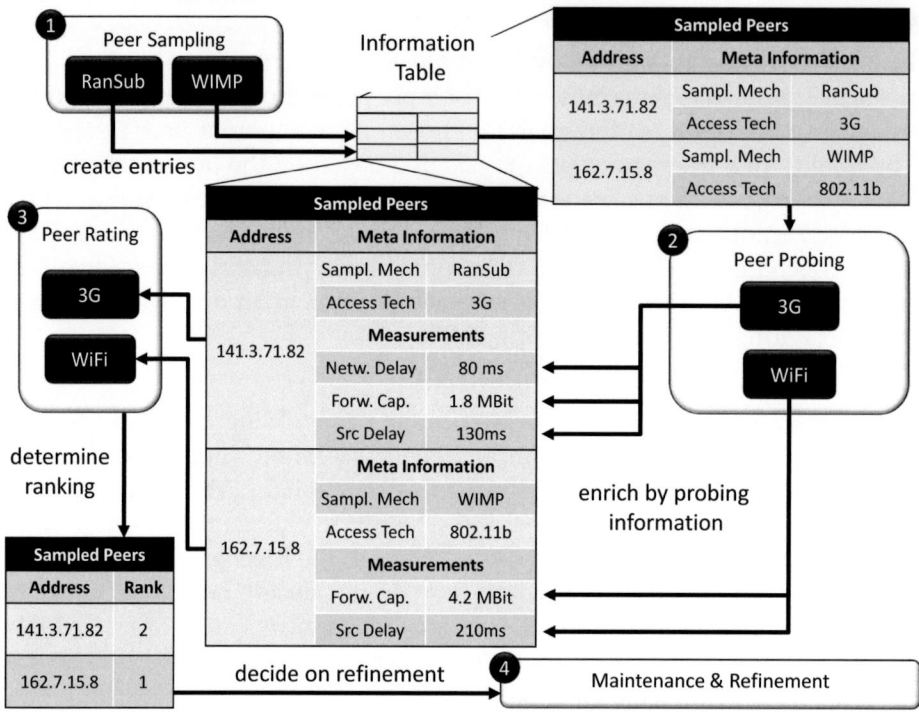

Figure C.2 Example Information Flow in a MOT-P Instance

- The set of Mechanisms to choose from has to exist in advance. The need to create dedicated Mechanisms for MOT-P comes with implementational overhead for developers. However, considering reusability of the Mechanisms, extensibility, and enhanced flexibility, this drawback will in long term be compensated with MOT-P.
- The choice of a specific Mechanism always has to be taken with respect to the remaining functional building blocks and their Mechanisms to some extent since part of the Mechanisms require specific information: Peer Rating Mechanisms, for instance, always require certain sets of information to evaluate the weighted sum heuristics. Therefore, the Mechanisms in Peer Probing have to provide these sets.

C.1.2   MOT-P's Chain of Information

In this section the information exchanged between Mechanisms and functional building blocks in MOT-P is focused. While the inner working of each Mechanism is freely designable, the expected flow of information in a MOT-P instance is fixed.

The collected sampled peers are written to an information table, consisting of peer addresses and meta information (cf. Figure C.2). Meta information is expressed by an unbounded set of *(key,value)* pairs, one set per address entry. In the figure the sampling mechanism used for each peer as well as the access technology of each sampled peer is stored as an example for meta information. Once per epoch the Mechanisms in Peer Probing read the information from the table in order to decide the measurement targets and which Mechanism to use for which peer's probing. In Peer Probing the original information table is enriched by probing information, also expressed by *(key,value)* pairs added to each peer entry (shown as the table in the center of the figure). This enriched table is used by the Peer Rating Mechanisms (i. e. one or more heuristic weighted sums). Which sum to use is determined by the meta information (3G or WiFi in the figure). The Mechanisms in Peer Rating calculate scalar values. As these values are directly comparable a rating ranking is calculated and added to the information table (for space limitations, only the ranks are shown in the figure). Finally, the Mechanisms in Maintenance & Refinement decide if and which parent peer is elected based on the ranking.

The information table provides a central database and also keeps information of predecessing epochs. These older entries can e. g. be used to calculate weighted average values, developing over time. To avoid growing space requirements caching strategies (like FIFO) can be used. The age of entries has to be stored and considered in this case to avoid taking decision on old measurements.

C.1.3   Tree-Based ALM with MOT-P

MOT-P can be used to build tree-based ALM protocols that follow different goals and show different behavior. It allows to choose its mechanisms more flexible than existing approaches, enhancing applicability and the number of scenarios it can be used in, including multihomed environments, for instance.

Table C.1 shows a compact comparison between MOT-P, AMMO, and XPORT, the latter two being the approaches that come closest to the overall goal of MOT-P. The comparison provides the functional building blocks and how the provided protocols implement them. In MOT-P all blocks are flexibly configurable, as described in this appendix. In AMMO and XPORT Peer Rating is configurable, while the remaining functional blocks are statically implemented: AMMO uses random subsets (RanSub [128]) for Peer Sampling, while XPORT relies on sampling the local neighborhood in the tree. For Peer Probing they use global probing relying on the random subsets and local tree probes, respectively. Regarding Maintenance & Refinement, AMMO uses an own mechanism (called *TreeMaint*), avoiding loops and ensuring validity of refinement decisions. XPORT uses a mechanism based on incremental local transformations in the tree in order to reduce global fluctuations.

While AMMO and XPORT already offer high applicability and configurability by providing flexible optimization, the remaining functional building blocks limit their extensibility to new and upcoming application cases. The locality in XPORT reduces efficiency in scenarios where a global search would be the better choice, while the TreeMaint mechanism in AMMO does not consider highly dynamic scenarios where further robustness is needed. Also, both approaches are limited to singlehomed scenarios where all peers are assumed to use a single access technology for Internet-wide communication. MOT-P, in contrast, can be used to adapt even to multihomed scenarios by using appropriate Mechanisms. Furthermore, the flexible Maintenance & Refinement functional block allows to employ different robustness enhancements in dynamic environments or leave them away in static environments in favor of lower overhead.

Protocol	Functional Building Blocks			
	Sampling	Probing	Rating	Maintenance
AMMO[192]	Fix:RanSub	Fix:Glob.Probe	Fix, Adapt	Fix:TreeMaint
XPORT[166]	Fix:Loc.Search	Fix:Loc.Probe	Fix, Adapt	Fix:Loc.Transf.
MOT-P	Free	Free	Free	Free
SARO[128]	RanSub	Global Probe	BW/Delay	Custom
DTA[118]	Local Tree	Local	Fanout/Delay	Custom
MeshTree[230]	Mesh	Mesh Probe	Cost/Delay	Custom

Table C.1 Comparable Approaches and exemplary statically designed Protocols

Due to its flexibility MOT-P can either be used to easily model a high number of existing tree-based ALM protocols by choosing the respective mechanisms or configure new kinds of protocols for scenarios that have not been fully considered yet. It is also usable for rapid prototyping of ALM protocols. Table C.1, in the lower part, provides examples how existing protocols with static functional building blocks can be implemented with MOT-P, mapping the respective functionality to each functional building block.

Example MOT-P ALM Scenarios

In this section a set of exemplary ALM application scenarios and corresponding MOT-P configurations is briefly described to provide insight in how MOT-P can be used to flexibly implement ALM protocols. As examples one small-scale scenario is chosen before MOT-P is also applied to the protocols presented in Chapter 5 and Chapter 6. Hence, the examples mainly differ in assumptions regarding the underlay network, the numbers of peers, and the peers' communication possibilities.

- **Small-scale Single-Homed Wired:** As a first example a case of live video streaming for a lecture is assumed. From a high-capacity PC located at a university a lecture video has to be disseminated to a group of students' home desktop PCs (< 50). The video should reach the peers with minimal delay and all peers are assumed to have wired Internet connections. For this case Peer Sampling can be configured with a single Mechanism that simply collects a complete list of all current peers from the source peer. Global knowledge about all peers can be collected, enabled through the limited number of participants. The benefit is that the final peer selection can be accomplished based on complete knowledge, allowing for highly efficient decisions. In the Peer Probing block a single Mechanism is used that directly measures network delay and available network capacity for each peer. Peer Rating uses two equally-weighted Objectives—dissemination delay and parent peer forwarding capacity—to choose a parent peer near to the source peer, concurrently avoiding to exceed peer forwarding capacity. Finally, Maintenance & Refinement Mechanisms accomplish final peer selection and reaction to churn (in case the parent peer is lost) by triggering reconnection or tree restructuring.

- **Large-scale Single-Homed Cellular (CMA):** In Chapter 5 CMA as a protocol to avoid cellular access network traffic congestions has been presented. The protocol parts can easily be modeled with MOT-P as follows. In Peer Sampling RanSub [128] is used as a single Mechanism to collect randomized subsets of peer in the tree. In Peer Probing network delay and access network traffic load state is queried for each peer in the formerly collected subset. Peer Rating considers the measured metrics in its Objectives, either using minimization or defined upper bounds, like discussed in the respective chapter. Maintenance & Refinement comprises the described Mechanisms regarding fluctuations, number of tree changes (*Inertia*, cf. Chapter 5), and offset for reaction.

- **Large-scale Multi-Homed Cellular/WiFi (CMA with WiFi Integration):** In Chapter 6 CMA has been enhanced by the consideration and integration of WiFi communication. With MOT-P this can be accomplished by extending the respective functional blocks configured in the predecessing example by dedicated WiFi-related Mechanisms (cf. Figure C.3): The Peer Sampling functional building block is extended by WIMP (cf. Section 6.1.3), implemented in a dedicated Mechanism. Together with

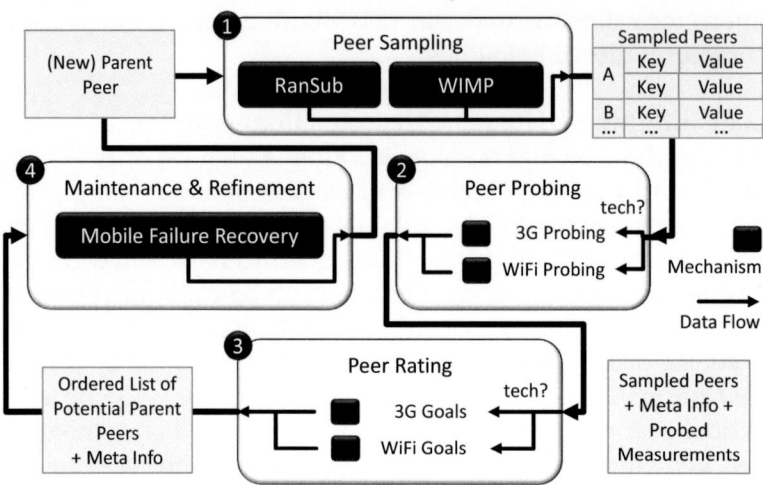

Figure C.3   CMA with WiFi Integration in MOT-P

RanSub it provides a joint set of sampled peers, consisting of random subsets based on the cellular tree and directly reachable WiFi peers, if available. In Peer Probing the sampled set of peers is measured against, collecting information about video dissemination delay, available forwarding capacities, and access network traffic load. How each peer is probed is decided based on the meta information, providing connectivity information (cellular or WiFi). In Peer Rating two different weighted sum heuristics are defined, one for each access technology. Maintenance & Refinement follows the same configuration as in CMA without WiFi consideration as described above.

C.2   Conclusion

In this appendix MOT-P as an approach for the design and provision of extensible and configurable tree-based ALM protocols has been presented. The need for such an approach has been concluded from the variety of existing specialized solutions that exist as well as from existing generic proposals. MOT-P exceeds these approaches by providing a decomposition of characteristic functional building blocks in tree-based distributed ALM protocols and allowing for the configuration of different Mechanisms inside each of these blocks.

Although the Mechanisms have to be designed and implemented in advance, their joint use clearly enhances the application scenarios of MOT-P, allowing combinations for e. g. multihoming support being added to existing protocols later, if needed. The overhead is compensated by the high reuse possibilities and easy extensibility of MOT-P. Furthermore, different optimization goals can be specified for different access technologies, supporting the consideration of technology-specific metrics and higher differentiation through more than one heuristic. A set of examples (including the presented protocols in this thesis) has been provided to give insight in how MOT-P can be used to implement existing and new ALM protocols.

Bibliography

[1] D. Abrahams and A. Gurtovoy. *C++ Template Metaprogramming: Concepts, Tools, and Techniques from Boost and Beyond (C++ in Depth Series)*, volume 5. Addison-Wesley Professional, Stoughton, Massachusetts, 2009.

[2] A. Adams, J. Nicholas, and W. Siadak. Protocol Independent Multicast - Dense Mode (PIM-DM): Protocol Specification (Revised). URL: `http://www.ietf.org/rfc/rfc3973.txt`, January 2005. IETF RFC 3973. Online Resource. Last Accessed: March 31, 2012.

[3] S. Agarwal and J. R. Lorch. Matchmaking for Online Games and Other Latency-sensitive P2P Systems. *ACM SIGCOMM Computer Communication Review (CCR)*, 39(4):315–326, August 2009.

[4] S. Agarwal and J. R. Lorch. Matchmaking for Online Games and Other Latency-sensitive P2P Systems. In *Proceedings of ACM Conference on Applications, Technologies, Architectures, and Protocols for Computer Communication (SIGCOMM '09)*, pages 315–326, Barcelona, Spain, August 2009. ACM Press.

[5] V. Aggarwal, O. Akonjang, and A. Feldmann. Improving User and ISP Experience through ISP-aided P2P Locality. In *Proceedings of IEEE INFOCOM Workshops 2008*, pages 1–6, Phoenix, Arizona, USA, April 2008. IEEE Computer Society.

[6] V. Aggarwal, A. Feldmann, and C. Scheideler. Can ISPS and P2P Users Cooperate for Improved Performance? *ACM SIGCOMM Computer Communication Review (CCR)*, 37(3):29–40, July 2007.

[7] B. Ahlgren, J. Arkko, L. Eggert, and J. Rajahalme. A Node Identity Internetworking Architecture. In *Proceedings of 25th IEEE Interna-

tional Conference on Computer Communications (INFOCOM '06), pages 1–6, Barcelona, Spain, April 2006. IEEE Computer Society.

[8] The Ariba Underlay Abstraction. URL: `http://www.ariba-underlay.org`. Website. Last Accessed: March 31, 2012.

[9] The New York Times: Customers Angered as iPhones Overload AT&T. URL: `http://www.nytimes.com/2009/09/03/technology/companies/03att.html`. Website. Last Accessed: March 31, 2012.

[10] A. Balasubramanian, R. Mahajan, and A. Venkataramani. Augmenting mobile 3G using WiFi. In *Proceedings of 8th International Conference on Mobile Systems, Applications, and Services (MobiSys '10)*, pages 209–222, San Francisco, California, USA, June 2010. ACM Press.

[11] A. Ballardie. Core Based Trees (CBT version 2) Multicast Routing. URL: `http://www.ietf.org/rfc/rfc2189.txt`, September 1997. IETF RFC 2189. Online Resource. Last Accessed: March 31, 2012.

[12] S. Banerjee and B. Bhattacharjee. A Comparative Study of Application Layer Multicast Protocols. URL: `http://www.cs.ucsb.edu/~almeroth/classes/W10.290F/papers/compare.pdf`. Online Resource (Unplublished Work). Last Accessed: March 31, 2012.

[13] S. Banerjee and B. Bhattacharjee. Analysis of the NICE Application Layer Multicast Protocol. URL: `http://www.cs.umd.edu/users/suman/pubs/cs-tr-4380.pdf`, June 2002. Technical Report UMIACS TR 2002-60 and CS-TR 4380. Department of Computer Science, University of Maryland, College Park, Maryland, USA. Online Resource. Last Accessed: March 31, 2012.

[14] S. Banerjee, B. Bhattacharjee, and C. Kommareddy. Scalable Application Layer Multicast. In *Proceedings of ACM Conference on Applications, Technologies, Architectures, and Protocols for Computer Communications (SIGCOMM '02)*, pages 205–217, Pittsburgh, Pennsylvania, USA, August 2002. ACM Press.

[15] S. Banerjee, B. Bhattacharjee, and C. Kommareddy. Scalable Application Layer Multicast. URL: `http://www.cs.umd.edu/Library/TRs/CS-TR-4373/CS-TR-4373.ps.zip`, 2002. Technical Report UMIACS TR 2002-53 and CS-TR 4373. Department of Computer Science, University of Maryland, College Park, Maryland, USA. Online Resource. Last Accessed: March 31, 2012.

[16] S. Banerjee, B. Bhattacharjee, and C. Kommareddy. Scalable Application Layer Multicast. *ACM SIGCOMM Computer Communication Review (CCR)*, 32(4):205–217, August 2002.

[17] R. Bartelmess. Untersuchung der Infrastruktur-Verzögerungen in zellulären Netzen, January 2011. Student Work at Institute of Telematics, Karlsruhe Institute of Technology (KIT). Advisor: Christian Hübsch and Martina Zitterbart.

[18] I. Baumgart. *Verteilter Namensdienst für dezentrale IP-Telefonie*. PhD thesis, Karlsruhe Institute of Technology (KIT), Germany, February 2011.

[19] I. Baumgart, B. Heep, and S. Krause. OverSim: A Flexible Overlay Network Simulation Framework. In *Proceedings of 10th IEEE Global Internet Symposium (GI '07) in conjunction with IEEE INFOCOM*, pages 79–84, Anchorage, Alaska, USA, May 2007. IEEE Computer Society.

[20] P. Baumung. Application-Layer Multicast in MANETs: To Broadcast or not to Broadcast? In *Proceedings of 5th Annual Conference on Wireless on Demand Network Systems and Services (WONS '08)*, pages 133–140, Garmisch-Partenkirchen, Germany, January 2008.

[21] P. Baumung. *P2P-basierte Gruppenkommunikation in drahtlosen Ad-hoc-Netzen*. PhD thesis, Universität Karlsruhe (TH), Germany, September 2008.

[22] P. Baumung, M. Zitterbart, and K. Kutzner. Improving Delivery Ratios for Application Layer Multicast in Mobile Ad hoc Networks. *Computer Communications*, 28(14):1669–1679, September 2005.

[23] Berlin: Wowereit plant kostenloses WLAN. URL: http://www.netzwelt.de/news/90278-berlin-wowereit-plant-kostenloses-wlan.html. Website. Last Accessed: March 31, 2012.

[24] S. Birrer and F. E. Bustamante. Resilience in Overlay Multicast Protocols. In *Proceedings of 14th IEEE Symposium on Modeling, Analysis, and Simulation of Computer and Telecommunication Systems (MASCOTS '06)*, pages 363–372, Monterey, California, USA, September 2006. IEEE Computer Society.

[25] Bittorrent. URL: http://www.bittorrent.com/. Website. Last Accessed: March 31, 2012.

[26] R. Bless, C. Hübsch, S. Mies, and O. Waldhorst. The Underlay Abstraction in the Spontaneous Virtual Networks (SpoVNet) Architecture. In *Proceedings of 4th EuroNGI Conference on Next Generation Internet Networks (NGI '08)*, pages 115–122, Krakow, Poland, April 2008. IEEE Computer Society.

[27] R. Bless, C. Mayer, C. Hübsch, and O. Waldhorst. SpoVNet: An Architecture for Easy Creation and Deployment of Service Overlays. In *Future Internet Services and Service Architectures*, pages 23–47. River Publishers, June 2011.

[28] R. Bless, O. P. Waldhorst, C. P. Mayer, and H. Wippel. Decentralized and Autonomous Bootstrapping for IPv6-based Peer-to-Peer Networks. Winning Entry of the IPv6 Contest 2009 by IPv6 Council, May 2009.

[29] B. H. Bloom. Space/Time Trade-offs in Hash Coding with Allowable Errors. *Communications of the ACM*, 13(7):422–426, July 1970.

[30] A. Broder and M. Mitzenmacher. Network Applications of Bloom Filters: A Survey. *Internet Mathematics*, 1(4):485–509, January 2004.

[31] R. G. Brown. *Smoothing, Forecasting and Prediction of Discrete Time Series*. Prentice-Hall Quantitative Methods Series, Prentice-Hall International Series in Management. Prentice-Hall, Englewood Cliffs, New Jersey, 1963.

[32] D. Camps-Mur, X. Pérez-Costa, and S. Sallent-Ribes. Designing Energy efficient Access Points with Wi-Fi Direct. *ACM Computer Networks*, 55(13):2838–2855, September 2011.

[33] J. Cano-Garcia, E. Gonzalez-Parada, and E. Casilari. Experimental Analysis and Characterization of Packet Delay in UMTS Networks. In *Next Generation Teletraffic and Wired/Wireless Advanced Networking*, volume 4003 of *Lecture Notes in Computer Science*, pages 396–407. Springer Berlin/Heidelberg, May 2006.

[34] M. Castro, P. Druschel, A.-M. Kermarrec, A. Nandi, A. Rowstron, and A. Singh. SplitStream: High-Bandwidth Multicast in Cooperative Environments. *ACM SIGOPS Operating Systems Review*, 37(5):298–313, October 2003.

[35] M. Castro, P. Druschel, A.-M. Kermarrec, A. Nandi, A. Rowstron, and A. Singh. SplitStream: High-Bandwidth Multicast in Cooperative Environments. In *Proceedings of 19th ACM Symposium on Operating Systems*

Principles (SOSP '03), pages 298–313, Bolton Landing, New York, USA, 2003. ACM Press.

[36] M. Castro, P. Druschel, A.-M. Kermarrec, and A. Rowstron. Scribe: A Large-Scale and Decentralized Application-Level Multicast Infrastructure. *IEEE Journal on Selected Areas in Communications*, 20(8):1489–1499, October 2002.

[37] S. Cheshire and M. Krochmal. Multicast DNS. URL: `http://tools.ietf.org/id/draft-cheshire-dnsext-multicastdns-14.txt`, February 2011. Working Draft. Last Accessed: March 31, 2012.

[38] Y. Choi, H. Wook Ji, J.-Y. Park, H.-C. Kim, and J. Silvester. A 3W Network Strategy for Mobile Data Traffic Offloading. *IEEE Communications Magazine*, 49(10):118–123, October 2011.

[39] Chsim: Wireless Channel Simulator for OMNeT++. URL: `http://www.cs.uni-paderborn.de/index.php?id=chsim&L=1`. Website. Last Accessed: March 31, 2012.

[40] Y. Chu, S. Rao, and H. Zhang. A Case For End System Multicast. In *Proceedings of ACM International Conference on Measurement and Modeling of Computer Systems (SIGMETRICS '00)*, pages 1–12, Santa Clara, California, USA, June 2000. ACM Press.

[41] Cisco Systems. Cisco Visual Networking Index: Global Mobile Data Traffic Forecast Update, 2010-2015. URL: `http://www.cisco.com/go/vni`. Website. Last Accessed: August 31, 2011.

[42] D. D. Clark. Toward the Design of a Future Internet. URL: `http://groups.csail.mit.edu/ana/People/DDC/FutureInternet7-0.pdf`, 2009. Technical Report, Version 0.7. Massachusetts Institute of Technology (MIT). Online Resource. Last Accessed: March 31, 2012.

[43] I. Clarke, O. Sandberg, B. Wiley, and T. Hong. Freenet: A Distributed Anonymous Information Storage and Retrieval System. In *Designing Privacy Enhancing Technologies*, volume 2009 of *Lecture Notes in Computer Science*, pages 46–66. Springer Berlin/Heidelberg, 2001.

[44] E. G. Coffman, Jr., M. R. Garey, and D. S. Johnson. Approximation Algorithms for Bin Packing: A Survey. In *Approximation Algorithms for NP-hard Problems*, pages 46–93, Boston, Massachusetts, USA, 1997. PWS Publishing Co.

[45] K. Collins, S. Mangold, and G.-M. Muntean. Supporting Mobile Devices with Wireless LAN/MAN in Large Controlled Environments. *IEEE Communications Magazine*, 48(12):36–43, December 2010.

[46] The 10 Most Connected Cities in the World. URL: `http://www.focus.com/briefs/most-connected-cities/`. Website. Last Accessed: March 31, 2012.

[47] T. H. Cormen, C. E. Leiserson, and R. L. Rivest. *Introduction to Algorithms*. MIT Press. MIT Press, McGraw-Hill Book Company, 1993.

[48] F. Dabek, R. Cox, F. Kaashoek, and R. Morris. Vivaldi: A Decentralized Network Coordinate System. *ACM SIGCOMM Computer Communication Review (CCR)*, 34(4):15–26, August 2004.

[49] F. Dabek, R. Cox, F. Kaashoek, and R. Morris. Vivaldi: A Decentralized Network Coordinate System. In *Proceedings of the ACM Conference on Applications, Technologies, Architectures, and Protocols for Computer Communications (SIGCOMM '04)*, pages 15–26, Portland, Oregon, USA, August 2004. ACM Press.

[50] F. Dabek, B. Zhao, P. Druschel, J. Kubiatowicz, and I. Stoica. Towards a Common API for Structured Peer-to-Peer Overlays. In *Peer-to-Peer Systems II*, volume 2735 of *Lecture Notes in Computer Science*, pages 33–44. Springer Berlin/Heidelberg, 2003.

[51] G. Dan, T. Hossfeld, S. Oechsner, P. Cholda, R. Stankiewicz, I. Papafili, and G. Stamoulis. Interaction Patterns between P2P Content Distribution Systems and ISPs. *IEEE Communications Magazine*, 49(5):222–230, May 2011.

[52] S. Deering and R. Hinden. Internet Protocol, Version 6 (IPv6) Specification. URL: `http://www.ietf.org/rfc/rfc2460.txt`, December 1998. IETF RFC 2460. Online Resource. Last Accessed: March 31, 2012.

[53] S. E. Deering. Host Extensions for IP Multicasting. URL: `http://www.ietf.org/rfc/rfc988.txt`, July 1986. IETF RFC 988. Online Resource. Last Accessed: March 31, 2012.

[54] S. E. Deering. Host Extensions for IP Multicasting. URL: `http://www.ietf.org/rfc/rfc1054.txt`, May 1988. IETF RFC 1054. Online Resource. Last Accessed: March 31, 2012.

[55] S. E. Deering. Host Extensions for IP Multicasting. URL: `http://www.ietf.org/rfc/rfc1112.txt`, August 1989. IETF RFC 1112. Online Resource. Last Accessed: March 31, 2012.

[56] S. E. Deering and D. R. Cheriton. Host Groups: A Multicast Extension to the Internet Protocol. URL: http://www.ietf.org/rfc/rfc966.txt, December 1985. IETF RFC 966. Online Resource. Last Accessed: March 31, 2012.

[57] S. E. Deering and D. R. Cheriton. Multicast Routing in Datagram Internetworks and Extended LANs. *ACM Transactions on Computer Systems,* 8(2):85–110, May 1990.

[58] J. Dinger and O. Waldhorst. Decentralized Bootstrapping of P2P Systems: A Practical View. In *Proceedings of IFIP International Conference on Networking,* volume 5550 of *Lecture Notes in Computer Science,* pages 703–715, Aachen, Germany, May 2009. Springer Berlin/Heidelberg.

[59] C. Diot, W. Dabbous, and J. Crowcroft. Multipoint Communication: A Survey of Protocols, Functions, and Mechanisms. *IEEE Journal on Selected Areas in Communications,* 15(3):277–290, April 1997.

[60] C. Diot, B. Levine, B. Lyles, H. Kassem, and D. Balensiefen. Deployment Issues for the IP Multicast Service and Architecture. *IEEE Network,* 14(1):78–88, February 2000.

[61] T. Do, K. Hua, N. Jiang, and F. Liu. PatchPeer: A Scalable Video-on-Demand Streaming System in Hybrid Wireless Mobile Peer-to-Peer Networks. *Peer-to-Peer Networking and Applications,* 2(3):182–201, 2009.

[62] Doxygen. URL: http://http://www.stack.nl/~dimitri/doxygen/. Website. Last Accessed: March 31, 2012.

[63] K. Egevang and P. Francis. The IP Network Address Translator (NAT). URL: http://www.ietf.org/rfc/rfc1631.txt, May 1994. IETF RFC 1631. Online Resource. Last Accessed: March 31, 2012.

[64] A. El-Sayed, V. Roca, and L. Mathy. A Survey of Proposals for an Alternative Group Communication Service. *IEEE Network,* 17(1):46–51, February 2003.

[65] eMule-Project.net - Official eMule Homepage. URL: http://www.emule-project.net. Website. Last Accessed: March 31, 2012.

[66] D. Estrin, D. Farinacci, A. Helmy, D. Thaler, S. Deering, M. Handley, V. Jacobson, C. Liu, P. Sharma, and L. Wei. Protocol Independent Multicast-Sparse Mode (PIM-SM): Protocol Specification. URL: http://www.ietf.org/rfc/rfc2117.txt, June 1997. IETF RFC 2117. Online Resource. Last Accessed: March 31, 2012.

[67] J. Fan and M. H. Ammar. Dynamic Topology Configuration in Service Overlay Networks: A Study of Reconfiguration Policies. In *Proceedings of 25th IEEE International Conference on Computer Communications (IN-FOCOM '06)*, pages 1–12, Barcelona, Spain, April 2006. IEEE Computer Society.

[68] L. Fan, P. Cao, J. Almeida, and A. Z. Broder. Summary Cache: A Scalable Wide-Area Web Cache Sharing Protocol. *IEEE/ACM Transactions on Networking (TON)*, 8(3):281–293, June 2000.

[69] L. Feeney and M. Nilsson. Investigating the Energy Consumption of a Wireless Network Interface in an Ad hoc Networking Environment. In *Proceedings of 20th IEEE International Conference on Computer Communications (INFOCOM '01)*, volume 3, pages 1548–1557, Anchorage, Alaska, USA, April 2001. IEEE Computer Society.

[70] R. Finlayson. IEEE 802.11 Standard Specifications. URL: `http://www.ieee802.org/11/`, 1999. Website. Accessed: March 31, 2012.

[71] R. Finlayson. The UDP Multicast Tunneling Protocol. URL: `http://tools.ietf.org/html/draft-finlayson-umtp-07.txt`, September 2002. IETF Draft. Online Resource. Last Accessed: March 31, 2012.

[72] S. Floyd, V. Jacobson, S. McCanne, C.-G. Liu, and L. Zhang. A Reliable Multicast Framework for Light-Weight Sessions and Application Level Framing. *ACM SIGCOMM Computer Communication Review (CCR)*, 25(4):342–356, October 1995.

[73] S. Floyd, V. Jacobson, S. McCanne, C.-G. Liu, and L. Zhang. A Reliable Multicast Framework for Light-Weight Sessions and Application Level Framing. In *Proceedings of ACM Conference on Applications, Technologies, Architectures, and Protocols for Computer Communication (SIGCOMM '95)*, pages 342–356, Cambridge, Massachusetts, United States, August 1995. ACM Press.

[74] Fon - A World of Free WiFi. URL: `http://corp.fon.com/en`. Website. Last Accessed: March 31, 2012.

[75] B. Ford. *UIA: A Global Connectivity Architecture for Mobile Personal Devices*. PhD thesis, Massachusetts Institute of Technology (MIT), September 2008.

[76] FreePastry. URL: `http://www.freepastry.org`. Website. Last Accessed: March 31, 2012.

[77] Freifunk - freie Netzwerke, freies WLAN, freie Funknetze im deutschsprachigen Raum. URL: `http://www.freifunk.net`. Website. Last Accessed: March 31, 2012.

[78] Gnutella Protocol Specification, Version 0.4. URL: `http://www.content-networking.com/papers/gnutella-protocol-04.pdf`. Online Resource. Last Accessed: March 31, 2012.

[79] Gnutella - Filesharing and Distributed Network. URL: `http://rfc-gnutella.sourceforge.net/`. Website. Last Accessed: March 31, 2012.

[80] L. Gong. JXTA: A Network Programming Environment. *IEEE Internet Computing*, 5(3):88–95, June 2001.

[81] D. A. Gratton. *Bluetooth Profiles: the Definitive Guide*. Prentice Hall Professional, 2003.

[82] S. Grau, M. Fischer, M. Brinkmeier, and G. Schäfer. On Complexity and Approximability of Optimal DoS Attacks on Multiple-Tree P2P Streaming Topologies. *IEEE Transactions on Dependable and Secure Computing*, 8(2):270–281, March 2011.

[83] C. Gui and P. Mohapatra. Efficient Overlay Multicast for Mobile Ad hoc Networks. In *IEEE Wireless Communications and Networking (WCNC '03)*, volume 2, pages 1118–1123, March 2003.

[84] K. Gummadi, R. Gummadi, S. Gribble, S. Ratnasamy, S. Shenker, and I. Stoica. The Impact of DHT Routing Geometry on Resilience and Proximity. In *Proceedings of ACM Conference on Applications, Technologies, Architectures, and Protocols for Computer Communications (SIGCOMM '03)*, pages 381–394, Karlsruhe, Germany, August 2003. ACM Press.

[85] D. Guo, J. Wu, H. Chen, Y. Yuan, and X. Luo. The Dynamic Bloom Filters. *IEEE Transactions on Knowledge and Data Engineering*, 22(1):120–133, January 2010.

[86] D. Haage and R. Holz. Optimization of Distributed Services with UNISONO (Extended Abstract). In *GI/ITG KuVS Fachgespräch NGN Service Delivery Platforms & Service Overlay Networks*, Berlin, Germany, November 2009.

[87] D. Haage and R. Holz. Towards Measurement Consolidation for Overlay Optimization and Service Placement. *Praxis der Informationsverarbeitung und Kommunikation (PIK)*, 33(1):12–15, April 2010.

[88] D. Haage, R. Holz, H. Niedermayer, and P. Laskov. A Cross-Layer Information Service for Overlay Network Optimization. In *Proceedings of GI/ITG Fachtagung Kommunikation in Verteilten Systemen (KiVS '09)*, pages 279–284, Kassel, Germany, March 2009. Springer Berlin/Heidelberg.

[89] D. Haage, R. Holz, H. Niedermayer, and P. Laskov. SpoVNet Bericht TP2 – AP 2.1: Anforderungsanalyse. SpoVNet Project Report, Universität Tübingen, 2009.

[90] D. Haage, R. Holz, H. Niedermayer, and P. Laskov. SpoVNet Bericht TP2 – AP 2.2 - 2.4: Spezifikation Rahmenarchitektur, Schnittstellenbeschreibung und Overlay-Organisation. SpoVNet Project Report, Universität Tübingen, 2009.

[91] D. Haage, R. Holz, H. Niedermayer, and P. Laskov. SpoVNet Bericht TP2 – AP 3.1 und 3.2: Messverfahren im Underlay und Overlay. SpoVNet Project Report, Universität Tübingen, 2009.

[92] D. Haage, R. Holz, H. Niedermayer, and P. Laskov. SpoVNet Bericht TP2 – AP 3.3: Korrelation zwischen Underlay und Overlay-Messungen. SpoVNet Project Report, Universität Tübingen, 2009.

[93] D. Haage, R. Holz, H. Niedermayer, and P. Laskov. SpoVNet Bericht TP2 – Sicherheitsmechanismen in CLIO/UNISONO. SpoVNet Project Report, Universität Tübingen, 2009.

[94] B. Han, P. Hui, V. A. Kumar, M. V. Marathe, G. Pei, and A. Srinivasan. Cellular Traffic Offloading through Opportunistic Communications: A Case Study. In *Proceedings of 5th ACM Workshop on Challenged Networks (CHANTS '10)*, pages 31–38, Chicago, Illinois, USA, September 2010. ACM Press.

[95] H. Hanano, Y. Murata, N. Shibata, K. Yasumoto, and M. Ito. Video Ads Dissemination through WiFi-Cellular Hybrid Networks. In *Proceedings of IEEE International Conference on Pervasive Computing and Communications (PerCom '09)*, pages 1–6, Galveston, Texas, USA, March 2009. IEEE Computer Society.

[96] A. Handa. Mobile Data Offload for 3G Networks. URL: `http://www.docstoc.com/docs/22754490/Mobile-Data-Offload-for-3G-Networks`, October 2009. Whitepaper. Online Resource. Last Accessed: March 31, 2012.

[97] M. Hosseini, D. T. Ahmed, S. Shirmohammadi, and N. D. Georganas. A Survey of Application-Layer Multicast Protocols. *IEEE Communications Surveys & Tutorials*, 9(3):58–74, July 2007.

[98] Y. hua Chu, S. G. Rao, S. Seshan, and H. Zhang. A Case for End System Multicast. *IEEE Journal on Selected Areas in Communications*, 20(8):1456–1471, October 2002.

[99] C. Hübsch. Considering Network Heterogeneity in Global Application Layer Multicast Provision. In *Proceedings of 8th Workshop on IP: Joint EuroNF, ITC, and ITG Workshop on Visions of Future Generation Networks (EuroView '08)*, Würzburg, Germany, July 2008.

[100] C. Hübsch. Considering Capacities in Application-Layer Multicast over Shared Access Networks. In *Proceedings of 8th Workshop on IP: Joint EuroNF, ITC, and ITG Workshop on Visions of Future Generation Networks (EuroView '10)*, Würzburg, Germany, July 2010.

[101] C. Hübsch, C. Mayer, S. Mies, R. Bless, O. Waldhorst, and M. Zitterbart. Reconnecting the Internet with ariba: Self-Organizing Provisioning of End-to-End Connectivity in Heterogeneous Networks. In *Proceedings of ACM Conference on Applications, Technologies, Architectures, and Protocols for Computer Communications (SIGCOMM '09)*, pages 131–132, Barcelona, Spain, August 2009. ACM Press.

[102] C. Hübsch, C. Mayer, S. Mies, R. Bless, O. Waldhorst, and M. Zitterbart. Reconnecting the Internet with ariba - Self-Organizing Provisioning of End-to-End Connectivity in Heterogeneous Networks. *ACM SIGCOMM Computer Communication Review (CCR)*, 40(1):131–132, January 2010.

[103] C. Hübsch, C. Mayer, S. Mies, R. Bless, O. Waldhorst, and M. Zitterbart. Using Legacy Applications in Future Heterogeneous Networks with ariba. In *Proceedings of IEEE International Conference on Computer Communications (INFOCOM '10)*, San Diego, California, USA, March 2010. IEEE Computer Society.

[104] C. Hübsch, C. Mayer, S. Mies, R. Bless, O. Waldhorst, and M. Zitterbart. ariba: Rahmenwerk für Overlay-basierte Dienste. In *Proceedings of Kommunikation in Verteilten Systemen 2011 (KiVS '11)*, Kiel, Germany, March 2011.

[105] C. Hübsch, C. Mayer, and O. Waldhorst. The Ariba Framework for Application Development using Service Overlays. *Praxis der Informationsverarbeitung und Kommunikation (PIK)*, 33(1):7–11, March 2010.

[106] C. Hübsch, C. Mayer, and O. Waldhorst. User-Perceived Performance of the NICE Application Layer Multicast Protocol in Large and Highly Dynamic Groups. In *Measurement, Modelling, and Evaluation of Computing Systems (MMB) and Dependability and Fault Tolerance*, volume 5987 of *Lecture Notes in Computer Science*, pages 62–77. Springer, Berlin/Heidelberg, 2010.

[107] C. Hübsch and O. Waldhorst. Enhancing Application-Layer Multicast Solutions by Wireless Underlay Support. In *Kommunikation in Verteilten Systemen (KiVS '09)*, pages 267–272, Kassel, Germany, March 2009.

[108] C. Hübsch and O. Waldhorst. On Shared Medium Capacity Awareness in Heterogeneous Application-Layer Multicast. In *Proceedings of 1st IEEE Workshop on Pervasive Group Communication (PerGroup '10) in conjunction with IEEE GLOBECOM*, pages 1503–1507, Miami, Florida, USA, December 2010. IEEE Computer Society.

[109] C. Hübsch and O. Waldhorst. Flexible Tree-based Application-Layer Multicast. In *Proceedings of 17th IEEE International Conference on Networks (ICON '11)*, pages 159–164, Singapore, December 2011.

[110] C. Hübsch and O. P. Waldhorst. Alleviating Network Load in Dense Urban Multi-access Application-Layer Multicast. In *Joint Workshop on Complex Networks and Pervasive Group Communication (PerGroup '11) in conjunction with IEEE GLOBECOM*, pages 105–109, Secember 2011.

[111] U. o. S. C. Information Sciences Institute. Internet Protocol. URL: http://www.ietf.org/rfc/rfc791.txt, September 1981. IETF RFC 791. Online Resource. Last Accessed: March 31, 2012.

[112] R. Iqbal, D. T. Ahmed, and S. Shirmohammadi. Distributed Video Adaptation and Streaming for Heterogeneous Devices. In *Proceedings of 6th IEEE International Conference on Pervasive Computing and Communications (PerCom '08)*, pages 492–497, Hongkong, China, March 2008. IEEE Computer Society.

[113] R. Iqbal and S. Shirmohammadi. A Cooperative Video Adaptation and Streaming Scheme for Mobile and Heterogeneous Devices in a Community Network. In *Proceedings of IEEE International Conference on Multimedia and Expo (ICME '09)*, pages 1768–1771, Piscataway, New Jersey, USA, July 2009. IEEE Computer Society.

[114] J. Jannotti, D. K. Gifford, K. L. Johnson, M. F. Kaashoek, and J. W. O'Toole, Jr. Overcast: Reliable Multicasting with an Overlay Network.

In *Proceedings of 4th Symposium on Operating Systems Design and Implementation (OSDI '00)*, pages 14–14, San Diego, California, USA, October 2000. USENIX Association.

[115] M. Jelasity and O. Babaoglu. T-Man: Gossip-based Overlay Topology Management. In *Proceedings of 4th International Workshop on Engineering Self-Organizing Applications (ESOA '06)*, volume 3910, pages 1–15, Hakodate, Japan, May 2006. Springer.

[116] M. Jelasity, A. Montresor, and O. Babaoglu. Gossip-based Aggregation in Large Dynamic Networks. *ACM Transactions on Computer Systems*, 23(3):219–252, August 2005.

[117] M. Jelasity, A. Montresor, and O. Babaoglu. T-Man: Gossip-based Fast Overlay Topology Construction. *ACM Computer Networks*, 53(13):2321–2339, August 2009.

[118] S. Jin, Y. Zhuang, L. Liu, and J. Wu. An Efficient Overlay Multicast Routing Algorithm for Real-Time Multimedia Applications. In *Advances in Data and Web Management*, volume 4505 of *Lecture Notes in Computer Science*, pages 829–836. Springer Berlin/Heidelberg, 2007.

[119] JiWire Mobile Audience Insights Report Q4 2011. URL: http://www.jiwire.com/sites/default/files/JiWire_MobileAudienceInsightsReport_Q42011_2.pdf. Online Resource. Last Accessed: March 31, 2012.

[120] K. Jones and L. Liu. What Where Wi: An Analysis of Millions of Wi-Fi Access Points. In *Proceedings of IEEE International Conference on Portable Information Devices (PORTABLE '07)*, pages 1–4, Orlando, Florida, USA, March 2007.

[121] Joost. URL: http://www.joost.com. Website. Last Accessed: March 31, 2012.

[122] M. Jurvansuu, J. Prokkola, M. Hanski, and P. Perala. HSDPA Performance in Live Networks. In *Proceedings of IEEE International Conference on Communications (ICC '07)*, pages 467–471, Glasgow, Scotland, June 2007. IEEE Computer Society.

[123] R. M. Karp. Reducibility Among Combinatorial Problems. In *50 Years of Integer Programming 1958-2008*, pages 219–241. Springer Berlin/Heidelberg, 2010.

[124] KaZaA. URL: http://www.kazaa.com. Website. Last Accessed: March 31, 2012.

[125] M. Kim, Y. Li, and S. Lam. Eliminating Bottlenecks in Overlay Multicast. In *NETWORKING 2005. Networking Technologies, Services, and Protocols; Performance of Computer and Communication Networks; Mobile and Wireless Communications Systems*, volume 3462 of *Lecture Notes in Computer Science*, pages 3–27. Springer Berlin/Heidelberg, 2005.

[126] G. G. Koch, M. A. Tariq, B. Koldehofe, and K. Rothermel. Event Processing for Large-Scale Distributed Games. In *Proceedings of 4th ACM International Conference on Distributed Event-Based Systems (DEBS '10)*, pages 103–104, Cambridge, United Kingdom, July 2010. ACM Press.

[127] A. Köpke, M. Swigulski, K. Wessel, D. Willkomm, P. T. K. Haneveld, T. E. V. Parker, O. W. Visser, H. S. Lichte, and S. Valentin. Simulating Wireless and Mobile Networks in OMNeT++: The MiXiM Vision. In *Proceedings of 1st International Conference on Simulation Tools and Techniques for Communications, Networks and Systems (SIMUTools '08)*, pages 1–8, Marseille, France, March 2008. ICST (Institute for Computer Sciences, Social-Informatics and Telecommunications Engineering).

[128] D. Kostić, A. Rodriguez, J. Albrecht, A. Bhirud, and A. Vahdat. Using Random Subsets to Build Scalable Network Services. In *Proceedings of 4th USENIX Symposium on Internet Technologies and Systems (USITS '03)*, pages 19–19, Seattle, Washington, USA, March 2003. USENIX Association.

[129] D. Kostić, A. Rodriguez, J. Albrecht, and A. Vahdat. Bullet: High Bandwidth Data Dissemination Using an Overlay Mesh. In *Proceedings of 19th ACM Symposium on Operating Systems Principles (SOSP '03)*, pages 282–297, Bolton Landing, New York, USA, 2003. ACM Press.

[130] D. Kostić, A. Rodriguez, J. Albrecht, and A. Vahdat. Bullet: High Bandwidth Data Dissemination Using an Overlay Mesh. *SIGOPS Operating Systems Review*, 37(5):282–297, October 2003.

[131] S. Kristiansen, M. Lindeberg, D. Rodriguez-Fernandez, and T. Plagemann. On the Forwarding Capability of Mobile Handhelds for Video Streaming Over MANETs. In *Proceedings of 2nd ACM SIGCOMM Workshop on Networking, Systems, and Applications on Mobile Handhelds (MobiHeld '10)*, pages 33–38, New Delhi, India, August 2010. ACM Press.

[132] S. Kristiansen, T. Plagemann, and V. Goebel. Towards Scalable and Realistic Node Models for Network Simulators. *ACM SIGCOMM Computer Communication Review (CCR)*, 41(4):418–419, August 2011.

[133] S. Kristiansen, T. Plagemann, and V. Goebel. Towards Scalable and Real-istic Node Models for Network Simulators. In *Proceedings of ACM Conference on Applications, Technologies, Architectures, and Protocols for Computer Communications (SIGCOMM '11)*, pages 418–419, Toronto, Ontario, Canada, August 2011. ACM Press.

[134] K. Lee, I. Rhee, J. Lee, Y. Yi, and S. Chong. Mobile Data Offloading: How Much Can WiFi Deliver? In *Proceedings of ACM Conference on Applications, Technologies, Architectures, and Protocols for Computer Communication (SIGCOMM '10)*, pages 425–426, New Delhi, India, August 2010. ACM Press.

[135] K. Lee, I. Rhee, J. Lee, Y. Yi, and S. Chong. Mobile Data Offloading: How Much Can WiFi Deliver? *ACM SIGCOMM Computer Communications Review (CCR)*, 40(4):425–426, August 2010.

[136] J. Li, J. Stribling, R. Morris, and F. M. Kaashoek. Bandwidth-efficient Management of DHT Routing Tables. In *Proceedings of 2nd Symposium on Networked Systems Design and Implementation (NSDI '05)*, volume 2, pages 99–114, Boston, Massachusetts, May 2005. USENIX Association.

[137] J. Li, J. Stribling, R. Morris, F. M. Kaashoek, and T. M. Gil. A Performance vs. Cost Framework for Evaluating DHT Design Tradeoffs under Churn. In *Proceedings of 24th IEEE International Conference on Computer Communications (INFOCOM '05)*, volume 1, pages 225–236, Miami, Florida, USA, August 2005. IEEE Computer Society.

[138] J. Liang and K. Nahrstedt. RandPeer: Membership Management for QoS Sensitive Peer-to-Peer Applications. In *Proceedings of 25th IEEE International Conference on Computer Communications (INFOCOM '06)*, pages 1–10, Barcelona, Spain, April 2006. IEEE Computer Society.

[139] J. Liebeherr and T. K. Beam. HyperCast: A Protocol for Maintaining Multicast Group Members in a Logical Hypercube Topology. In *Proceedings of 1st International Workshop on Networked Group Communication (NGC' 99)*, pages 72–89, Pisa, Italy, November 1999. Springer Berlin/Heidelberg.

[140] J. Liebeherr, J. Wang, and G. Zhang. Programming Overlay Networks with Overlay Sockets. In *Group Communications and Charges. Technology and Business Models*, volume 2816 of *Lecture Notes in Computer Science*, pages 242–253. Springer Berlin/Heidelberg, 2003.

[141] J. Lin. Multiple-Objective Problems: Pareto-optimal Solutions by Method of Proper Equality Constraints. *IEEE Transactions on Automatic Control*, 21(5):641–650, October 1976.

[142] J. Lin and S. Paul. RMTP: A Reliable Multicast Transport Protocol. In *Proceedings of 5th IEEE International Conference on Computer Communications (INFOCOM '96)*, volume 3, pages 1414 –1424 vol.3, San Francisco, California, USA, March 1996. IEEE Computer Society.

[143] Y. Liu, Y. Guo, and C. Liang. A Survey on Peer-to-Peer Video Streaming Systems. *Peer-to-Peer Networking and Applications*, 1(1):18–28, 2008.

[144] Y. Liu, X. Liu, L. Xiao, L. Ni, and X. Zhang. Location-Aware Topology Matching in P2P Systems. In *Proceedings of 23rd IEEE International Conference on Computer Communications (INFOCOM '04)*, volume 4, pages 2220–2230, Hongkong, China, March 2004. IEEE Computer Society.

[145] Y. Liu, Z. Zhuang, L. Xiao, and L. Ni. AOTO: Adaptive Overlay Topology Optimization in Unstructured P2P Systems. In *Proccedings of IEEE Global Telecommunications Conference (GLOBECOM '03)*, volume 7, pages 4186–4190, San Francisco, California, USA, December 2003. IEEE Computer Society.

[146] Bittorrent Live. URL: `http://live.bittorrent.com/`. Website. Last Accessed: March 31, 2012.

[147] Vision: London wird weltgrößter WLAN-Hotspot. URL: `http://www.netzwelt.de/news/82781-vision-london-weltgroesster-wlan-hotspot.html`. Website. Last Accessed: March 31, 2012.

[148] M. O. Lorenz. *Methods of Measuring the Concentration of Wealth*, volume 9, pages 209–219. Publications of the American Statistical Association, June 1905.

[149] The Positif and MAC framework for OMNeT++. URL: `http://www.consensus.tudelft.nl/software.html`. Website. Last Accessed: March 31, 2012.

[150] Y. Mao, B. T. Loo, Z. Ives, and J. M. Smith. MOSAIC: Unified Declarative Platform for Dynamic Overlay Composition. In *Proceedings of ACM International Conference On Emerging Networking Experiments And Technologies (CoNEXT '08)*, pages 883–895, Madrid, Spain, December 2008. ACM Press.

[151] B. Mathieu, M. Song, A. Galis, L. Cheng, K. Jean, R. Ocampo, M. Brunner, M. Stiemerling, and M. Cassini. Self-Management of Context-Aware Overlay Ambient Networks. In *Proceedings of 10th IFIP/IEEE International Symposium on Integrated Network Management (IM '07)*, pages 749–752, Munich, Germany, May 2007. IEEE Computer Society.

[152] C. P. Mayer. *Hybrid Routing in Delay Tolerant Networks*. PhD thesis, Karlsruhe Institute of Technology (KIT), Karlsruhe, Germany, January 2012.

[153] P. Maymounkov and D. Mazieres. Kademlia: A Peer-to-Peer Information System Based on the XOR Metric. In *Peer-to-Peer Systems*, volume 2429 of *Lecture Notes in Computer Science*, pages 53–65. Springer Berlin/Heidelberg, 2002.

[154] S. Mies and O. Waldhorst. Autonomous Detection of Connectivity. In *Proceedings of IEEE International Conference on Peer-to-Peer Computing (P2P '11)*, pages 44–53, Kyoto, Japan, September 2011. IEEE Computer Society.

[155] S. Mies, O. Waldhorst, and H. Wippel. Towards End-to-End Connectivity for Overlays Across Heterogeneous Networks. In *Proceedings of IEEE International Conference on Communications Workshops (ICC '09)*, pages 1–6, Dresden, Germany, June 2009. IEEE Computer Society.

[156] S. Mies and H. Wippel. Providing End-to-End Connectivity Across Heterogeneous Networks. In *Proceedings of 8th Workshop on IP: Joint EuroNF, ITC, and ITG Workshop on Visions of Future Generation Networks (EuroView '08)*, Würzburg, Germany, July 2008.

[157] C. K. Miller. *Multicast Networking and Applications*. Addison Wesley, Reading, Massachusetts, USA, 1999.

[158] Mobility Framework for OMNeT++. URL: `http://mobility-fw.sourceforge.net/`. Website. Last Accessed: March 31, 2012.

[159] R. Moskowitz, P. Nikander, and P. Jokela. Host Identity Protocol. URL: `http://www.ietf.org/rfc/rfc5201.txt`, April 2008. IETF RFC 5201. Online Resource. Last Accessed: March 31, 2012.

[160] J. Moy. Multicast Extensions to OSPF. URL: `http://www.ietf.org/rfc/rfc1584.txt`, March 1994. IETF RFC 1584. Online Resource. Last Accessed: March 31, 2012.

[161] Napster. URL: `http://www.napster.com`. Website. Last Accessed: March 31, 2012.

[162] T. S. E. Ng and H. Zhang. Predicting Internet Network Distance with Coordinates-Based Approaches. In *Proceedings of 21st Annual Joint Conference of the IEEE Computer and Communications Societies (INFOCOM '02)*, pages 170–179, New York City, New York, USA, June 2002. IEEE Computer Society.

[163] Nobbies Mobilfunkseiten. URL: http://www.nobbi.com. Website. Last Accessed: March 31, 2012.

[164] J.-R. Ohm. Advances in Scalable Video Coding. *Proceedings of the IEEE*, 93(1):42–56, January 2005.

[165] Z. Ouyang, L. Xu, and B. Ramamurthy. Diverse Community: Demand Differentiation in P2P Live Streaming. *Peer-to-Peer Networking and Applications*, 4(1):23–36, 2011.

[166] O. Papaemmanouil, Y. Ahmad, U. Çetintemel, J. Jannotti, and Y. Yildirim. Extensible Optimization in Overlay Dissemination Trees. In *Proceedings of the ACM International Conference on Management of Data (SIGMOD '06)*, pages 611–622, Chicago, Illinois, USA, June 2006. ACM Press.

[167] P. Parnes, K. Synnes, and D. Schefström. Lightweight Application Level Multicast Tunnelling using mTunnel. *Computer Communications*, 21(15):1295–1301, October 1998.

[168] A. Passarella, F. Delmastro, and M. Conti. XScribe: A Stateless, Cross-layer Approach to P2P Multicast in Multi-hop Ad hoc Networks. In *Proceedings of 1st International Workshop on Decentralized Resource Sharing in Mobile Computing and Networkingn (MobiShare '06), in conjunction with ACM Mobicom '06*, pages 6–11, Los Angeles, California, USA, September 2006. ACM Press.

[169] C. Perkins. IP Encapsulation within IP. URL: http://www.ietf.org/rfc/rfc2003.txt, October 1996. IETF RFC 2003. Online Resource. Last Accessed: March 31, 2012.

[170] L. L. Peterson and B. S. Davie. *Computer Networks - A Systems Approach*. Morgan Kaufmann Publishers Inc., San Francisco, California, USA, 2003.

[171] PlaceEngine. URL: http://www.placeengine.com/en. Website. Last Accessed: March 31, 2012.

[172] I. Poese, B. Frank, B. Ager, G. Smaragdakis, and A. Feldmann. Improving Content Delivery Using Provider-Aided Distance Information. In *Proceedings of 10th Annual Conference on Internet Measurement (IMC '10)*, pages 22–34, Melbourne, Australia, November 2010. ACM Press.

[173] PPLive.com. URL: http://www.pplive.com. Website. Last Accessed: March 31, 2012.

[174] PPS.tv. URL: http://www.pps.tv. Website. Last Accessed: March 31, 2012.

[175] J. Prokkola, M. Hanski, M. Jurvansuu, and M. Immonen. Measuring WCDMA and HSDPA Delay Characteristics with QoSMeT. In *Proceedings of IEEE International Conference on Communications (ICC '07)*, pages 492–498, Glasgow, Scotland, June 2007. IEEE Computer Society.

[176] H. Prömel and A. Steger. *The Steiner Tree Problem. A Tour Through Graphs, Algorithms and Complexity*. Vieweg Verlag, Wiesbaden, Germany, 2002.

[177] T. Qiu, G. Chen, M. Ye, E. Chan, and B. Zhao. Towards Location-aware Topology in both Unstructured and Structured P2P Systems. In *Proceedings of IEEE International Conference on Parallel Processing (ICPP '07)*, page 30, Xi'an, China, September 2007. IEEE Computer Society.

[178] T. Qiu, F. Wu, and G. Chen. A Generic Approach to Make Structured Peer-to-Peer Systems Topology-Aware. In *Parallel and Distributed Processing and Applications*, volume 3758 of *Lecture Notes in Computer Science*, pages 816–826. Springer Berlin/Heidelberg, 2005.

[179] M. Ramalho. Intra- and Inter-domain Multicast Routing Protocols: A Survey and Taxonomy. *IEEE Communications Surveys & Tutorials*, 3(1):2–25, First Quarter 2000.

[180] S. Ratnasamy, P. Francis, M. Handley, R. Karp, and S. Shenker. A Scalable Content-addressable Network. *ACM SIGCOMM Computer Communication Review (CCR)*, 31(4):161–172, August 2001.

[181] S. Ratnasamy, P. Francis, M. Handley, R. Karp, and S. Shenker. A Scalable Content-addressable Network. In *Proceedings of ACM Conference on Applications, Technologies, Architectures, and Protocols for Computer Communications (SIGCOMM '01)*, pages 161–172, San Diego, California, USA, August 2001. ACM Press.

[182] S. Ratnasamy, M. Handley, R. Karp, and S. Shenker. Topologically-aware Overlay Construction and Server Selection. In *Proceedings of 21st*

Annual Joint Conference of the IEEE Computer and Communications Societies (INFOCOM '02), volume 3, pages 1190–1199, New York, New York, USA, June 2002. IEEE Computer Society.

[183] S. Ratnasamy, M. Handley, R. M. Karp, and S. Shenker. Application-Level Multicast Using Content-Addressable Networks. In *Proceedings of 3rd International COST264 Workshop on Networked Group Communication (NGC '01)*, pages 14–29, London, United Kingdom, November 2001. Springer London.

[184] S. Ren, L. Guo, S. Jiang, and X. Zhang. SAT-Match: A Self-adaptive Topology Matching Method to Achieve Low Lookup Latency in Structured P2P Overlay Networks. In *Proceedings of 18th International Parallel and Distributed Processing Symposium (IPDPS '04)*, page 83, Santa Fe, New Mexico, USA, April 2004. IEEE Computer Society.

[185] S. Rhea, D. Geels, T. Roscoe, and J. Kubiatowicz. Handling Churn in a DHT. In *Proceedings of the USENIX*, pages 1–14, Boston, Massachusetts, USA, June 2004. USENIX Association.

[186] S. Rhea, B. Godfrey, B. Karp, J. Kubiatowicz, S. Ratnasamy, S. Shenker, I. Stoica, and H. Yu. OpenDHT: A Public DHT Service and Its Uses. *ACM SIGCOMM Computer Communication Review (CCR)*, 35(4):73–84, August 2005.

[187] S. Rhea, B. Godfrey, B. Karp, J. Kubiatowicz, S. Ratnasamy, S. Shenker, I. Stoica, and H. Yu. OpenDHT: A Public DHT Service and Its Uses. In *Proceedings of ACM Conference on Applications, Technologies, Architectures, and Protocols for Computer Communications (SIGCOMM '05)*, pages 73–84, Philadelphia, Pennsylvania, USA, August 2005. ACM Press.

[188] I. Rhee, N. Balaguru, and G. N. Rouskas. MTCP: Scalable TCP-like Congestion Control for Reliable Multicast. *Computer Networks*, 38(5):553–575, April 2002.

[189] L. Rizzo. Pgmcc: A TCP-friendly Single-rate Multicast Congestion Control Scheme. In *Proceedings of ACM Conference on Applications, Technologies, Architectures, and Protocols for Computer Communications (SIGCOMM '00)*, pages 17–28, Stockholm, Sweden, August 2000. ACM Press.

[190] L. Rizzo. Pgmcc: A TCP-friendly Single-rate Multicast Congestion Control Scheme. *ACM SIGCOMM Computer Communication Review (CCR)*, 30(4):17–28, August 2000.

[191] A. Rodriguez, C. Killian, S. Bhat, D. Kostić, and A. Vahdat. MACEDON: Methodology for Automatically Creating, Evaluating, and Designing Overlay Networks. In *Proceedings of 1st Symposium on Networked Systems Design and Implementation (NSDI '04)*, pages 20–20, San Francisco, California, USA, March 2004. USENIX Association.

[192] A. Rodriguez, D. Kostic, and A. Vahdat. Scalability in Adaptive Multi-Metric Overlays. In *Proceedings of 24th International Conference on Distributed Computing Systems (ICDCS '04)*, pages 112–121, Tokyo, Japan, March 2004. IEEE Computer Society.

[193] A. I. T. Rowstron and P. Druschel. Pastry: Scalable, Decentralized Object Location, and Routing for Large-Scale Peer-to-Peer Systems. In *Proceedings of IFIP/ACM International Conference on Distributed Systems Platforms (Middleware '01)*, pages 329–350, Heidelberg, Germany, November 2001. Springer Berlin/Heidelberg.

[194] Cirrus - Use RTMFP For Developing Real-Time Collaboration Applications. URL: `http://labs.adobe.com/technologies/cirrus/`. Website. Last Accessed: Match 31, 2012.

[195] H. F. Salama, D. Reeves, and Y. Viniotis. An Efficient Delay-Constrained Minimum Spanning Tree Heuristic. URL: `http://rtcomm.csc.ncsu.edu/papers/DCMinSpanTree.pdf`, 1996. Unpublished Work. Online Ressource. Last Accessed: March 31, 2012.

[196] K. Savetz, N. Randall, and Y. Lepage. *MBONE: Multicasting Tomorrow's Internet*. IDG Books Worldwide Inc., Foster City, California, USA, 1st edition, 1995.

[197] J. Schiller. *Mobilkommunikation*. Addison-Wesley, 2000.

[198] D. Schmidt. Analyse eines hierarchischen Multicast-Ansatzes in Anwendungsschicht, April 2008. Diploma Thesis at Institute of Telematics, University of Karlsruhe (TH). Advisor: Christian Hübsch and Martina Zitterbart.

[199] K. Shudo, Y. Tanaka, and S. Sekiguchi. Overlay Weaver: An Overlay Construction Toolkit. *Computer Communications*, 31(2):402–412, February 2008.

[200] Singapore Offers Free Wi-Fi in Public Areas. URL: `http://www.ida.gov.sg/News%20and%20Events/20061013120532.aspx?getPagetype=20`. Website. Last Accessed: March 31, 2012.

[201] CAIDA: The Cooperative Association for Internet Data Analysis. URL: http://www.caida.org/tools/measurement/skitter/. Website. Last Accessed: March 31, 2012.

[202] T. Sohn, A. Varshavsky, A. LaMarca, M. Chen, T. Choudhury, I. Smith, S. Consolvo, J. Hightower, W. Griswold, and E. de Lara. Mobility Detection Using Everyday GSM Traces. In *UbiComp 2006: Ubiquitous Computing*, volume 4206 of *Lecture Notes in Computer Science*, pages 212–224. Springer Berlin/Heidelberg, 2006.

[203] Spontaneous Virtual Networks (SpoVNet). URL: http://www.spovnet.de. Website. Last Accessed: March 31, 2012.

[204] R. Steinmetz and K. Wehrle. *Peer-to-Peer Systems and Applications*. Number 3485 in Lecture Notes in Computer Science. Springer, 2005.

[205] A. Stepanov and M. Lee. The Standard Template Library, 1994. Technical Report. Hewlett-Packard Laboratories.

[206] M. Stiemerling. System Design of SATO and ASI. Deliverable D12-F.1, Ambient Networks Project, 2006.

[207] M. Stiemerling and S. Kiesel. A System for Peer-to-Peer Video Streaming in Resource Constrained Mobile Environments. In *Proceedings of 1st ACM Workshop on User-provided Networking: Challenges and Opportunities (U-NET '09)*, pages 25–30, Rome, Italy, December 2009. ACM Press.

[208] M. Stiemerling and S. Kiesel. Cooperative P2P Video Streaming for Mobile Peers. In *Proceedings of 19th International Conference on Computer Communications and Networks (ICCCN '10)*, pages 1–7, Zurich, Switzerland, August 2010. IEEE Computer Society.

[209] I. Stoica, D. Adkins, S. Zhuang, S. Shenker, and S. Surana. Internet Indirection Infrastructure. *IEEE/ACM Transactions on Networking*, 12(2):205–218, April 2004.

[210] I. Stoica, R. Morris, D. Karger, M. F. Kaashoek, and H. Balakrishnan. Chord: A Scalable Peer-to-Peer Lookup Service for Internet Applications. *ACM SIGCOMM Computer Communication Review (CCR)*, 31(4):149–160, August 2001.

[211] B. Stroustrup. *The Design and Evolution of C++*. ACM Press/Addison-Wesley Publishing Co., New York, New York, USA, 1994.

[212] T. Strufe. *A Peer-to-Peer-Based Approach for the Transmission of Live Multimedia Streams*. PhD thesis, Technical University Ilmenau, Germany, Ilmenau, Germany, 2007.

[213] D. Stutzbach and R. Rejaie. Understanding Churn in Peer-to-peer Networks. In *Proceedings of 6th ACM SIGCOMM Conference on Internet Measurement*, pages 189–202, Rio de Janeiro, Brazil, October 2006. ACM Press.

[214] E. Tan, L. Guo, S. Chen, and X. Zhang. CUBS: Coordinated Upload Bandwidth Sharing in Residential Networks. In *Proceedings of 17th IEEE International Conference on Network Protocols (ICNP '09)*, pages 193–202, Princton, New Jersey, USA, October 2009. IEEE Computer Society.

[215] S.-W. Tan, G. Waters, and J. Crawford. A Survey and Performance Evaluation of Scalable Tree-based Application Layer Multicast Protocols. URL: http://www.cs.kent.ac.uk/pubs/2003/1679/, July 2003. Technical Report No. 9-03. University of Kent, Canterbury, Kent, UK. Online Resource. Last Accessed: March 31, 2012.

[216] A. Tanenbaum, S. Wetherall, and J. David. *Computer Networks*. Pearson, Boston, USA, 5th edition, 2011.

[217] H. Tang, M. Janic, and X. Zhou. Hopcount in the NICE Application Layer Multicast Protocol. In *Proceedings of IEEE/SMC Multiconference on Computational Engineering in Systems Applications*, pages 1020–1026, Beijing, China, October 2006. IEEE Computer Society.

[218] C.-L. Tsao and R. Sivakumar. On Effectively Exploiting Multiple Wireless Interfaces in Mobile Hosts. In *Proceedings of 5th International Conference on Emerging Networking Experiments and Technologies (CoNEXT '09)*, pages 337–348, Rome, Italy, December 2009. ACM Press.

[219] G. Valadon, F. L. Goff, and C. Berger. A Practical Characterization of 802.11 Access Points in Paris. In *Proceedings of 5th Advanced International Conference on Telecommunications (AICT '09)*, pages 220–225, Venice/Mestre, Italy, May 2009. IEEE Computer Society.

[220] G. Valadon, F. Le Goff, and C. Berger. Daily Walks in Paris: A Practical Analysis of Wi-Fi Access Points. In *Proceedings of 3rd International Conference on emerging Networking Experiments and Technologies (CoNEXT '07)*, pages 63:1–63:2, Venice, Italy, December 2007. ACM Press.

[221] A. Varga and R. Hornig. An Overview of the OMNeT++ Simulation Environment. In *Proceedings of 1st International Conference on Simulation*

Tools and Techniques for Communications, Networks and Systems & Work-shops (SIMUTools '08), pages 1–10, Marseille, France, March 2008. ICST (Institute for Computer Sciences, Social-Informatics and Telecommunications Engineering).

[222] V. Vishnumurthy and P. Francis. On Heterogeneous Overlay Construction and Random Node Selection in Unstructured P2P Networks. In *Proceedings of 25th IEEE International Conference on Computer Communications (INFOCOM '06)*, pages 1–12, Barcelona, Spain, April 2006. IEEE Computer Society.

[223] Vodafone Germany. URL: `http://www.vodafone.de/`. Website. Last Accessed: March 31, 2012.

[224] L. Vu, I. Rimac, H. Volker, M. Hofmann, and K. Nahrstedt. iShare: Exploiting Opportunistic Ad hoc Connections for Improving Data Download of Cellular Users. In *Proceedings of 1st IEEE Workshop on Pervasive Group Communication (PerGroup '10)*, Miami, Florida, USA, December 2010.

[225] D. Waitzman, C. Partridge, and S. E. Deering. Distance Vector Multicast Routing Protocol. URL: `http://www.ietf.org/rfc/rfc1075.txt`, November 1988. IETF RFC 1075. Online Resource. Last Accessed: March 31, 2012.

[226] O. Waldhorst, C. Blankenhorn, D. Haage, R. Holz, G. Koch, B. Koldehofe, F. Lampi, C. Mayer, and S. Mies. Spontaneous Virtual Networks: On the Road towards the Internet's Next Generation. *it — Information Technology Special Issue on Next Generation Internet*, 50(6):367–375, December 2008.

[227] O. P. Waldhorst, R. Bless, and M. Zitterbart. Overlay-Netze als Innovationsmotor im Internet – Spontane virtuelle Netze: Auf dem Weg zum Internet der Zukunft. *Informatik Spektrum*, 2(288):171–185, March 2010.

[228] F. Wang, Y. Xiong, and J. Liu. mTreebone: A Hybrid Tree/Mesh Overlay for Application-Layer Live Video Multicast. In *Proceedings of 27th International Conference on Distributed Computing Systems (ICDCS '07)*, page 49, Toronto, Ontario, Canada, June 2007. IEEE Computer Society.

[229] Z. Wang and J. Crowcroft. Quality-of-Service Routing for Supporting Multimedia Applications. *IEEE Journal on Selected Areas in Communications*, 14(7):1228–1234, September 1996.

[230] S. wei Tan, G. Waters, and J. Crawford. MeshTree: A Delayoptimised Overlay Multicast Tree Building Protocol, 2005. Technical Report. University of Kent. IEEE Computer Society, Washington, DC, USA.

[231] WiGLE - Wireless Geographic Logging Engine. URL: http://wigle.net. Website. Last Accessed: March 31,2012.

[232] R. Wittmann and M. Zitterbart. *Multicast Communication: Protocols and Applications.* Morgan Kaufmann Publishers Inc., San Francisco, California, USA, 1999.

[233] K. Woyach, D. Puccinelli, and M. Haenggi. Sensorless Sensing in Wireless Networks: Implementation and Measurements. In *Proceedings of 4th International Symposium on Modeling and Optimization in Mobile, Ad Hoc and Wireless Networks (WiOpt '06)*, pages 1–8, Boston, Massachusetts, USA, April 2006.

[234] H. Xie, Y. R. Yang, A. Krishnamurthy, Y. G. Liu, and A. Silberschatz. P4P: Provider Portal for Applications. *ACM SIGCOMM Computer Communication Review (CCR)*, 38(4):351–362, August 2008.

[235] H. Xie, Y. R. Yang, A. Krishnamurthy, Y. G. Liu, and A. Silberschatz. P4P: Provider Portal for Applications. In *Proceedings of the ACM Conference on Data Communication (SIGCOMM '08)*, pages 351–362, Seattle, Washington, USA, August 2008. ACM Press.

[236] M. Yang and Z. Fei. A Proactive Approach to Reconstructing Overlay Multicast Trees. In *Proceedings of 23rd Annual Joint Conference of the IEEE Computer and Communications Societies (INFOCOM '04)*, volume 4, pages 2743–2753, Hongkong, China, March 2004. IEEE Computer Society.

[237] J. Yao, Y. Duan, J. Pan, and K. chan Lan. Implementation of a Multihoming Agent for Mobile On-board Communication. In *Proceedings of IEEE Vehicular Technology Conference (VTC '06)*, volume 2, pages 896–900, Montreal, Canada, May 2006. IEEE Computer Society.

[238] W.-P. Yiu, X. Jin, and S.-H. Chan. Challenges and Approaches in Large-Scale P2P Media Streaming. *IEEE Multimedia*, 14(2):50–59, June 2007.

[239] H. Yoon, J. Kim, F. Tan, and R. Hsieh. On-demand Video Streaming in Mobile Opportunistic Networks. In *Proceedings of 6th Annual IEEE International Conference on Pervasive Computing and Communications (PerCom '08)*, pages 80–89, Hongkong, China, March 2008. IEEE Computer Society.

[240] Zattoo. URL: http://www.zattoo.com. Website. Last Accessed: March 31, 2012.

[241] M. Zhang, L. Zhao, Y. Tang, J.-G. Luo, and S.-Q. Yang. Large-scale Live Media Streaming over Peer-to-PeerNetworks through Global Internet. In *Proceedings of ACM Workshop on Advances in Peer-to-Peer Multimedia Streaming (P2PMMS '05)*, pages 21–28, Singapore, November 2005. ACM Press.

[242] Y. Zhu and B. Li. Overlay Multicast with Inferred Link Capacity Correlations. In *Proceedings of 26th IEEE International Conference on Distributed Computing Systems (ICDCS '06)*, page 54, Lisboa, Portugal, July 2006. IEEE Computer Society.

[243] Y. Zhu and B. Li. Overlay Networks with Linear Capacity Constraints. *IEEE Transactions on Parallel and Distributed Systems*, 19(2):159–173, February 2008.

[244] S. Zhuang, K. Lai, I. Stoica, R. Katz, and S. Shenker. Host Mobility using an Internet Indirection Infrastructure. *Wireless Networks*, 11(6):741–756, November 2005.

[245] H. Zimmermann. OSI Reference Model–The ISO Model of Architecture for Open Systems Interconnection. *IEEE Transactions on Communications*, 28(4):425–432, April 1980.

Nomenclature

LCC .... Link Capacity Correlation
LHB .... Leader Heartbeat Message
LTE .... Long Term Evolution
LTE-A .... Long Term Evolution Advanced
LTM .... Location-aware Topology Matching
MAC .... Media Access Control
MACEDON .... Methodology for Automatically Creating, Evaluating, and
                                             Designing Overlay Networks
Mbone .... Multicast Backbone
mDNS .... Multicast-based DNS
MIP .... Multi-NIC IP
MOSPF .... Multicast Open Shortest Path First
MOT-P .... Multi-objective Tree-based Protocols
MOVi .... Mobile Opportunistic Video-on-Demand
MS .... Mobile Station
MSC .... Mobile Services Switching Center
MTCP .... Multicast TCP
Mtunnel .... Multicast Tunneling Protocol
NAT .... Network Address Translation
NIC .... Network Interface Card
NICE .... NICE is the Internet Cooperative Environment
NICE-WLI .... NICE with Wireless Integration
OF .... Offset
OO .... Optimization Objective
P2P .... Peer-to-Peer
P4P .... Provider Portal for Applications
PaDIS .... Provider-aided Distance Information System
PAN .... Personal Area Network
PCF .... Point Coordination Function
PDF .... Probability Distribution Function
PGMCC .... Pragmatic General Multicast Congestion Control
PIM-DM .... Protocol Independent Multicast Dense Mode
PIM-SM .... Protocol Independent Multicast Sparse Mode
PROP .... Peer-exchange Routing Optimization Protocols
RF .... Responsibility Factor
RFC .... Request for Comments
RFCOMM .... Radio Frequency Communication
RMTP .... Reliable Multicast Transport Protocol
RNC .... Radio Network Controller
RNS .... Radio Network Subsystem
ROAM .... Robust Overlay Architecture for Mobility

RP .... Rendezvous Point
RTMFP .... Real-time Media Flow Protocol
RTS/CTS .... Request To Send/Clear To Send
RTT .... Round-trip Time
SAM .... Shared Access Medium Domain
SATO .... Service-aware Adaptive Transport Overlay
SBF .... Standard Bloom Filter
SC .... Supercluster
SCTP .... Stream Control Transmission Protocol
SDMA .... Space Devision Multiple Access
SDP .... Service Discovery Protocol
SGSN .... Serving GPRS Support Node
SNR .... Signal-to-Noise-Ratio
SpoVNet .... Spontaneous Virtual Networks
SRM .... Scalable Reliable Multicast
SSID .... Service-Set Identifier
STL .... Standard Template Library
SVC .... Scalable Video Coding
TCP .... Transmission Control Protocol
TDMA .... Time Devision Multiple Access
UDP .... User Datagram Protocol
UE .... User Equipment
UIA .... Unmanaged Internet Architecture
UMTP .... UDP Multicast Tunneling Protocol
UMTS .... Universal Mobile Telecommunications System
URI .... Uniform Resource Identifier
VLR .... Visitor Location Register
VoD .... Video-on-Demand
WCDMA .... Wideband Code Division Multiple Access
WIMP .... Wireless Multi-Access Proximity Probing
XPORT .... Extensible Optimization in Overlay Dissemination Trees

Index